Investigating Home and Family

Also available from Oxford University Press:

All about Children: an introduction to child development
 Dorothy Baldwin   ISBN 0 19 832715 3
All about Health: an introduction to health education
 Dorothy Baldwin   ISBN 0 19 832719 6

INVESTIGATING
Home and Family

Dorothy Baldwin

Oxford University Press 1990

Oxford University Press, Walton Street, Oxford
OX2 6DP

Oxford   New York   Toronto
Delhi   Bombay   Calcutta   Madras   Karachi
Petaling Jaya   Singapore   Hong Kong   Tokyo
Nairobi   Dar es Salaam   Cape Town
Melbourne   Auckland

and associated companies in
Ibadan   Berlin

Oxford is a trade mark of Oxford University Press

© D. Baldwin 1989

ISBN 0 19 832750 1

Typeset by MS Filmsetting Limited, Frome,
Somerset
Printed in Hong Kong

Acknowledgements

The author and publishers are grateful to the
following for permission to reproduce GCSE exam
questions: London and East Anglian Group;
Midland Examining Group; Northern Examining
Association (Associated Lancashire Schools
Examining Board, Joint Matriculation Board, North
Regional Examinations Board, North West Regional
Examinations Board, Yorkshire & Humberside
Regional Examinations Board); Scottish
Examination Board; Southern Examining Group;
Welsh Joint Education Committee. The WJEC
GCSE paper is graded in order of difficulty, and the
questions quoted from it were originally numbered
as follows: 1 (a)(p. 35), 1 (b)(p. 47), 11B (a–c)(p. 83),
6 (a)(p. 95, first part), 11B (d)(p. 95, second part),
2 (a)(p. 107), 11A (p. 119), 3 (p. 143, parts a and b),
6 (b)(p. 143, part c), 4 (p. 167), 10B (c)(p. 191).

The table on p.49 is reproduced with the permission
of the Controller of HMSO.

Thanks are also due to K. Dreher for original
illustrations.

The publishers would like to thank the following for
permission to reproduce photographs and other
copyright material.

Aga-Rayburn p. 151 (right); Allsport pp. 135, 138
(left), 194 (bottom); Apple Computer (UK) Ltd.
p. 139; Ardea pp. 36 (bottom middle, centre right
and bottom right), 60 (top right), 64 (bottom); ASH
p. 191 (all); Bank of Scotland p. 17 (bottom left);
Barnaby's Picture Library p. 153 (left); BBC Hulton
Picture Library pp. 34 (top, and bottom right), 40
(top); Anthony Blake pp. 137 (both), 197 (top left);
Janet and Colin Bord p. 38; Pat Brindley p. 132 (left);
BAAF/Trefor Jarrett Ball p. 46; Bryant Homes pp.
70 (bottom), 125; Camera Press pp. 153 (right), 194
(top); J Allan Cash pp. 17 (centre), 48 (centre), 120
(left), 123 (top and bottom); Martyn Chillmaid pp.
14 (top), 22, 24 (all), 152, 168 (top); Country Homes
(Anglia) Ltd. p. 121 (top); Chubb Fire Security Ltd.
p. 182 (both); Bruce Coleman Ltd. pp. 36 (top
middle, centre middle, and top right), 60 (bottom),
61 (top); Creda p. 151 (centre); Debenhams Fitch
and Company p. 91 (top); Department of Health
p. 189; Eurisol p. 142; Format Partnership pp. 25 (top
right), 48 (top), 64 (top), 202 (bottom right); Paul
Glendall p. 60 (top left); Richard and Sally Greenhill
pp. 18 (right), 25 (middle right, bottom right and far
left), 36 (top left, centre left and bottom left), 42
(both), 43, 52 (left), 70 (top), 86 (top and bottom),
108 (bottom left, middle and right), 111 (middle),
112 (bottom); Habitat p. 161; Halifax Building
Society p. 76 (centre); Robert Harding pp. 18 (left),
25 (top left), 108 (top), 120 (top centre, and bottom
right), 148 (right), 197 (bottom left and right); Help
the Aged p. 56 (right); Hobart p. 65; Camilla Jessel
p. 177; Roger Jeffcoate p. 52 (right); The Littlewoods
Organization p. 80 (bottom); London Fire and Civil
Defence Authority p. 89 (both); Sorin Masca p. 56
(left); Tony Mays pp. 94 (bottom), 116 (top), 120
(top right), 127; Milk Marketing Board p. 193; Bill
Meadows p. 61 (bottom); Morgan Horowskyj
Architects pp. 121 (bottom), 122 (top); Mothercare
p. 158 (top); National Medical Slide Bank p. 188;
Neff UK Ltd. p. 40 (bottom); Network pp. 120
(bottom centre), 202 (top, and bottom left), 203;
Oxfam p. 91 (bottom); Permutit p. 62 (top); Phab
p. 56 (centre); Photo Co-op pp. 25 (middle left), 168
(bottom); Picturepoint pp. 44 (left), 76 (left), 171;
The Post Office p. 76 (right); Rentokil p. 128 (all);
Royal School for the Deaf, Derby p. 68; ROSPA
p. 180 (both); Science Photo Library p. 71; Sharp
p. 151 (top); Shelter p. 111 (top and bottom); Sophie
Nursery Products p. 158 (bottom); The Spastics
Society p. 44 (right); St John Supplies p. 187;
Sporting Pictures pp. 99 (both), 138 (right); Thames
Water pp. 62 (bottom), 63; John Topham p. 48
(right); Tower p. 133; Valor p. 132 (centre);
Walden's Wiltshire Foods Ltd. p. 59; John
Walmsley pp. 13, 17 (top, and bottom right), 53, 77,
81 (bottom), 96, 97 (bottom), 112 (top), 141 (both),
172, 174, 175, 179, 183 (all), 185; The Wellcome
Institute Library p. 25 (bottom left); Charlotte
Whitaker p. 66; Elizabeth Whiting Associates pp. 2
(bottom left), 144 (both), 166; Zanussi p. 151 (left).

Additional photography by Chris Honeywell and
Rob Judges.

The illustrations are by: Andrew Aloof Associates,
Peter Burrows, Helen Charlton, Elitta Fell, Gecko
Ltd., Tina Jane Hancocks, Zoe Hancox, Debbie
Hinks, Jane Hughes, Alan Marks, David Mitcheson,
Nigel Paige, Julie Tolliday, Lynne Willey, Clare
Wright, and Melvyn Wright.

Contents

Preface

Home and Family brings together in one book all the material required by the various GCSE Home Economics syllabuses for courses on the family and the home. It is also designed to be used as a written and practical text for the other Home Economics courses at this level. Students who are interested in any area of family and home life may wish to study this course without taking examinations.

The book will be of real value to teachers in the classroom, especially those working with groups, and those tackling the GCSE examinations for the first time. Students are introduced step by step to the GCSE approach of analysing problems, identifying the available resources, testing out the information and applying it in the appropriate manner. Each chapter starts with a clear statement of the objectives it covers, and ends by referring students back to this to check what they have achieved.

The many suggestions for practical work and investigative tasks allow much room for choice. The experienced Home Economics teacher will find they can be readily adapted to suit their own and the students' needs. Many require little planning; only a few involve long-term advanced preparation. There are two symbols which appear throughout the text;   ◯   for discussion and   ◗   for investigative tasks.

Questions, including some from GCSE papers, are provided in every chapter to reinforce understanding in both practical and written work. They give a wide variety of extended topics from which the teacher may select, according to the needs and abilities of the students. The language used will be readily accessible to most students. Written work can be undertaken unaided, while the teacher is engaged in practical work or with special groups.

The opening chapters explore different values, attitudes, and life styles in some depth. This will enable students to develop a clearer understanding of why some choices are more appropriate than others. These chapters are also of value in raising the issues which help to develop and extend personal growth.

For the student

The study of Home Economics covers a wide area of human activity: family, home, food, textiles, and child development. Each of these themes *interacts* with the others: they all affect one another. Family and home is your main theme. It is the study of choices available to people in their personal and domestic lives, and of the skills needed to make those choices. As you work through this book, relate your choices, where possible, to the wider themes of Home Economics.

You need *information* to identify human needs and match them to material resources. Some can be found in this book: check the index. Some can be sought from agencies: check the address pages. Some will be obtained from your own investigations and practical work. Once you have identified the information, you can test it out.

All your tasks, whether practical or written, need careful *planning*. Concentrate on *organization* and *management* skills. Tools have to be chosen and handled correctly. Records of your work must be kept, and your plans reviewed in the light of their progress. If this is unsatisfactory, you need to alter your plans slightly, or switch them altogether. This is the process of learning by practical application.

When you have sought out and tested the information, you can solve the problem or make the decision. Information on its own gives you facts and figures' *Knowledge* includes the ability to use the information properly: *to apply it in the appropriate manner*.

As no two people are the same, there is no such thing as one 'right' choice. There may be many choices which all seem suitable. There may be none which is exactly right. Some may fit a short-term need, but will not give long-term satisfaction, and vice versa. Checking with the wider Home Economics themes can help with your choice.

However, *some choices are more appropriate than others*. The skills of problem solving and decision making are like detective work, and anyone can learn them. When you have made your choice, give the reasons for it. Good reasons gain good marks even if there are more appropriate choices.

Each chapter is broken down into single-page units. Most units contain at least one practical or investigative task. It is important you record your findings as you go along. They are not in the text, and you could forget them when you come to revise.

The questions at the end of each unit help you practise what you have learned. The last ones are more difficult, and may extend the topic area to wider themes. Try to answer as many as you can. Choose work from the suggestions for individual study, investigations, and practical assignments. Examination questions are at the end of each chapter.

We hope you enjoy this study. When you leave home, the choices about your future life are your own. Practise and learn these skills now.

1 An introduction to your work

By the end of this chapter, you should be able to:

- analyse a simple statement or problem.
- identify and use classroom resources.
- investigate a human need.
- plan a simple task.
- know your values.
- accept the effect of culture on values.
- understand how they affect choice and behaviour.
- distinguish between a value and a fact.
- acknowledge other values.
- check your values.
- improve your discussion skills.
- understand the function of goals.
- think about your priorities.

Human needs

Each individual has physical, mental, emotional and social needs. They must be met if the individuals are to be properly nurtured and grow and develop to their full potential.

Which of these two people do you think needs more sleep?

A physical need is for sleep. Teenagers are sometimes short of sleep. How can you find out how much sleep you actually need? What happens to your mind when you are very tired? What about your emotions – are you more, or less, cheerful without sleep? Are you likely to enjoy the company of others when you are in this state?

It is not really possible to divide a person into separate needs. For example, if you sleep well, your body feels fitter. What happens to your mental, emotional and social state?

- Human needs are interdependent – each is affected by the others, and they all affect the well-being of the whole person.

How can you find out if the above statement is true? Part of your work is concerned with learning how to **analyse** (examine, test) information. You can then decide whether to act on it, or not. In what way might this help you to become a more effective manager of your life?

---

1 Using a thesaurus, find some synonyms for these words: nurtured, potential, interdependent, effective, choice.
2 Describe your feelings when you are **a** hungry, **b** confused by information, **c** angry, and **d** lonely. Now state some actions you might take to remove each feeling effectively.

3 Find out how many hours the average teenager needs to sleep.
4 Sometimes, the word 'psychological' is used to refer to a human need which is both mental and emotional. Create a sentence about human needs showing the use of this word.

What is a resource?

A resource is anything which meets a need.

- 'When you get stuck, the teacher will help out.'
- 'I know I can do it, if I practise enough.'
- 'It was Farida's quick thinking that saved the day.'
- 'His grandmother is an expert at growing plants.'
- 'I haven't got two pairs of hands.'

Can a person be a resource? Identify the human resources in each of the above statements (knowledge, ability, energy, skill, patience, hard work, time, and so on). Are human resources available all the time? Which sentence answers this?

Material resources are non-human things. Complete the following:

A raincoat meets the need for protection.
A dictionary meets the need for information.
A light bulb meets the need for . . .
Name three material resources in your classroom. Which needs do they meet?
Name three material resources in a bathroom and state the physical needs they meet.

What material resources does this photograph show?

Is there a limit to material resources? Joe is tired and thirsty. He has enough money for his bus fare, or to buy a drink, but not both. Joe has to decide on his priorities – is he more tired or more thirsty? A priority is any person or thing which has first claim on your resources at a particular time.

Has Joe any alternative choices? Is there a drinking fountain nearby? Might some older person offer him a lift home? Before you can make choices, you need to find out what alternative resources there are. You must also study the consequences of deciding on those resources. Would it be wise for Joe to accept a lift from a stranger?

You must solve the problem in the best way possible for Joe.

---

1 If you were shipwrecked on a desert island, would you choose to have **a** another person with you and nothing left of the luxury liner, or **b** all the contents of the luxury liner and to be on your own? Why?

2 What is meant by a priority? What kind of information would you need before you could decide on Joe's priority? (For example, you would need to know his degree of tiredness/thirst, the length of his walk home, the chance of a lift, and so on.)

3 When we describe a person as resourceful, what do we mean?

4 Draw up a list of all the material resources you use when making a cup of tea. Name the human resources also involved.

Investigating human needs

- The function of the family is to meet basic human needs.

Do you agree with this statement? How can you find out what are basic human needs?

The following task has been planned by your teacher.
Collect: germinating seeds, sand, pots, watering can, fertilizer, and labels.
a Plant seeds with fertilizer. Water. Label pots.
b Repeat **a** but withhold fertilizer.
c Keep a weekly record of your findings.
d After two weeks, withhold water from some pots in both groups.
e Study the nutrients in the fertilizer. Discuss plant growth without nitrogen, phosphorus, and potassium.
f What else did you find essential to maintain life?

Is air (oxygen) a basic human need?
N.B. Students with breathing problems should not do the following tasks.
Collect: a partner to work with, and a stop watch.
a In turn, hold your breath for a full minute.
b Describe your partner's face towards the end.
c Record your own feelings.
d Compare your findings with your partner's.

▶ **Collect:** plastic bags for fruit, and for clothing.
a Examine and describe both sorts of bag.
b Read any safety warnings.
c In what way are these warnings of vital importance to people who look after small children?
If someone breathes in with a plastic bag against his or her mouth or nose, the plastic forms a tight seal over the airways. An older person can easily pull it off. A toddler may not have the strength to do so.
d Do you consider the safety warnings adequate? Create one of your own.

1 Why was the first task carried out on plants, not people? Do you think it could have been carried out on animals, and why?
2 Equate (make a link between) the nutrients in the fertilizer and the need for these nutrients in the human diet. Study a food chart and list five foods rich in these nutrients.
3 A baby must be held with one hand supporting the back, neck, and head. Equate this statement with the reason why infants under the age of one year are not given pillows to sleep on.
4 State the ways in which the information on this page helps people to become more effective parents.

Planning an investigation

The human needs are for hygienic food storage. The human resources are the time and energy of the three students. The material resources are the cleaning agents required.

List the material resources your teacher collected to prepare for the first task on p. 14. Find out the answers to these questions:

a Were the seeds bought? If so, when was the shopping trip planned? Discuss the human resources involved to buy them – time, travel, energy, and so on.

b Was the fertilizer bought at the same time? Why?

c What would have happened to the investigation if the teacher had not checked the contents label for the named nutrients?

d When and how were the other resources collected?

e Roughly estimate the total costs of the material resources.

f When were the seeds germinated? How long did it take?

g Make a rough estimate of the total planning time involved.

h What would have happened to this lesson if the teacher had not planned it fully? Do you consider planning an important skill? Why?

The function of planning is to achieve a desired end – an **objective** or **goal**. What was the objective of this investigation?

Guidelines for planning include:

- Analyse the human needs, the problem or objective.
- Identify the resources involved – equipment, time, energy.
- Research (seek) facts which apply to the situation.
- Consider different ways to use all the information.
- Plan one course of work – draw or list what you will do.
- Rehearse the plan – has anything been forgotten or overlooked?
- Control the plan – test it out, recording each stage.
- Evaluate the results – discuss any surprises or mishaps.
- If necessary, choose and test a different plan.
- Evaluate the whole plan, from the beginning to the end.

An alternative plan might have been to show that warmth is essential for growth and development.

Collect: a sunny window ledge, and a fridge.

Plan a similar investigation with germinating seeds. Identify each step involved in the planning process. Evaluate your plan.

The fridge now needs cleaning. Three students begin the task without planning their work. Three other students draw up a plan for the task on the blackboard. The rest of the class watches. Discuss any problems met by the two groups.

1 Devise a simple plan to carry out a normal household task without using the 'normal' resources; for example, making toast without an electric toaster or grill.

2 Create your own plan for defrosting and cleaning a fridge.

What are values?

Values are the ideas or beliefs by which people live. They are the things you judge to be important in life. They can be to do with material things, such as valuing wood rather than plastic, or they can be to do with non-material things, such as valuing truth, beauty, and loyalty rather than lies, ugliness, and betrayal.

You have two pens, A and B. B does not write well.

- 'I value pen A because it writes so well.'
- 'I value pen B because it was given to me by a very special person.'

Which of these values comes from intellect and which from emotions?

You lose both pens and want to buy another. Would you choose:

a a pen that writes well?
b a pen just like pen B?
c a pen that writes well and reminds you of pen B?

Do you think it is more, or less, effective to use both intellect and emotions when making choices? Why?

Collect: portions of diced apple and broken biscuits. Sufficient portions are needed for each student to select freely.
a Each student chooses and eats one.
b Which values did you base your choice on – a sweet tooth? nourishing diet? healthy teeth? body weight? other?

Your values are basic to any kind of choice or decision you make. They affect your behaviour and the way you expect others to behave.

---

1 Investigate some of your values by writing statements to complete the following list. You may want to write down quite a bit for some answers and just a short statement for others. Put a star beside the values you think might change as you get older. Keep the list somewhere private and study it again **a** when you have completed the chapter, and **b** when you have completed the course.

- I do/do not value a tidy room because
- I do/do not value television because
- I do/do not value saving money because
- I do/do not value good manners because

- I do/do not value home cooking because
- I do/do not value smoking because
- I do/do not value fashion in clothing because
- I do/do not value parties because
- I do/do not value a member of my family because
- I do/do not value being corrected because
- I do/do not value helping others because
- I do/do not value exercise because
- I do/do not value learning more about myself because

2 Choose one value and state in what ways it affects **a** your behaviour, and **b** the way you expect other people to behave.

Different values

Dawn values buying and arranging flowers to adorn her room. Judy values growing flowers and thinks it is wicked to cut them.

Who is right? Does your 'geography' affect the kind of values you hold?

Sally admires bankers and is studying economics. Pete thinks bankers are robbers and should all be shot. Does your family 'history' affect some values you hold?

Using the correct resources, write the meaning of and some synonyms for the word 'culture'.

● Values differ from one culture to the next.

Do you agree with this statement? Why?

Values are statements of opinion. A statement of opinion is sometimes called a **value judgement**. Values are not facts. Facts can be tested to find out if they are true or not. Divide the following into value judgements or facts in class.

● Cut flowers on a table always cheer people up.
● Women are hopeless at business.
● Men are, on average, physically stronger than women.
● Boys have more courage than girls.
● Speaking with food in your mouth is rude.
● If you try to talk while swallowing, you risk choking.
● You need oxygen from the air you breathe in.
● Every cloud has a silver lining.
● All small children should be taught to swim.
● Savers can earn interest on their money.
● The function of a roof is to protect against the weather.
● Some poor people live in homes with leaky roofs.
● It is always the builder's fault if the roof leaks.
● We live in a democratic society.
● People are proud to live in a democracy.

This is where Dawn lives.

Here is Judy's home.

1 Imagine you hold Judy's values about cutting flowers. Name alternative choices you might suggest to help Dawn brighten up her drab room.
2 The flowers satisfied Dawn's **aesthetic** need. Using resources, write two separate sentences which show the meaning of the word 'aesthetic'.
3 Explain the difference between a value and a fact.

This is Sally's mother's workplace.

Here is where Pete's mother works.

Values and prejudice

Case study

Two-year-old Jenny is taken shopping for shoes. The choice comes down to colour – black or red. Jenny cannot decide.

'Boths,' she lisps. 'No, red. Yes, red. I want to go home.'

Her parents are cross. 'Stupid child! If she can't choose, she shall have neither.'

From what you have learned about values, discuss why Jenny is unable to choose between two colours.

Prejudice means 'pre-judging' and 'finding guilty' people who are 'different'; people whose values are not the same as yours. Is it any less 'savage' to pierce a hole for a ring in the ear than for a bone in the nose? Is it, in fact, 'savage' to do either of these things? Some doctors think it is brutal to pierce any healthy human flesh.

People make value judgements all the time. There is nothing wrong with them, as long as the person knows they are opinions and not facts. Compare the following value judgements:

- 'You haven't eaten real food till you eat at my place!'
- 'People who enjoy cabbage/salad/curry make me sick. They must be animals to eat such disgusting stuff.'

'People who put needles in their noses are backward savages.'

'People who put rings in their ears are backward savages.'

Which of these two value judgements do you think shows real prejudice? Spend some time discussing the reasons for your answer.

Collect: assorted dishes of different ethnic foods.
a Sort them into those you like and those you loathe.
b Try to work out the reasons for your choices.
c Is this prejudice or a matter of taste?

---

1 Many famous chefs say the British have the worst food in the world. Write about the way this statement makes you feel.

2 The girls in a class tease another girl because her clothes are old. What kind of values do these girls hold? Do you agree with them, and why? Write about the way this statement makes you feel.

3 Yesterday, three white youths attacked and badly beat up a black youth just because he was black. What do you think were the values held by the three youths? How did these values affect their choice of behaviour? Write about the way this statement makes you feel.

Checking your values

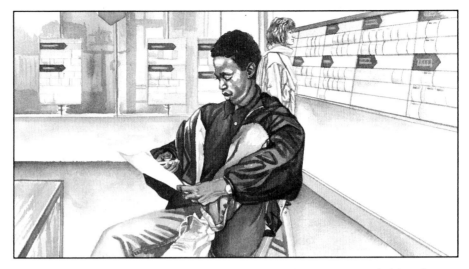

'I'm hopeless,' boasts Rudy. 'I can never manage to be on time.' Rudy likes the idea of being a 'free spirit'. He cannot be bothered with such fussy little things as time.

Do you think Rudy's value is likely to help him lead an effective life? Why? The way to check your values is to work through this list:

a Is it a value you hold from free choice?
b Are you aware of the consequences of your value?
c Do you know about the alternative choices you have?
d Are you aware of the consequences of those choices?
e Do you feel comfortable with your value?
f Are you ready and willing to talk about it in public?
g Is it an important part of your life?
h Are you comfortable knowing that your value affects your behaviour and the choices you have to make in life?

Many people hold values they never think about. They simply feel they are right for them. The purpose of checking your values is to find out if they are the right ones for you. Are they going to help you lead a more effective life? If so, is there any point in changing them? If not, what other choices do you have?

Rudy checks his value (**a** in the list) and realizes he chose it at the age of five. An uncle he admired very much did not bother with time and the five-year-old boy wanted to be just like him. Now, Rudy realizes any value made at that age is hardly a grown-up free choice. So he continues to **b**.

b One consequence of being late has been losing the chance of a job he really wanted. He continues to **c**.
c What was Rudy's alternative choice?
d Is the consequence of this choice likely to help him in life?

Rudy was feeling happy up till now. Then his checking problems began . . . (see next page).

Ask one member of the class to choose a material value, such as preferring to save money rather than spend it. Go down the checking list for this value, trying to answer each question in great detail. Discuss the class results.

---

1 Turn back to the work you did on p. 16. Study your personal list of values again. Choose one 'like' and one 'dislike' value from it. Check each in turn with the above list.

2 Did you enjoy this work, and why?
3 In what way, if any, do you think it might help you to lead a more effective life?

Resisting change

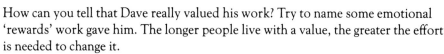

Dave's win of £541 000 'will not change his way of life,' he insists.

Dave Hokham, age 54, turned up at work yesterday after winning a fortune on the pools. He donned the protective apron and goggles he has worn for the last 25 years.

'Isn't it daft!' he beamed. 'I've dreamed of being rich all my life. But I don't want to lose my work mates. And I wouldn't know what to do with myself at home all day. Besides,' he added after a pause, 'I'm needed here. This is where I belong.'

How can you tell that Dave really valued his work? Try to name some emotional 'rewards' work gave him. The longer people live with a value, the greater the effort is needed to change it.

Collect: a hard plastic nailbrush, and a softer bendy one.

a Scrub the delicate skin near your cuticles with each.
b Record your results and the type of brush you prefer.
c Which brush is likely to be more effectively used, and why?

Change is a slow process. It often causes pain. The more Rudy (see p. 19) thinks about the job he lost and all the past trouble he caused by being late, the more he is unable to face change. Besides, he still likes the idea of being a free spirit. And his friends would sneer if he suddenly started being on time.

Name two satisfactions (emotional rewards) Rudy comforts himself with. What reward could he offer himself to take the place of those he will lose if he does change?

For behaviour to change, the person must feel some satisfaction. It is thought one of the reasons why people stop exercising is that they do not notice an immediate change in their body shape. Do you think this could be true of dieting as well? Why?

1 Study the following statements. Which do you think will contribute to making a family be **a** more happy, and **b** less happy, and why?
- 'We were all hit as children. I'll certainly slap mine around.'
- 'I want to be like my Gran; she's cheerful all the time.'
- 'I like teasing my sister and making her cry.'
- 'I only steal from Mum's purse if I think she's being mean.'

2 What rewards do you think the speaker's Gran gets from being cheerful all the time? Choose another statement and write down **a** what rewards you think the speaker gets from it, and **b** what rewards the speaker might get if he or she changed behaviour.

Conflicting values

Case studies

A doctor has enough medicine to treat only one of seven patients dying of a rare disease. The patients are: a nurse who cares for the disabled; an employer who provides work for hundreds; a pop star; a philanthropist: an artist; an unemployed parent; a five-year-old child. The doctor chooses the person he considers most useful to society. He gives the medicine to the artist as her work brings beauty into people's lives.

Do you agree with the doctor's choice? Why? Discuss the values and priorities involved, and the way they affect behaviour. Choose one of the remaining six people to receive the medicine and discuss the reasons for your choice. Then list all seven people in the order you think they should receive the medicine. Discuss your reasons.

Fatimah has an evening and Saturday job. She is warned by her teacher that she needs this time to study for her exams. Fatimah values the independence her wages bring. Money is short at home. Her parents give her what they can and she hates to ask for more. But she also values the chance to continue her education in the hope of getting a better job later on.

Fatimah must choose between what she needs now and what she needs in the future. Write as much as you can about what you would do in her place. Be prepared to discuss your priorities in class. Listen carefully while each student discusses Fatimah's problem. Then decide whether you want to change your opinion; add some factors to it, or take some away.

Mark goes shopping for a black and red shirt. His new friend tells Mark to buy the green one. Mark values his first choice, and green does not suit his skin tones. But he also values having a new friend. He buys the green shirt though he really dislikes it.

Is Mark likely to wear the shirt? Why do you think his new friend gave him such bad advice? Write about Mark's conflict of values and discuss them in class.

---

1 What do you think is the main function of having a class discussion? Did you learn much about values different from your own? Write in some detail about one student's values which you had not thought about before. Did you change any of your values? If so, how did you feel – sad? not too bad? really pleased about what you had learned?

2 Did you find discussing your ideas in class easy, not too hard, or very difficult? Think of a difficult choice you made recently and write in detail about it. Practise discussing the problem and the reasons for the choice you finally made at home, or with a friend. In what ways might the skills of open discussion help you to be more effective in your career?

3 What personal resource do you think Mark lacks?

Your goals

Using resources, create your own definition of a goal.

Make a list of some goals you would like to achieve in the next year. They might include:

- passing an exam.
- winning a sports award.
- improving your body shape.
- increasing your energy level.
- making new friends.
- meeting people of the opposite sex.
- going to college.

- passing a job interview.
- getting a place of your own.
- opening a bank account.
- becoming happier.
- getting on better with your family.
- changing some values.
- becoming a more effective person.

a Goals can be short-term or long-term. They need to be fairly realistic and attainable. The above goals are long-term. Do you think they are realistic? Write down those you think you may never be able to achieve, and why.

b Goals are limited by resources. Choose three of the above goals and discuss some human resources you need to develop in order to achieve them – time, energy, hard work, and so on.

c To achieve a goal you must commit yourself to it fully. This does not mean you neglect the other sides of your life. But a goal is not really a goal unless you are committed to achieving it. It stays a want, a wish, a vague longing which gets you nowhere.

During the teens, it seems there are hundreds of different goals to choose between. Make a list of the goals you would like to achieve **i** by the end of today and **ii** by the end of this week.

d It is thought that having too many goals at once can be distracting, and that people find they cannot commit themselves fully to any particular one. Write about whether you agree or disagree with these ideas.

---

1 In what ways do you think that knowing your goals can help in any decisions you make about your future?

2 It is thought that values underlie most human behaviour, and that goals and goal-setting are directly related to values. Prepare a full class discussion on this.

Further work on Chapter 1

→ 'I wish I could stop smoking.'

1 Teenagers often have no free choice about smoking. They begin because of pressure from their friends.

Analyse this statement in class.

2 Many studies show that the majority of smokers wish they could stop. They are not comfortable with their choice and they fear the consequences of their behaviour.

Using resources, find out and write about **a** the addictive power of nicotine, **b** the physical consequences of smoking, and **c** the dangers from passive smoking.

3 Each birthday, a member of your family values a home-made present. You have no money to buy any resources. Plan a suitable gift using only the resources which are free, or that you already have – cardboard, string, paint, boxes, cotton wool, wild flowers, and so on. You may choose to make up your gift as a practical assignment.

4 Children have certain basic needs. They need to feel loved and secure, to be provided with new experiences, to have responsibilities and to be praised for their efforts. Explain why these needs are important and say how they would be provided for when bringing up a family. *(Northern Examining Association)*

5 A child begins to develop values and attitudes in the early years at home with the family. Give and explain an example of how values and attitudes may be influenced by:
   a the religious beliefs of the family.
   b the culture of the family. *(London and East Anglian Group)*

Now look again at the objectives at the beginning of the chapter, and check that you have achieved them.

2 *Changes in people*

By the end of this chapter, you should be able to:
- use role-play as a learning resource.
- plan a visit to an outside agency.
- carry out a simple survey.
- analyse and interpret data.

Roles

Here are some roles one individual, Sonia, plays in a day. Name the people in the opposite role to Sonia's (for example, when she is a student the opposite role is that of teacher).

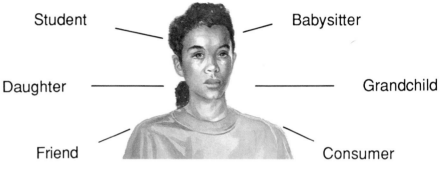

Student — Babysitter
Daughter — Grandchild
Friend — Consumer

- A **role** is a part you play, depending on whom you are with.

Analyse this statement by acting out various roles.

Collect: two students who enjoy acting (one to play Sonia and one the opposite role). Working in groups, create a short, realistic scene for each role played by 'Sonia' during one day.

Observe and record how 'Sonia's' behaviour (choice of words/tone of voice/body movements) changes with each different person. Why is this?

People **interact** with (act upon) one another, They **influence** (alter and affect) each other's behaviour. Would it be appropriate (fitting/suitable) behaviour for Sonia to interact with her grandmother in the same way as with a child? Why is this?

Role-play:
a a frightened elderly person being helped across the road
b a shy teenager at a job interview
c a child trying to get a busy adult's attention.

Was the interaction difficult or easy? The way people interact depends upon how they perceive (think of) their role and the role of the other person. Have you learned anything from watching different role-plays? If so, discuss what it is.

Identify the roles defined by uniforms and symbols.

Some students dislike role-play, saying it is boring/embarrassing/time wasting. But role-play has an important function in learning. It helps you **empathize** with other people's situations. It makes you feel what it is really like to 'be in their shoes'. Did you learn anything from watching the different role-plays? Do you think there is value in empathy, and why?

1 Find and draw four other symbols which define particular roles.
2 Explain the meaning of the following: role, interact, appropriate behaviour, empathize, sensitive, symbol.
3 Think of and write about one situation in which your behaviour was inappropriate; and explain why.

The life cycle

'All old people are frail and need help.'

The life cycle

Individuals can be put into groups: the elderly, the young, the disabled, and so on. Families can be defined by their roles: the parent, the child, the sibling, the cousin. Defining people by their roles makes the study of families easier. But there is a disadvantage. Study the picture on the left and find out what it is.

'Stereo' means solid or stiff. To **stereotype** people is to put solid, stiff labels on them, and to insist they are all the same. What is your opinion of the stereotype teenager as a football hooligan?

---

1 At what stage in the life cycle are you now? When do you expect to move on to the next stage? Name some new skills you might need to help you become effective in your new role.

2 At some stages in the life cycle, you depend upon others for your welfare.

Name these stages. At what stages do you think others will be dependent upon you?

3 Change is inherent in the human condition.

Analyse this statement.

Growth and development

The graph shows the growth of twins, Ingo and Ingrid.

a Until what age do the twins grow at the same rate?

b What is their age when they are both the same height again?

c Between what ages is Ingrid taller than Ingo?

d How tall is each of the twins at age 20?

e Find and name two minerals needed in the diet for the growth of bones. State two foods rich in these minerals.

f Most graphs on growth show similar data (information). **Data** are facts from which conclusions can be drawn. What conclusion, if any, can you draw about the average **gender** (sex) difference in adult heights? How did you come to your conclusion? What further data would you look for to test your conclusion?

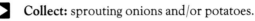

Collect: sprouting onions and/or potatoes.

a Identify the new shoots which are growing.

b Measure them, and count the number of leaves and roots. Record and draw.

c Measure and count again after one week.

d What are you measuring – growth? development? both?

Growth is an increase in size, mainly progress in body structure. Though there is a wide natural range in the stages of growth, they can be fairly accurately predicted. They can be measured in terms of height, weight, proportion of cartilage to bone (which gives the age of growing bone), and so on.

● Each individual is unique in his or her rate of growth.

Devise a class measuring task to test the accuracy of this statement.

Development is an increase in complexity. It involves progress in the body, the mind, and the emotions – the whole personality. The various stages of development can be predicted, but are not easily measured. Why do you think this is? Do you think each individual is unique in his or her pattern of development? Why do you think this?

In healthy growth and development, the whole personality progresses at a predictable rate and with a predictable outcome. If things go wrong, one part of the personality may develop while another stays immature, or the whole personality can regress.

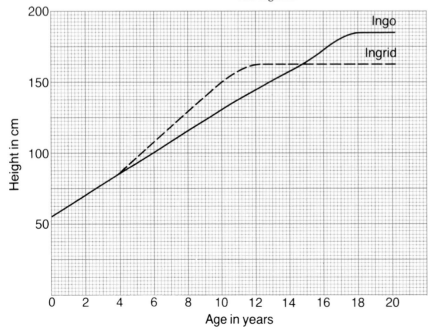

1 Why might it be useful for parents to expect that each individual is unique in his or her rate of growth and development?

2 'Failure to thrive' is the term used when a child is not growing at the predicted rate. What is the importance of being able to measure early stages of growth?

3 At what age did growth stop for the twins? Do you think development also stops at this age? Why?

4 Using resources, find out why Ingrid and Ingo would have been the same sex if they were identical twins.

Milestones of development

Milestones are guidelines for what a child can be expected to do at a certain stage of development. In all human development, there is a natural progression from one stage to the next.

● Each stage of development is built on the experience of the previous stages.

Analyse this statement by studying the diagrams below.

→ Plan a visit for child observation (see p. 28). This can be done at: a well-baby clinic, a child or health centre, school if a parent and child visit, or home if there is a small child.

a Select a choice of dates and times.
b Contact and make arrangements for the visit.
c Obtain school/home permission.
d Choose and arrange transport.
e Identify what is to be learned from the visit.
f Identify resources needed – notebook, sketch pad, tape-recorder, camera, lunch, and so on.
g Recognize factors influencing your choice of plan.

→ 1 Using child development books as your resource, find out the milestones for speech.
2 You cannot obtain permission for your intended visit over the telephone. Plan a letter to your local health education officer asking if it could be arranged. Evaluate your plan to make sure the officer knows precisely who you are, the purpose of your visit, and any other relevant details. Write your letter for class and teacher evaluation.

Child observation

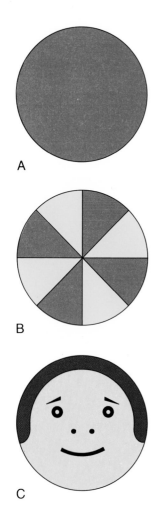

A

B

C

Page 27 suggests how you might set this observation up.

Observe and record how a baby (aged 3 months plus) reacts to these pictures. From your findings, state whether you think a baby values the human face or not.

Observe and record both the parent's and baby's reaction to one of the following: **a** ask a parent to don sunglasses or a similar disguise, **b** briefly separate the child from the parent, and **c** briefly separate the child from his or her favourite toy or comfort blanket, or stop the baby sucking his or her thumb. From your observation, state whether you think **a** the child values the parent's presence, **b** the parent values the child's, and **c** the child values familiar or unfamiliar things. From your findings, what conclusions can you draw about a child's emotional needs?

Try to observe how a crying baby reacts when it is **a** picked up, **b** fed, **c** changed, and **d** given an injection. What conclusions can you draw about a baby's physical needs?

What do you think is the function of **a** toys which rattle, **b** brightly-coloured toys, and **c** mobile toys? Devise a small task to show a baby needs mental **stimulation**.

Note the interaction between a toddler and parent. Is it close or distant, relaxed or tense? Observe how parents try to control toddlers. Note some words, phrases, facial expressions, and body movements used.

Can children manage their own lives effectively? Name some functions of controlling a child, and the parent's goals.

Note the number of resources needed for a child – pushchair, tissues, feed or drink bottle, toys, and so on. Are all the resources used? What conclusions can you draw about **a** the parent's need to plan an outing, and **b** some costs involved in meeting a child's needs?

Note the proportion of mothers to fathers. On average, which gender seems more involved in practical parenting?

Note whether any parents seemed tired. Observe how often they move in caring for the child.

Observe any interaction between toddlers. Is it easy? Does bullying or squabbling break out? If so, how is this dealt with? What conclusions can you draw about a toddler's social needs?

Note the clothing of the children. Was it the parent or the child who valued neatness or cleanliness? Why?

Observe the naturally wide range of milestones of growth and development in perfectly normal children.

---

1 Sort out your notes and write about the needs of infants under these headings: physical, mental, emotional, and social.

2 Do you consider parenting an easy or demanding role? Discuss some needs of adults which you think parents might have to forgo, and why.

Role models

Interaction happens by communication. It can be verbal or non-verbal. The parent knows what the child means by holding out the cup. In return, the child looks for a way to return the favour. He has watched older members of the family pass food to one another. He works out that the parent might like a cake so he passes the plate. He does not wait to be asked. His parent smiles, praises, and encourages him. The child gets the rewards of happy feelings: he is clever, good, useful – an important member of the family. His self-esteem (the image he has of himself) rises. On whom is the child modelling his behaviour?

Which of the following values do you think the child is learning: sensitivity, empathy, impatience, fairness, co-operation, greed? What might have happened if the parent ignored the cup?

Working in groups, devise and plan a task in which one person refuses to co-operate. Discuss the outcome in terms of physical, mental, emotional, and social needs. What value, if any, do you think there might be in learning to co-operate with others?

While passing the plate, the child knocks over the milk. It stains the beautifully laundered tablecloth. Children's motor skills (movements) are not fully co-ordinated. Parent X tells the child off. Parent Y smiles wryly, and shows the child how to mop up the mess.

What do you consider was each parent's goal in his or her choice of behaviour? What lessons do you think the child might learn from the behaviour of **a** parent X, and **b** parent Y? Which parent do you consider the more effective role model, and why?

---

1 Plan a visit to a department store, and examine the tableware resources in the home economics room. Choose the equipment you would use to lay a table for a child's meal, giving reasons for your choice.

2 Each stage of development is built on the experience of earlier stages. Discuss the emotional impact of an uncaring role model on a child's future self-esteem.

The adolescent

Two case studies

Ephra, aged 16, feels her life is full of unfair pressures. Her family want her to do well in her exams, career choices, and judo classes. Her friends want her to go to parties, where there are drugs, drinking, and opportunities for sexual encounters. She feels inner pressures from the changes in her looks and body shape at puberty – from not knowing what she really wants or who she really is. Ephra becomes so anxious she can no longer interact socially, and she cuts herself off from her family and friends. She is suffering from an identity problem.

a Why do you think some people have identity problems in the teens? Is change easy (p. 20)?

b Why does Ephra think these pressures are 'unfair'?

c What can she do about finding out her values and setting herself goals? Would these things help, and why?

Edward, aged 16, had an unhappy childhood. He is now so angry that he only thinks about revenge. He tries drugs, makes a girl he hardly knows pregnant, and takes up drinking in a big way because he likes the feelings of power the alcohol gives him. He has been arrested once for violence. The next time it will be prison.

a Whom is Edward really punishing?

b Are his goals short-term or long-term?

c Are they helping him to lead an effective life, and why?

Now imagine Ephra and Edward in six years' time. They are happily married with a new baby. They hope to be a success at parenting. Their goals are to:

● want the best for their baby, always.
● love the baby and build up its self-esteem.
● protect the baby from people or things which can harm it.
● forgive the baby when it does silly or wrong things.
● cheer the baby up when it is miserable.
● help the baby deal with its angry feelings.
● encourage the baby in its development from one stage to the next.

The average teenager does not face such extreme problems. But developmental changes can make people unhappy. Ephra and Edward were taught to 'parent' themselves. Work through each of their problems, discussing how self-parenting helped them cope.

Write down some personal problems which make you anxious. Now 'parent yourself' by checking with the above list. Does it help? Is change a fast or slow process? Do you think you might need to parent yourself fairly often? Why?

The young adult

Marriage vows are made in front of a registrar, who represents the law. Two witnesses must be present. The law makes the marriage contract legal and binding. The married couple become a single unit in society, and have rights and obligations towards each other and their children. Over 50 per cent of all marriages take place in a Register Office, and about 35 per cent of all marriages in the UK are remarriages.

These are some vows made by couples who marry in a place of worship.

Christian
Those whom God hath joined together, let no man put asunder.

Hindu
O virtuous, I have accepted thee thoughtfully and so hast thou accepted me. Out of the fullness of love I accepted thee and so hast thou accepted me.

Islam
She: I marry you according to the Islamic way with the dowry agreed upon in the presence of the witnesses here. He: I accept marrying you.

Judaism
Behold. You are consecrated to me by this ring, according to the laws of Moses and Israel.

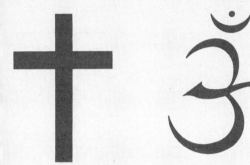

 Collect: samples of marriage vows, and sample marriage certificates.
a Discuss the marriage vows in some detail.
b Copy and fill in your 'ideal' sample marriage certificate.

The 1986 report *Babies and Money*, by the Family Policy Studies Centre, states that the time devoted to bringing up two children can mean the loss of £135 000 in the mother's lifetime earnings. What does this actually mean?
How many children would you like, and why?

1 Marriage today is about sharing – a home, money, home-making, and childcare.
Do you agree with this statement? Why? List some things you would expect to share with a **spouse** (see p. 36). Should they be discussed before or after marriage? Why?

2 List some personal goals you would expect from marriage.

 3 Plan to make a wedding item – invitations, buttonholes, table decorations, clothing, or food. Cost your item and compare it with the shop price. Show the planning process. You may choose to make up the item as a practical assignment.

4 Adults who have not learned to 'parent themselves' find it difficult to parent their children.
Analyse this statement.

5 Using resources, find and explain the meanings of 'monogamy' and 'polygamy'. Write a brief essay about marriage customs in an ethnic group which is different to your own.

The middle-aged

'It's been a good life – so far!' Janice smiled. 'We raised four children. Hard work, but fun. We were always short of money. I worked part-time to help out. They've left home now and we were looking forward to having the place to ourselves – the empty-nest syndrome, they call it. Peace and quiet, I call it. Being able to spend time and money on ourselves for a change!'

Then her face grew sad. 'But this new technology. We've both lost our jobs. What's more, his poor old mother – her health is failing so we've taken her in. I mean, that's what families are for, aren't they? And our eldest – she's divorced and has no-one to care for the baby. Guess who's doing that! And you're not as strong as you were when you were young.'

She grinned, bravely this time. 'You think life's going to get easier when you're middle-aged. But look at us!'

Greta and Ken, both age 80, live in a small flat close to the family. Their grandchildren visit daily to make sure they are all right.

Michael, age 15, enjoys his grandmother's company. She does all the household chores, and is there to greet him after school.

Maureen, age 17, turns the music up loud to annoy her grandfather. She dislikes him because he's always ill and her mum is worn out looking after him.

There are over one million carers in Britain – people who look after their older relatives. The majority of carers are daughters or daughters-in-law who are no longer young themselves.

Seventy per cent of people over the age of 65 live with their families. Twenty-four per cent live independent lives in their own homes.

1 What is meant by 'the empty-nest syndrome'? Describe the kind of life style Janice hoped for in middle age. Why do you think she longed for it so much?

2 Working in groups, imagine a day in her life now. Create a list of some of the work she will have to do during one period of 24 hours.

3 Do you agree with her statement, 'that's what families are for'? Why?

4 Choose one of the scenes pictured above, and role-play **a** positive and **b** negative family interaction.

The elderly

A group of students wanted data (information) on the number of their grandparents still living. They did a class survey by asking how many students had:

A no grandparents
B one grandparent
C two grandparents
D three grandparents
E four or more grandparents
F don't know

The answers they gave were:

C	F	D	D	E	B
E	A	E	A	B	C
D	D	C	E	A	D
D	C	D	E	D	E
E	D	E	D	C	D

They presented their findings as follows:

No. of grandparents	A	B	C	D	E	F
No. of students	3	2	5			

Copy out and complete this table.

They could have presented their findings like this:

3 students had no grandparents still living
2 students had one grandparent still living
5 students

Complete this presentation.

Is the second method quicker or slower than the first method? Does it use more or less space? Is it harder or easier to understand? Which method of presenting the data do you prefer? Why?

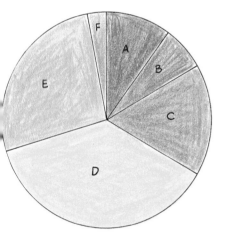

Key
A: no grandparents
B: one grandparent
C: two grandparents
D: three grandparents
E: four or more grandparents
F: don't know

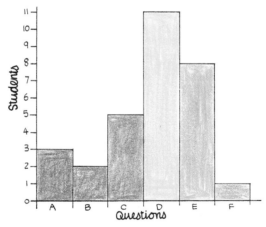

Key
A: no grandparents
B: one grandparent
C: two grandparents
D: three grandparents
E: four or more grandparents
F: don't know

The same data can be presented as a pie chart, and as a bar chart (or histogram).
In most surveys, there are usually a few 'don't knows'. Here, some family members may have lost touch. When you do any survey, do not try to insist on answers from the 'don't knows'. Be polite. Be sensitive to the feelings of others. Do not waste their time.

1 How many students took part in the class survey?
2 Collect your own data on the number of grandparents still living.
3 Present this data in as many forms as you can.
4 Some people consider surveys an invasion of privacy.

Discuss this statement.

Life expectancy

Slums like this have been cleared.

Life expectancy is the average time people can expect to live. One of the things on which it depends is the year in which people are born.

A 1950 class survey of grandparents still living showed:

No. of grandparents	A	B	C	D	E	F
No. of students	7	12	6	2	0	3

Compare these data with those of your own survey from the previous page. What conclusion, if any, can you draw from the comparison? Explain the reasons for your conclusion.

In Britain in the seventeenth century, life expectancy was only 35 years. This was partly due to high infant mortality (the death of babies in the first year of life). Today, life expectancy is 77 years for women and 70 for men. If there are grandchildren, a woman can expect to live 23 more years after the birth of her last grandchild; a man, 14 years. Why women live longer than men is not fully understood.

The population of Britain, as in all western countries, is growing much older: life expectancy has increased, so there are more people living to greater ages.

---

1 Do you think it likely there are now many more great-grandparents still living? Why? Devise a way to find out if your hypothesis (guess) is correct.
2 Name the stages in the life cycle when people are likely to be dependent on others for their physical needs (see p. 25). What impact do you think the great change in life expectancy has on family resources?
3 Do an individual study on the effects of poor living conditions on individual health in the nineteenth century.

Better health care is more widely available.

Sanitation has improved.

Further work on Chapter 2

1 Visit a nursery or play-group to observe the interaction between the adults and children. Do you think it is easy to be a role model? Why?
2 Teenagers may deliberately choose a role model while they are searching for their adult identity. Which values would you look for in a role model?
3 Study the chart below and answer the following questions:

Population aged 65+ (in thousands)						
Year	all 65+	% of pop.	all 75+	% of pop.	all 85+	% of pop.
1901	1734	4.7	507	1.4	57	0.15
1951	5332	10.9	1731	3.5	218	0.45
1981	7985	15.2	3052	5.7	552	1.03
Estimates for the future based on today's number of elderly						
2001	8546	15.2	4005	7.1	1029	1.8
2021	10005	17.6	4335	7.7	1202	2.1

a What was the total number of people aged 65+ in i 1901, and ii 1981?
b What was the total number of people aged 75+ in the same years?
c What is the total estimated number of people aged 85+ in the year 2001?
d In 1901, what percentage of the population was i 65+, ii 75+, and iii 85+?
e State the percentages for these age groups in 1981.
f What are the estimated percentages for these age groups in the year 2001?
g 'Who cares for the carers?' Contact the National Council for Carers and their Elderly Dependents, and do an individual study on your findings.

4 Your role in the home can be described as:
  i your relationship with your brother or sister.
  ii the part you play in family life at home.
  iii the way you behave. *(Welsh Joint Education Committee)*
5 Briefly explain *two* ways in which parents can influence children to take up certain sex roles and give examples of each.
6 Research has shown that elderly people like to continue living in a home of their own as long as possible. Discuss why this should be. *(London and East Anglian Group)*
7 Why is it impossible to state the exact age at which a baby will walk?
(Southern Examining Group)

Now look again at the objectives at the beginning of the chapter, and check that you have achieved them.

3 *The changing family*

By the end of this chapter, you should be able to:

- analyse more difficult statements.
- interpret more advanced data.
- consider the value of relationships.
- acknowledge the place of technology in change.

- understand the impact of change in women's roles.
- consider some effects of change on family values.

The family

What do the groups in each of these three sets of photographs have in common that makes them families?

What is a household?

A household is:

a any group of people who live together and share household expenses, and
b any person living in a home of his or her own (including rented housing).

In this book, the words 'family' and 'home' refer to any kind of household group.

---

1 Using resources, look up and write down the meanings of: spouse, sibling, and cohabitee.

2 Using resources, list as many groups as you can think of who can be called 'kin'. Now divide your list into two columns for **a** people you are fond of, and **b** people who will help you in times of need. Do some people appear in both lists? Why?

3 Learn both the definitions of a household given above.

The structure of the family

Work out some of the relationships in this family tree.

The nuclear family is made up of mother, father, and at least one child who live together in one home. The extended family includes all other relations, whether they live in the same house, the same street, or very far away. Most people belong to at least two families in their life time – the one into which they are born, and the one they create when they grow up and leave home.

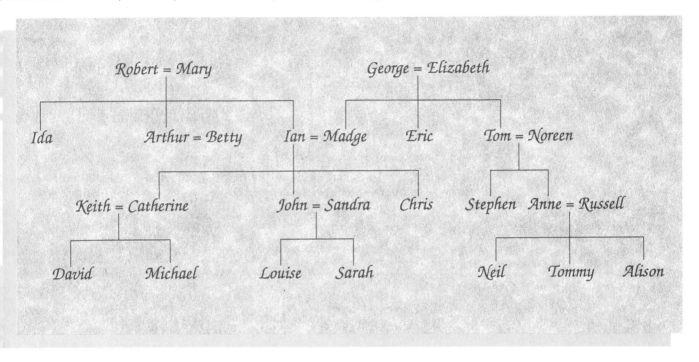

In the seventeenth century, because life expectancy in western countries was much less than it is today (see p. 34), widowhood and widowerhood were common, and children were often raised in one-parent homes. Remarriage for the third, fourth or fifth time was not unusual. Children frequently had step-parents, step-siblings, half-siblings, and in-laws, some of whom they hardly knew.

Analyse the chart in detail. What are the most noticeable trends? What conclusions can you draw from the chart as to the probable future trends in family life?

Within the different family structures are further differences, such as:
- the happy family and the unhappy,
- the poor family and the well-off,
- the employed family and the unemployed, and
- the rural, the suburban, and the urban family.

People in households in Britain: by type of household and family in which they live

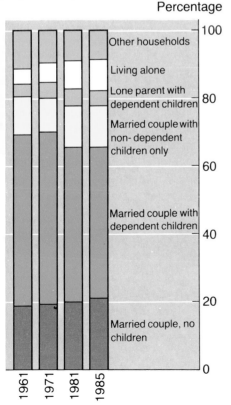

1 Cliff lives with his sister, mother, second cousin, and grandfather. Does he live in a nuclear or an extended family?

2 Find out where **a** rural, **b** suburban, and **c** urban families live. Which type is your family?

3 Which of the further differences in families do you consider most important? Be prepared to discuss your choice in class.

4 To a large extent, family structure depends upon the society people live in.

Do you agree with this statement? Why?

The value of relationships

Support is like these props, which hold up a damaged tree. In what way can friends or family help support damaged feelings?

An American survey in 1976 asked over 100 000 people to list in order of priority the things which made them most happy. These are called **positive life events.** The data are shown on a scale of 0 to 100.

Positive life events	Males 21−	21+	Females 21−	21+
Getting married or engaged	47.0	73.5	71.3	71.4
Falling in love	75.7	72.9	87.0	73.1
Birth of a child	41.4	57.8	60.5	70.1
Making a new friend	63.0	58.3	75.6	73.4

Taking a holiday, visiting family or friends, and recovering from a serious illness were also high on the scale. Getting a new job and winning a lot of money came much lower down.

Do you consider the above things are positive life events – that is, would they make you happy? Notice the gender differences in the ratings. Why do you think the birth of a child has the lowest score? Think about this carefully before you reply.

Draw up a list of your own positive life events and put them in your own order of priority on a scale of 0 to 100.

A British study in 1976 found the most stressful life events on a scale of 0 to 20 were:

Death of a child	19.5	Death of spouse	19.1
Being sent to prison	17.8	Serious money problems	17.6
Unfaithful spouse	17.3	Criminal court case	16.9
Getting divorced	16.3	Losing a job	15.9

Look up the meanings of the word **stress**. Under the headings 'physical', 'mental', 'emotional' and 'social', list the ways you feel before a stressful event, such as entering an exam. Compare your list with the rest of the class. Why do you think stress can affect any part of you? (See 'interdependence', p. 12.) Too much stress going on for too long damages people's health. It is a major factor in heart attacks, headaches, stomach upsets, anxiety attacks, and depression (loss of self-esteem).

1 Which of the stressful life events are to do with relationships? Identify some ways in which the other events might also affect a family.

2 Other research found that teenagers and widowed, divorced, and elderly people often feel lonely. What is the connection between this and family life?

3 It was also found that most teenagers stop feeling lonely in early adult life. What is likely to be the cause of this?

4 Discuss the function of support in a relationship, and the connection with the fact that, on average, lonely people are ill more often than people in close relationships.

Are relationships easy?

- 'I can do it', insists the 5-year-old, struggling with shoes.
- 'Let me decide!', insists the teenager, struggling to be adult.
- 'That's the way I am', insists the adult, struggling to be on time for work.

Autonomy means self-government. On reaching the age of majority, each person has the right to govern (rule) her or himself. Within certain limits, people are free to choose the way they behave. They then take full responsibility for the choices they make.

The family is an autonomous group in society. But families work best when there is co-operation between the members. Each person has to fit his or her needs into the family's needs. At times, this is difficult. There are bound to be conflicts of interest. If each person co-operates, these conflicts can be sorted out.

Happiness in marriage

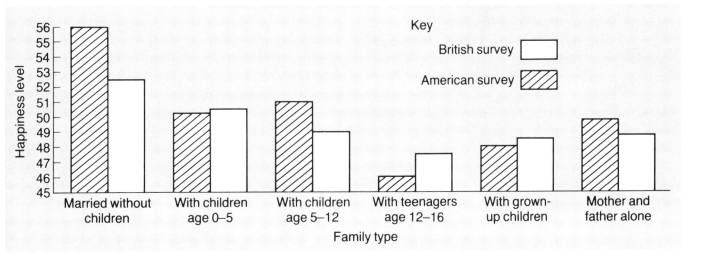

- The low point in family happiness happens when the teenager's natural struggle for autonomy conflicts with the parent's natural anxiety about the adolescent's future.

Do you agree with this statement? Why? At what stage of life are the parents? What kind of problems might they be having (p. 32)? Name the stages of dependency. Do you long to be independent (autonomous)?

As the teenager becomes an adult, co-operation and affection return. One survey found that over 55 per cent of young women said that their mother was now their best friend.

Are spouses interdependent? Make a list of some of the things they are likely to depend on each other for. Early marriages tend not to last. Could there be any connection between this and the need for independence? What about early parenthood? How might a young person who longed for independence feel about becoming a parent too soon?

---

1 What is meant by 'co-operation between family members'? Give one example of family co-operation you know, and respect.

2 Which data show that having children brings worries and problems as well as happiness? Try to name several kinds of stress new parents are likely to face.

3 Why do you think grandparents (mother and father alone) are happier on their own? What kind of stresses might there be when grown-up children live at home?

4 To some extent, we are all dependent.

Discuss this, in relation to the changing roles in the life cycle.

Investigating technology in the home

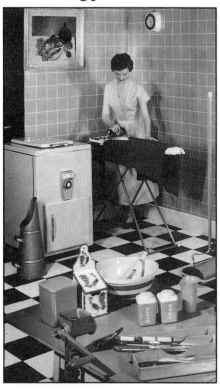

Technology is the application of practical science and its products, especially engines and machines.

Collect: a paring knife, a blender, a vacuum cleaner, a steam iron, etc. Plan, carry out and evaluate an investigation (see p. 15) into the advantages and disadvantages of working with one of the above and its old-fashioned equivalent. Some factors to consider include:

a the time involved.
b the energy involved.
c the costs involved.
d the skills required.

e any health risks.
f the safety factors.
g the standard of hygiene involved.
h general effectiveness.

'In my day, a woman's place was in the home.'
'Women are frail creatures, not fit for a man's work.'

How much physical effort is involved in the 'woman's work' in the kitchen on the left? Do you consider a woman's place is in the home? Why?

1 What do you think is meant by **'quality of life'**, as shown in these two pictures? Working in groups, list all the changes in material resources you can find.
2 The quality of life includes non-material resources. Do you think technology can contribute to people being more or less happy in their relationships? Why?

3 Change usually happens first in material resources. This produces a later change in non-material values.

   Analyse this statement in relation to 'a woman's place'.

Social change

In 1970, the Equal Pay Act was passed. It was updated in 1984. What does this Act mean? It was followed in 1975 by the Sex Discrimination Act. Using resources, look up the word '**discrimination**', and create your own definition. The Equal Opportunities Commission (EOC) was set up with legal powers to enforce both these Acts. The EOC's function is to make sure that jobs and life in general are more equal between women and men.

It is unlawful to discriminate on the grounds of sex in:

- pay – women and men have a right to equal pay for broadly similar work.
- terms of employment – women and men have a right to equal working hours, holidays, and bonuses.
- career prospects – women and men have a right to an equal chance at promotion.
- marital status – married women and men have equal employment rights with single people.
- advertising – job descriptions must be for both sexes.
- education – the same choice of subjects and career advice must be available for male and female students.
- housing – provision of homes must be equally available.
- finance – credit, mortgage, or loans must be offered on equal terms.
- goods, services, and facilities – these must be equally provided.

In 1976, the Race Relations Act made it unlawful to discriminate against any person because of race, colour, or nationality at birth. This is to help people from different ethnic groups in such areas as employment, housing, and so on.

All these Acts are trying to stop one group of people being unfair to another group. Which group of people was discriminated against by both sex and race? What effects might these Acts have in the home, and why?

1 Rita and Jim are doing broadly similar work in a clothing factory. Rita has a shorter lunch break than Jim; she receives less pay; she will be sacked if she marries or becomes pregnant. List the ways in which the factory is behaving unlawfully.

2 Rita's friend, Shaun, says there is no point in making a fuss. Do you agree with Shaun, and why?

3 Is the Equal Pay Act working? Turn to p. 75 for some recent data on this. Comment on your findings. Make a connection between the work on this page and that on p. 18. Discuss.

4 As an individual study, investigate what Rita can do to make her job equal. Contact the EOC or your local council.

New family roles

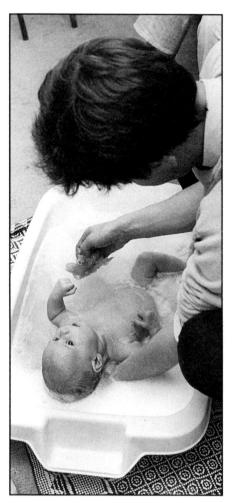

Many women today have dual careers. They raise their families and earn money in full- or part-time jobs outside the home. Anyone who works outside the home is called **economically active** (earning money). A full-time home-maker is called **economically inactive** – what does this mean? These rather clumsy words are meant to raise the status of the home-maker; to acknowledge that running a family and home is active, hard work which is unpaid.

Some mothers give top priority to their parenting role. Instead of having a dual career, they choose to stay at home and raise their families. This means they lose the rewards of a pay packet and the companionship of friends at work. What other rewards do you think they might gain instead?

● Today's fathers share in the work of childcare.

How could you find out if this statement is true?

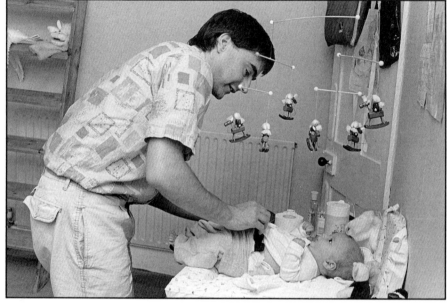

A case study

Beth and her partner are **cohabitees**. Their baby was unplanned and Beth is unhappy at the thought of having to give up her career for childcare. Her partner persuades Beth it is better for the baby if she stays at home. Beth agrees, but finds she cannot interact happily with the baby – it reminds her of the career she has lost and the happy times she had at work. She thinks her partner should stay at home, as he earns far less than she does. Beth does not explain this to him as she is afraid he will be cross.

Do you think either Beth or her partner is being fair to the other? Why? Discuss Beth's situation, and the quality of care she is likely to give her new baby. What other options can you suggest she might try?

---

1 Working in groups, draw up a list of some activities the average home-maker with three children, ages 1, 4, and 12, will undertake in one morning. List them in the order you think they might be done. Now, roughly estimate the time they are likely to take. From your findings, discuss some further reasons why mothers may choose to stay at home while their children are very young.

2 Do you think the status of the full-time home-maker should be raised? Why?

The one-parent family

About 160 000 divorces happen every year in the UK. In 1986, about 44 per cent of divorcing couples were childless – what percentage had offspring? It is estimated that one in four children will be in a one-parent family at some stage of their lives.

A case study

The Kroners have two children, ages 6 and 2. Their seven-year marriage is unhappy. Both parents are trying to decide on their priorities. Should they:

a put their own needs first and get divorced?
b stay together for the sake of the children?

● There are no 'wrong' or 'right' answers.

Analyse this statement.

The children of a divorce may live with either parent, or with another family member. The judge takes their welfare as the top priority. Where possible, older children may decide which parent they will live with. Is change easy (p. 20)? What kind of loss happens to a child when parents divorce? Is it likely that divorce is a very stressful event in a child's life? Why?

Mr Kroner was earning £350 a week. Mrs Kroner was a full-time home-maker. She was granted custody of the children and awarded **maintenance** – money for their financial support. Mr Kroner has moved out of the family home. What extra costs does he face? What happens to the material resources of the whole Kroner family after the divorce?

Some problems of one-parent families include:

a lack of sufficient funding.
b lack of good pre-school facilities.
c lack of company, support, time, and energy.

Mr Kroner remarries and has a baby by his new wife. She already has three children and no means of supporting them, as her ex-husband has left the country. The first Mrs Kroner is looking for good day-care facilities for her younger child so she can get a job, but can find none. Her older child hates being a half-sibling to the new baby, and step-sibling to the three children. He refuses to visit his father, truants from school and fights with his mother. Both families need support from the community (see Chapter 4).

➜

1 Investigate the different kinds of day-care facilities for pre-school children in your area.

2 Write about some of the stresses suffered by one-parent families. Contact: Gingerbread, and the National Council for One-Parent Families.

Disability in the family

About 3 per cent of the population aged 0 to 16 years is handicapped. Some handicaps are very mild, and do not slow down or interfere with a child's ability to grow and develop. They do not affect a child or older person's quality of life.

The definition of a serious handicap is a continuing disability of the body, mind, or emotions. This means the handicap is unlikely to get better and does affect the milestones of growth and development. It also affects the person's quality of life.

Collect: different screw-top jars, tin-openers, heavy saucepans, a toothbrush in bubble packaging, nuts in a vacuum pack, a milk carton, and medicine containers (including the child-proof kind). Plan, carry out, and evaluate an investigation into the ways in which modern packaging of foods and other goods can affect the quality of life of a disabled person. (Might it help if you stiffen the fingers of one hand while actually carrying out the plan? Why?)

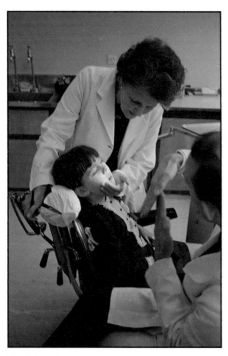

This little girl stammers, but she will probably soon grow out of it.

This little boy has cerebral palsy. He cannot control the constant movements of his limbs.

1 Working in groups, suggest ways in which a packaging of your choice could be made more accessible to people with disabilities.

2 Write a letter to your local Genetic Counselling Clinic asking them for information on which handicaps can be inherited.

3 Do an individual study on one of the following conditions in children: partial sight or hearing, diabetes, cerebral palsy, Down's syndrome.

Violence in the family

The sad truth of family violence

WOMAN STABS HUSBAND

Accused of murdering his wife

LIFE SENTENCE FOR KILLING BABY JEMMA

People can be cruel to each other with words or actions, inside families as well as outside. Domestic violence is often linked to stress, or a low self-image. In a way, it is passing on the hurt you feel about yourself to someone else – punishing the other person for your own painful feelings. Analyse this by exploring **a** stress, and **b** low self-image through role-play.

Collect: press reports of family violence.

a Select two which might have been caused by the above factors.
b Create small plays of situations which could have led up to that violence.
c Role-play the scenes up to (but not including!) the violence.
d Discuss the stresses the violent person was under.
e Discuss what the person with a low self-image could have done instead of resorting to violence.

● In many cases of family violence, the violent person is in such a muddle about his or her own feelings as to be only partly aware of his or her wrongdoing.

Do you agree with this statement? Why?

However, there are a few sadists – people who enjoy giving pain. There are also people who sexually abuse children. The crime of incest (sexual intercourse between people who are closely related) is not new. Nor is the sexual abuse of a child by a person not related but well known to the child – a friend, a neighbour, or a step-parent.

Child abuse includes deaths, serious or moderate harm, and failure to thrive (p. 26) due to neglect. Neglect is not just lack of physical care for the child. It can also include lack of love, company, and happy feelings; too much criticism, coldness, and emotional starvation. Why do these things also affect a child's growth and development (pp. 12, 26)?

Sexually abused children find it difficult to talk about what is happening. Adults can teach them that the private areas of their body are not to be touched. All children need to know they have the right to say, 'No. That's not allowed. I am going to tell.'

---

1 A stranger has been molesting children in the park. Your sibling, aged 9, asks to play there with a friend before bedtime. Which of the following options would you choose, and why?

a Refuse, and tell him or her your parents would not allow it.
b Agree, as two children should be safe together.
c Distract your sibling by turning on the television set.
d Suggest you both play his or her favourite board-game instead.
e Agree, but frighten your sibling thoroughly first by talking about the child-molester.
f Go with your sibling and his or her friend, and join in their running-about games.
g Choose a different option which suits you both better.

2 Do an individual study on violence in the family. Contact the National Society for the Prevention of Cruelty to Children (NSPCC).

Fostering and adoption

Usually, Ranee was a loving mother. But her problems suddenly became so great she found herself shouting at the children non-stop. 'Next thing, I'll be hitting them. Or neglecting them,' she thought, 'and I'm not having that. But how can I sort my life out when I have to spend all my time looking after them?'

When families get into difficulties, their children can be **fostered** – boarded out. This gives the adults time to sort out their problems. Using resources, find and write out the definition of 'confinement'.

The words 'unsatisfactory home conditions' do not necessarily mean the adults are being cruel. They may be training for new work skills, going through a difficult divorce, or simply needing a break from childcare. 'Other circumstances' include older children who are in 'moral danger'. They may have fought with their families; run away from home; or committed – or be at risk of committing – various criminal offences.

Circumstances in which children came into care, 1977 and 1983

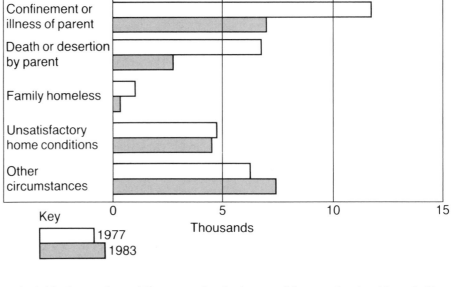

Key
1977
1983

A child who is adopted becomes a legal relation of the new family. About half a million children have been adopted over the last fifty years. The peak year was in 1968, with 27 000 adoptions. Just under 9000 adoptions took place in 1986. Couples who are **infertile** (unable to have children) find there are now few babies waiting to be adopted. This change is due to:
a improved family planning methods.
b more terminations of pregnancy (abortions).
c more single-parent families – more unmarried mothers bring up their own child.

Will you be my foster parent?

1 Graham, age 8, is being fostered while his mother is in hospital. He thinks he is being given away – **adopted**. How would you:
   a explain the difference to him?
   b comfort and reassure him?
   c evaluate your success at this?
   d find out his skills and plan to help him make his mother a 'get well' gift?
   What might be the value (if any) of Graham making a gift rather than buying one?

2 Plan a visit to the family planning clinic or write a letter asking a speaker to discuss birth control.

3 On remarriage, a step-parent may ask to adopt the child or children from the partner's first marriage. Discuss some stresses there may be between step-parents and step-children.

Further work on Chapter 3

1 Family life is not only about relationships. It is also about the time, energy, and skills needed to do a great deal of hard work. Write about some of the advances in technology which have taken some of the 'work' out of housework.

2 The role of each family member is no longer clearly defined. Analyse this statement, and discuss some stresses changes in roles can bring.

3 Social changes can be brought about by technological and scientific advances. Some families benefit from them; others find they bring great stress.

   Discuss these statements.

4 Draw a circle round the people listed below who can be described as *kin*.
   neighbours (not related by blood or marriage)
   aunts
   mothers
   cousins
   grandfathers
   friends   *(London and East Anglian Group)*

5 Suggest *one* cause of conflict in the home between parents and teenagers.
                                                              (Welsh Joint Education Committee)

6 Give one example of a physical handicap.
   Give one example of a mental handicap.
   State two problems which might be experienced by the family in:
      physical handicap
      mental handicap

7 What is a 'family'?   *(Northern Examining Association)*

8 What is meant by the term 'nuclear family'?
   Define 'joint custody'.
   Define 'care and control'.
   Define 'access'.   *(Southern Examining Group)*

Now look again at the objectives at the beginning of the chapter, and check that you have achieved them.

Community support

By the end of this chapter, you should be able to:

- understand the need for community support.
- know something of the work of local authorities.
- recognize the interdependence of society and families.
- accept the need for participation in community life.

The welfare services

A welfare state is one in which the government is mainly responsible for looking after the needs of its citizens. In Britain, the government has a legal obligation to provide services such as health care, education, housing, social security, and public health. These services are called **statutory**, as they have been passed by law (statute). Each citizen has a right to them. The government departments responsible include:

- the Departments of Health and of Social Services (formerly one department, the DHSS) – responsible for the National Health Service (NHS), social services.
- the Department of Employment – responsible for Jobcentres, paying unemployment benefit.
- the Department of Education and Science (DES) – responsible for schools, colleges.
- the Department of the Environment – responsible for housing, public health.
- the Home Office – responsible for community relations, law and order.

The money to finance (pay for) the welfare state comes from the people, in taxes and National Insurance contributions (p. 89). The people depend upon the government to provide their welfare needs. This is another example of interdependence – each group depends upon and supports the other. A few people try to evade their taxes; to get away with not paying them. Tax evasion is a serious offence.

Decision making and consequences

1 Do you think it right that people are forced to pay taxes? Before you make a decision, you need to look at the consequences of that decision. The consequences of being caught in tax evasion are **a** an extremely heavy fine, or prison, and **b** having to pay all the back taxes which are owed. Now think of the consequences to an individual who is not caught evading taxes – what are they? Now study the above pictures and discuss what some of the consequences would be if everybody got away with evasion. And the final question – are you prepared to accept those consequences? Why?

2 Do you value the welfare state? Why?

Some welfare needs

A	1971	1981	1986	1991	2001	2011	2025	Social and economic needs
People aged:								
Under 1	120	97	100	109	101	95	101	Maternity services, health visiting, preventative medicine
1–4	127	94	100	108	110	98	105	Day care, nursery education
5–15	121	113	100	97	110	104	101	Compulsory education
16–19	85	105	100	84	80	92	78	Further and higher education, training employment
15–44 (females)	86	95	100	100	95	91	89	Maternity services
20–49	90	94	100	105	101	99	94	Employment, housing, transport
50–59/64[1]	109	104	100	98	115	123	130	Pre-retirement training, early retirement
60/65[2]–74	98	102	100	99	94	107	122	Retirement pensions
75–84	73	90	100	105	109	106	132 }	Retirement pension, health care, home helps, sheltered
85 or over	68	84	100	124	164	186	191 }	housing, retirement homes

[1] 59 for females, 64 for males
[2] 60 for females, 65 for males

Source: Social Trends 18

B	Age	Males	Females
	0–1	578	472
	1–4	218	192
	5–15	136	123
	16–24	140	136
	25–44	154	160
	45–64	236	225
	65–74	498	454
	75+	945	1159

(Data do not include maternity costs.)

The number 100 in the 1986 column is called an index. It acts as a base on which to compare past and future needs. It is used to make **projections** (estimates) about future needs, based on the changes in the population of different age groups. Make a connection between the above age groups and the stages of the life cycle (p. 25).

To use the National Health Service, you must first be registered with a family doctor. Other services provided by the NHS include sight, hearing, and speech tests; family planning; child health care; and school medical care. Health education officers (HEOs) are an important resource for health information.

Chart B shows the annual costs of NHS by age and sex in 1984, in £s per person.

1 From chart A, answer the following:
  a Was the birth rate expected to rise between 1986 and 1991? Name three welfare needs of the 0–4s.
  b How old now are the children who were born in 1971? Which welfare services are they likely to use in 2001?
  c In 1984, 702 000 babies were born. Is this more, or less, than in 1971? The 'baby boom' of the 60s ended in the early 70s. Which data show this? What is happening to the number of schools needed now, and why?

2 From chart B, answer the following:
  a Which two age groups cost most in health care? Why do you think this is?
  b Which seems to be the 'healthier' sex? How do you account for the data changes in the 75+ group?
  c Some groups must pay towards dental and prescription charges. Using HEO resources, find out which groups, and the amount paid.

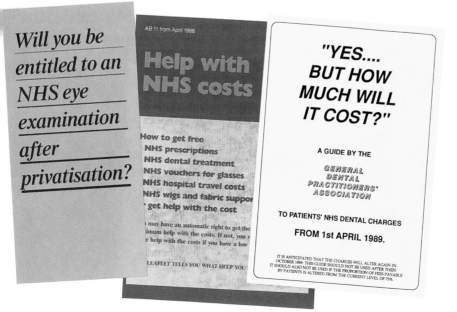

Some welfare benefits

Social security (SS) is money to provide people with a basic income when they cannot earn enough for themselves or their families, or when they have retired. These moneys are called **benefits**.

Find out and create your own definition of the word 'support'. Income support (IS) and family credit (FC) can be claimed by any person whose income and/or benefit is too low to live on. The social security officer must first be satisfied that the person's income is below an appropriate level. Some people find this offensive or embarrassing – why do you think it is required?

Collect: leaflets on various benefits.

a Choose child, maternity, or one-parent family benefit. Find out how much it is worth, how often and where it is paid, what conditions are attached to receiving it, and any reasons why the payments may be stopped. Write up your findings and be prepared to present the information in class.

b Do you consider your chosen benefit is enough to live on? Why? What further help can an individual or family apply for if the payments are not adequate?

The poverty trap

Before the major overhaul of the social security system in April 1988, some families in low paid work were worse off than if they had been on full unemployment benefits. An extra £1 in earnings could lead to a big increase in taxes and a drop in benefits. Families with children and single parents were often the worst affected. Does the system now help people in low paid work more effectively?

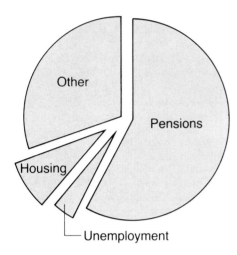

Expenditure on social security benefits, 1987–8

For more information, dial 0800 666555.

1 Which is the largest group of people to receive social security benefits? What are these benefits called? Is this group likely to get larger or smaller in the next twenty years? What effect do you think this change in a population group is likely to have on the future cost of the welfare state?

2 Find and write about the conditions for statutory sick pay.

3 Look up the meaning of the word 'benefit'. Do you consider it an accurate description of a pension? Why?

What is a community?

One sort of community is a group of people living in one area. In Britain, the area for each community is managed (run) by its own **local authority.** The local authority has a statutory duty to look after the welfare of the community by providing the following services:

a your personal needs – medical and dental care, housing, schools and career guidance, and personal social services.

b your protection needs – police, fire, ambulance, coastguard, and consumer protection.

c a healthy environment – street cleaning, refuse collection, public toilets, control of pollution, and so on.

d leisure and other amenities – museums, playgrounds, parks, libraries, sports centres, and so on.

Collect: a street map of your neighbourhood.

a Mark in any local authority services you already know.

b Using the scale, work out the distance of these services from your home. Which of these services do you or your family use?

c Using the school as your starting point, work out the distance to the nearest hospital, the town or county hall, the junior school, the library, and a park with swings. Discuss the purpose of becoming familiar with your own community.

1 Find some local authority services in the above picture.

2 Plan to find out more about your community. You will have to use your own resources of time, energy, comfortable walking shoes, notepad, and so on. Where do you think might be the best place to start, and why? A model of the community could be made as a special assignment.

Community care for disabled people

The Chronically (long-term) Sick and Disabled Persons Act states that each local authority has a statutory duty to:

a keep a register of all sick and disabled people.

b keep them informed of all the help they can get.

c provide meals inside or outside the home, if needed.

d provide a home help, health visitor, home nurse, and ambulance, if needed.

e provide a telephone, pay the rental, and add special attachments, if needed.

f provide a television set and pay for the licence, if needed.

g provide a radio, if needed.

h provide holidays, if needed.

i provide day-care and luncheon clubs, if needed.

j check public buildings have ramps for wheelchairs, suitable toilets, and so on.

Pick out those services which are provided 'if needed'. These are not statutory – they are called **permissive.** This means the social worker has permission to decide whether or not they are really needed. Do you think it a sensible idea to have these services as permissive? Why? (See p. 58.)

Home adaptations – a stair lift

Personal aids – an adapted home computer

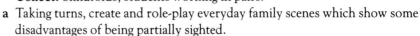

Collect: blindfolds, students working in pairs.

a Taking turns, create and role-play everyday family scenes which show some disadvantages of being partially sighted.

b Notice and record any behaviour changes. Was the interaction between you and your partner too sensitive, insensitive, appropriate? Comment on your findings.

c What human resources might a partially sighted person need to develop in order to cope?

d Name some material resources which might improve the quality of life in a blind person's kitchen.

---

1 Investigate adaptations of public buildings in your local community. Which privately owned buildings, such as shops, offices, and homes, have made these adaptations? In what ways do slopes and ramps also help **a** a new parent, and **b** an elderly person? Why?

2 Name one television programme and one radio programme which you think are likely to stimulate the mental needs of the disabled.

3 Do an individual study on one special aid for a disabled person. Contact the Royal Society for Disability and Rehabilitation.

Sheltered housing

Sheltered housing is the name for small units of bungalows or flats which are **purpose built** (specially designed) for the elderly or disabled. The homes are grouped together and **wardens** look after the residents. At night, there are alarms to call the warden if a resident gets into difficulties. Government guidelines lay down standards of space, design, heating, and fittings. These include:

a non-slip surface on all floors.
b heating at 21°C throughout.
c rise of stairs not too steep.
d firmly fixed stair rails on both sides.
e stairs narrow enough so both rails can be held.
f lever handles on doors, not knobs.
g grip rails for toilet and bath.
h door to toilet and bathroom open outward.

1 Investigate mobility. Measure the width and rise of some stairs. Stiffen one leg at the knee. Timing yourself, climb the stairs, then descend. Which is more difficult, to go up or down? Did you need the rails? Were they too far apart?
Time yourself again walking normally, and compare the results. From your findings, comment on some of the government guidelines above.
2 Working in pairs, devise a task to show the need for either **f**, **g**, or **h**.
3 Investigate sheltered housing. Plan your visit first (p. 27). Check the site for lack of noise. Is it purpose built or adapted? Is it far from or near the local community? Is there a garden and/or a space for taking exercise? How can you find out whether the inside fittings conform to government guidelines? Note the furnishings and fabrics, and kitchen equipment – are they attractive, easy to clean, and fit for their purpose? Collect information on the safety factors. Draw a plan of the layout – is there easy access to all the rooms?

Chat with the residents. Are they encouraged to shop, prepare meals, and generally live independent lives? Ask their opinion of the accommodation. Find out who is responsible for running the home and what social functions are available.

When you return to school:
a Discuss some ways in which the material resources met human needs.
b Select one negative aspect of your findings and suggest a solution to the problem. Be prepared to discuss this in class, giving reasons for your choice.
c Evaluate your investigation in terms of **i** any adaptations to your plan, **ii** the success of your interaction with a resident or staff member, and **iii** the amount of information you gained.
d Relate the results of your investigation to the care of a disabled child in the family. Discuss under the separate topics of food, textiles, family, and home.

Some community resources

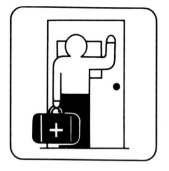

Health visitors are nurses with special training in family health. They visit **vulnerable groups** in the community – pre-schoolers, the disabled, and the elderly. Why are these groups called 'vulnerable'?

Home nurses visit the elderly and sick to give drugs, change dressings on wounds, and give general nursing care.

Social workers have special training in personal problems. They help to sort out practical, personal, and social problems.

Home helps do housework and shopping for the housebound. Without their help, many families could not stay in their own homes.

Ambulance crews take people to hospital. Many have training in First Aid techniques.

Childminders must be registered with the social services, who assess individually how many children each minder may care for.

Trained children's nurses provide care for babies over 6 months old. Day nurseries open long hours to help working parents.

Teachers work in schools for children with special educational needs, whose handicap is too disabling for regular school.

Physiotherapists work with the victims of road accidents, and with people recovering from strokes, to regain mobility (use of limbs).

Chiropodists help the elderly to stay mobile by treating their foot problems.

---

1 Terry crashes his motor bike and loses mobility in his legs for a year. He shares a flat with two friends in full-time jobs. List all the community resources Terry will need until he is mobile again.

2 Advances in science and technology, together with changes in roles, make it difficult for the family to provide for the whole range of human needs. Society helps out with human and material resources.

Discuss this statement.

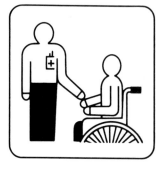

The personal social services

The personal social services are for individuals – not for large groups. For example, education is a service for all children; it becomes a personal social service when a disabled child needs a special kind of wheelchair to travel on the bus to school. The aim of the personal social services is to improve the quality of life for the individual. They also try to keep families together and the elderly or disabled in their own homes.

A case study

Wendy and her three children are a one-parent family. She lives with her mother, who is recovering from an operation. Her young baby has Down's Syndrome, and needs constant care. Her divorced husband has stopped paying maintenance. Wendy is exhausted from coping with her problems. She goes to the doctor saying that she cannot sleep.

a Why cannot Wendy sleep, through she is tired all the time?

b What social security benefits is Wendy entitled to?

c Is money alone likely to improve her quality of life? Why?

A social worker is put on Wendy's case. The baby is given a day nursery place, and Wendy's mother attends a day centre for elderly folk. What relief from stress do you think this brings Wendy? She is also provided with new bedding, clothes for the children, a washing machine, and help with heating costs.

Wendy is encouraged to join a local group of single parents. In times of stress, many people find the best support is to meet others with the same problems. Why do you think this is?

d List all the human needs the social worker is attempting to meet.

e Why is Wendy likely to be more effective as an individual and as a parent if these needs are met?

Had Wendy been cruel to her children, they would have been **taken into care**. That means putting them in a 'place of safety' – a foster parent's or children's home. If the social worker suspected abuse but there was no proof, the children would have been put on the **'at risk' register**. This means the family would be regularly visited by both the social worker and the health visitor.

Social Security and children in the care of a local authority

---

1 Using resources, find out how much it costs per week to keep:

a a baby at a children's home.

b a baby in a day nursery.

c a child in a foster home.

Discuss all the reasons why one aim of the personal social services is to keep people in their own homes.

2 You suspect a neighbour's child is suffering from abuse. What steps can you take to help (see above and p. 45)?

The voluntary services

The community uses paid workers to run its services, but there are never enough resources to go around. Anyone can participate in the life of the community by joining the voluntary services. You can become an unpaid helper, often working closely with local authority staff to improve the quality of life in the community.

Citizens Advice Bureau (CAB) is a free information service, often run by voluntary helpers. In 1985–6, they helped with over a million social security problems. They give advice on housing, family, personal, employment, and legal problems. Of their enquiries, 17 per cent were to do with consumer problems (Chapter 8).

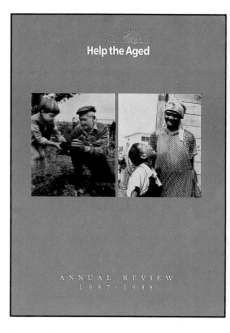

The Samaritans give a telephone service for people with personal problems, some of whom are unhappy enough to think of suicide. The service provides a 'listening ear'.

Age Concern and Help the Aged act as **pressure groups** (p. 58) to improve the quality of life for old people. They also offer practical help and advice.

The Physically Handicapped and Able-Bodied (PHAB) run social events to help both groups get together and enjoy themselves.

Community service volunteers (CSV) help young people to help others. Visits are arranged to a mental hospitals, where the young can be company for lonely and confused people, b homes for handicapped children, to help with play, meal times, baths, and bedtimes, c sheltered housing, to organize outings and entertainment for the elderly, d homes, to help people from abroad develop language skills, and e overseas projects, to help with famine relief or to organize a water supply.

1 Choose one of the following, or any voluntary service with a main office or local branch near you. Plan a visit and full investigation of its services: CAB, Shelter, Gingerbread, Young People's Counselling and Advisory Services, Save the Children, Alcoholics Anonymous, National Marriage Guidance Council, British Red Cross Society.

2 The voluntary services not only fill the gaps in the welfare state. They also meet a human need for helping others.

Discuss this statement.

Who pays for community support?

The government is responsible for collecting taxes and supporting the welfare departments (p. 48). How does the government get into power? What can you do if you do not like their policies – if, for example, you disagree with the way they spend your taxes? What age must you be? Find out the percentage of people who voted in the last general election.

The local authority raises money from the people in its area in a tax called a **community charge**. Most people over the age of 18 must pay the same amount. However, local services are so costly that the community charge does not cover all the expenses. The government helps out by giving back some of your taxes to the local authority as a **block grant**.

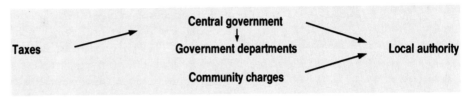

The local authority is made up of local people. They are called **councillors**, and are **elected** (voted into power) by the community every four years. But fewer people use their right to vote in local and county elections than in general elections. In many areas, the turnout of voters is well below 50 per cent.

Yet the decisions taken by a local authority directly affect the health and happiness of the community. They decide which services are most needed, which will get the most money and other resources, which will suffer cut-backs if there is not enough money to go around, and so on.

One local authority's expenditure for 1988–9

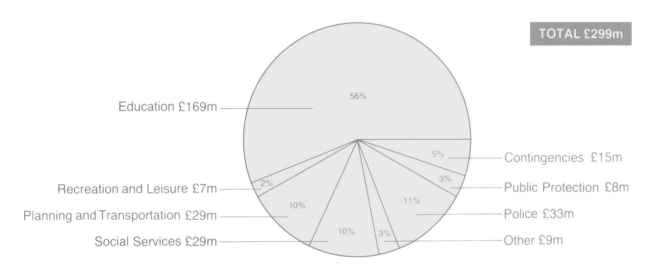

TOTAL £299m

- Education £169m — 56%
- Recreation and Leisure £7m — 2%
- Planning and Transportation £29m — 10%
- Social Services £29m — 10%
- 3%
- Contingencies £15m — 5%
- Public Protection £8m — 3%
- Police £33m — 11%
- Other £9m

Collect: a community charge bill.
Discuss the meaning and implications of its contents.

Collect: last year's data on the ways in which a local authority divides up its resources between the various departments.
a How much money is spent on actually running the local authority?
b How many staff are employed?
c Do a full class project on the work which is carried out at your town or county hall.

● The choices a local authority makes about spending community charges can improve the quality of life of individuals and families to a great extent.

Discuss this statement.

Taking part in community life

The road to better paths

Madam,
This year shows an increase of £1,000,000 in the County Council's budget for road maintenance. This increase was largely due to the Labour Group's insistence that the council has been failing in its duty to repair roads and footpaths properly for many years. Despite this increase the rise in rates will still be less than the level of inflation.

However, the Labour Group recognises that the county council must do more. We regret it has not been possible to provide more resources, but we will continue to try and improve the situation.

In the meantime residents in Marlborough Road, Park Road, Warwick Road, Gatteridge Street, Orchard Way, Bird Close, Leigh Grove, Prescott Avenue and others will be relieved to know that at least part of their footways will be relaid this year.

Should any other local resident feel that repairs to their road or footpath are needed then they should write to me or any other Labour councillor and we'll see if work can be arranged to put it right.
Jack Steer,
Labour Spokesman
Environmental Committee.

FURTHER to the comments of your correspondent on the alleged lack of leisure-time facilities in the town (issue February 16), why do we not maximise on the use of one of the most under-exploited facilities already exisiting in and around Banbury.

Pubs are nowat liberty to stay open all day, but it appears that seldom is their mid-shift clientele sufficient to justify doing so.

Surely the opportunity is there to provide a fuller service to attract customers. Provision of tea and coffee, with snacks and pastries, etc, would draw in ppers, tourists and passers-by. Money is made relatively easily by these means as a complementary service to the sale of alcohol, and many customers would appreciate the choice.

And why not attract customers by implementing a two-shift staffing system and organising a regular mid-morning or afternoon event — a quiz, a concert, a fashion show or a discussion group — so that the public house once again regains its former image as a versatile social centre for the inhabitants of the town? There must be enough shift

---

'I can't bear people who complain about things!'

Turn back to p. 52. Look at some of the services which are permissive. What happens if you really believe:

a your elderly parents need meals on wheels
b a friend with a handicapped child needs a holiday
c your housebound uncle cannot afford a television set

– and your social worker does not? Would you: shrug and say it is tough luck? believe the authorities always know what is best and do nothing? insist on having the person's case investigated?

The community charge is a new tax in place of local rates. The Ratepayers' Association was a **pressure group** which kept close watch over how their rates were spent. They put pressure on the local authority to improve their services. They also looked for ways to keep the costs of the rates down.

Individuals and families are not isolated (cut off) units in the community. They can participate strongly in the decisions taken by their local authority. They have the right to question, to argue, to object, and to insist on the support they need. In a perfect world, this would not be necessary. But do you think you are perfect, honestly? And if not, why do you think other people are?

Collect: the letters page from local press over four weeks.

a Cut out and study the complaints about local services.
b Group them according to their separate departments (p. 51).
c Do any services receive constant criticism? If so, which?
d Choose one criticism which is fairly easy to investigate, and find out all you can about it. Is there sufficient reason for the complaint? Why?
e Choose one thing about any community service which you think could, and should, be improved. Write a letter in which you **i** state what is wrong, **ii** give reasons for your criticism, **iii** suggest an improvement, **iv** give reasons for your suggestion, and **v** state the costs and any drawbacks there might be.

I'VE BEEN reading with interest the comments in the Oxford Mail about the "pornographic rubbish" on view at the Museum of Modern Art. The subjects of the painting could not be described as either — however the quality is another matter.

Sue Coe may have a problem if she thinks all men are brothel-creeping rapists but I think she has a bigger problem in the skill she shows as an artist — this sort of skill can be found in any second or third-form art class.

What I object to is the amount of time given to this exhibition. Britain is full of talented artists who are crying out for their work to be seen.

Perhaps David Elliott (director of MoMA) could find some of them and put some skill and content on the walls of MoMA.

M. J. KELLY
Coniston Avenue,
Headington

Social work has been chosen here as it is not too difficult to investigate. But any department can be poorly administered (run). The Commissioners for Local Administration investigate complaints of injustice caused by poor administration in local authorities in England, Scotland, and Wales.

---

1 Do you think more people should participate in local elections? Why?

2 Society is made up of institutions, some of which can help people, and some of which can harm them. Any service which affects your life needs to be explored, identified, and understood. Each person can develop resources to help him or her participate in community life.

Discuss this point of view.

Further work on Chapter 4

➦ **1 Collect:** information and a menu from Meals on Wheels.
   a List various groups of people needing this service.
   b Name various groups of people who supply the service.
   c Find out how the food is kept hot.
   d Select one meal and list the nutrients it contains. Do you consider them satisfactory? Why?
   e Find out the costs of the meal for one week for one person. Compare them with a rough estimate of the costs of a home help preparing the meals at a disabled person's home. Comment on your findings.
   f Do you consider the money spent on the Meals on Wheels service should be more, less, or the same? Why? What would be the consequences to your community charges if more money were spent? Are you prepared to accept those consequences?
   g Is the food presented in an appetizing manner? What suggestions would you make to add to the appeal of the meal without raising the costs?

2 Plan, prepare, cook, and deliver a meal to a person of your choice. Evaluate your work from beginning to end.

3 A nation which looks after the welfare of its children has its heart in the right place.

Discuss this statement. Then re-read p. 43 and the problems of the two Kroner families. List all the services which can offer support. Give as much detail as possible of **a** the financial, and **b** the practical support they are entitled to. What voluntary agencies might also be able to offer some solutions to the personal problems of the parents?

➦ **4** Do an individual study on the work of the Women's Royal Voluntary Service (WRVS).

5 Suggest ways in which elderly people may be helped with difficulties relating to all aspects of living at home as long as possible.
Briefly evaluate one of the ways you have suggested, in the light of course work.

(London and East Anglian Group)

6 Give the name of one voluntary group that offers assistance to one-parent families.
State *two* ways in which this group can help. *(Northern Examining Association)*

Now look again at the objectives at the beginning of the chapter, and check that you have achieved them.

INDIVIDUAL MEALS & SWEETS

Wiltshire meat and vegetables are the basis of the Company' large range of individual meals.

Nourishing traditional meals of Roast Beef and Yorkshire Pudding, Casserole of Lamb and Vegetables, Braised Liver and Onions, and Waldens' own Wiltshire Sausages in a rich gravy, are among the firm favourites.

Welfare Meals are in two sizes attractively presented in silver foils – simplicity itself for Meals on Wheels. From a choice of sweets, a substantial individual baked fruit bread pudding or a light lemon sponge make a well rounded meal.

Waldens' years of experience in the food industry ensure well-balanced nutritious meals.

5 *A healthy environment*

By *the end of this chapter, you should know:*

- the relationship between health and the environment.
- more facts about public hygiene.
- that it is people who produce pollution.

- the value of conservation.
- that changes in technology can increase and decrease pollution.

Pollution 1

Waste products from factories can pollute the environment.

In a health context, the **environment** means 'the conditions which influence growth and development'. A **pollutant** is any substance in the environment which harms living things. Environmental health officers monitor the level of pollution in the community.

Radiation

Natural radiation comes from the sun and outer space. It is at a low level and does not cause harm. Artificial radiation from nuclear power stations and X-rays is at a higher level and is therefore a carcinogen – that is, it can cause cancer. Radiographers and all staff working with radioactive material must be protected from the rays. Why do you think pregnant women are rarely given an X-ray?

Nuclear power stations use the energy from radiation to generate electricity. This produces radioactive waste which must be disposed of safely. It is dumped at sea in concrete and steel containers, or buried deep in the ground – a landfill. People have natural fears about the risk of a leak.

1 Karim has hurt his ankle, and wants an X-ray. Would you **a** rush him to the hospital, or **b** tell him to wait until the swelling either persists or goes down? Why? How would you ease his pain? Resource: First Aid manual.

2 When was the last radioactivity scare? What was it about? You may like to do a full class project on this topic.

3 Do an individual study on water pollution caused by **a** farm pesticides, or **b** factory waste.

Pollution 2

Smoke comes from the burning of fuels in homes and factories, and in the engines of cars and aeroplanes. Smoke contains particles of carbon dust which settle as a dirty film on the land, blackening the buildings and damaging people's lungs.

Sulphur dioxide is a choking gas, also produced by burning fuels. In damp air it forms sulphuric acid, which falls as **acid rain**. It can be carried some distance from the source. When it falls on towns, it corrodes metal and stone, and affects people's lungs. Britain is a major offender.

Carbon monoxide is a highly poisonous gas produced by petrol and diesel engines. It can cause headaches and stomach cramps in small doses. Why are people in homes near flyovers or busy roads at special risk?

Lead is also given off from cars' exhausts, when they are using leaded petrol, and is in some water pipes and types of paint. When lead enters the body, it cannot be broken down and removed. It collects and, if the level rises, it causes damage to the brain – especially in growing children. Plants growing by the roadside also contain lead.

Coal dust and asbestos are factory pollutants which damage workers' lungs. Asbestos is no longer used in new buildings, and it has been removed from the walls and ceilings of schools.

Decision-making pressures
A pressure group urged the government to reduce the amount of lead in petrol. One reason why lead is added is to prolong the life of the engine. An equally strong pressure group from the motor industry put up the following arguments: was the government aware of some of the consequences? For example, with a shorter engine life, fewer families would be able to afford to own a car. Manufacturers, delivering goods to the shops by lorry, might pass on the extra costs to the family. The price of public transport, aeroplane tickets, and parcels sent by post might all soar. Was the government prepared to accept these consequences? Were they aware that rising costs made the voters cross? And if a government loses popularity, what are the likely consequences at the next election?

1 Find out how many tonnes of poisonous gases Britain produced last year. Resource: *Social Trends*.
2 How many petrol stations now sell unleaded petrol, and how does its price compare with leaded petrol? Would you be prepared to pay more for everything, if necessary, so that the amount of lead in petrol could be reduced still further?

3 Decision making can involve human needs, material resources, values, priorities, goals, and conflicting choices all at the same time.

Discuss this statement.

Clean water

% of 4-year-olds with no tooth decay		
Year	Boys	Girls
1964	45	38
1971	65	74

Rain is collected in reservoirs and pumped to filtration plants. When it is clean, **chlorine** is added to kill off any germs. The purity (and taste) are tested before the water is pumped into huge sealed pipes called **mains**. These run under the roads, bringing clean water to homes and other buildings.

In 1964, **fluoride** was added to a city's water supply. Study the findings of two surveys into the health of children's teeth in that city, given on the left.

What conclusions can you draw about fluoride and dental health? If you were a councillor, would you vote to have fluoride added to the local water supply? Why?

Some citizens objected. They felt their rights to a clean water supply were being attacked. They feared that once one substance could be added to water, it might lead to other – perhaps less useful and more harmful – things being added without their consent.

a Discuss this point of view.
b Find out whether your water supply has added fluoride.

> **Collect:** rainwater, bottled water, two used tea towels, and some soap.
> a Make a copy of the chart below.
> b Wash towels separately and record your findings on the chart.

	Rainwater Y/N	Bottled water Y/N
Feels softer on the skin		
More energy needed to remove dirt		
Less rinsing needed		
Clinging scum left on sink		

As rain seeps down through the earth in chalk or limestone areas, it dissolves **calcium** and other minerals in the soil. These make water 'hard'. When hard water is heated above 60°C, the minerals settle out and are deposited as scaling in the pipe. Hard water is thought to be better for bone growth, and to protect against heart disease. Soft water absorbs lead from old pipes – modern pipes avoid this serious health risk.

> **Collect:** water, a heat source, and a thermometer.
> a Find out if water heated to 60°C feels hot enough for a bath.
> b How could you solve the problem of scaling in pipes?

Scaling inside a hot-water tank

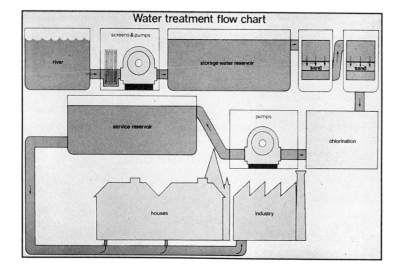
Water treatment flow chart

screens & pumps
river
storage water reservoir
sand   sand
service reservoir
pumps
chlorination
houses
industry

> 1 Collect advertisements for mineral water. Why is it called this? Why is rainwater soft?
> 2 Find out **a** what is used to stop a kettle scaling, and **b** the costs of installing a water softener in the home.
> 3 Name one advantage and one disadvantage of living in a hard water area.

Sewage disposal

Sewage is the name for liquid waste. It includes urine and faeces from the toilet, used water from sinks and baths, and liquid waste from factories. All sewage leaves through a trap; an S- or U-bend in a pipe. The fresh water acts as a seal, stopping any unpleasant odour (smell) from the drains coming back.

Collect: buckets of water.
You are in charge of twenty children and five parents at a play-group, and are told all water will be cut off for the next two hours.
a Devise a task to show how you can keep the children's toilets fresh and hygienic.
b Work out how many buckets you would fill with fresh water to meet the drinking and washing needs of the whole group.

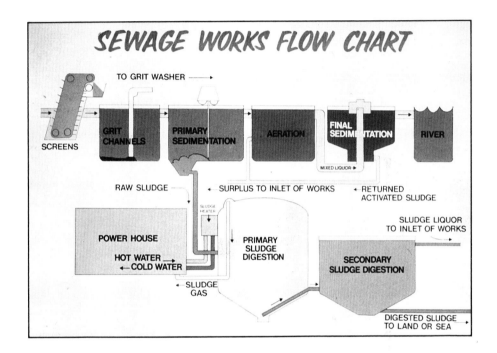

The liquid waste flows into sealed sewer pipes which spread under the street and lead to the sewer treatment works. The raw sewage passes through metal grills which remove rubbish – glass, rags, boxes, etc. The screened sewage goes into grit tanks, moving slowly to give the grit and heavy rubbish time to sink to the bottom. In the sedimentation tanks, it stays still to allow the solid waste – now called **sludge** – to separate out from the liquid. The top liquid goes into open biological filter tanks. Air and microbes break down the waste particles and destroy the harmful germs. The treated liquid is called **effluent**. It is pumped into rivers or the sea. Air and microbes are also used to destroy the germs in the sludge. The sludge is then dried, and some is used as fertilizer, but most is dumped in the sea.

Sanitation includes a clean water supply and the hygienic disposal of waste. **Cholera** is a serious water-borne disease which no longer affects western countries because of good sanitation. But it can be brought back from other countries by tourists and business travellers. If you were in a cholera area, would you **a** put ice-cubes in your drinks, **b** buy bottled water, or **c** eat fresh food washed in local water? Why?

---

  1 Find, then mark on the map of your community, three street manhole covers. What is their function?
2 Put the following in their correct order of use: sewage treatment works, trap, grit tank, biological filter, screening, sedimentation tank.

Refuse disposal

In 1987, the average British family dustbin held:
142 kg (312 lb) of paper – the remains of six trees!
141 kg (310 lb) of food waste
51 kg (112 lb) of metal
51 kg (112 lb) of glass
41 kg (90 lb) of plastic
Name three items made of each material that are used in the home.

Refuse is dumped at sea, burned in incinerators, or buried in landfills. Dumping pollutes beaches; burning produces ash and smoke; landfills waste precious land. Not only do we have more refuse, we now have plastic refuse which will not **degrade** (break down).

Recycling means saving things and using them again. In Britain, the amount of paper used each year destroys a forest the size of Wales. Over 1500 million empty drink cans which could be recycled are thrown away every year. It takes a great deal of energy to produce paper from trees, and cans from steel or aluminium. The more materials we use and throw away, the more we rob the earth of its natural resources.

Some local authorities provide metal, paper, and bottle banks. It is not cost efficient to collect refuse from each home, and many people do not use recycling banks. Suggest an answer to this problem.

Collect: items which would normally be thrown away.
a Work out ways in which each can be altered or restored to be of further use.
b Do you consider conservation an important issue? Why?

---

1 Investigate street refuse disposal.
  a Find out what kind of street bin is used. Do you consider it is **i** fit for its purpose, **ii** safe and hygienic, **iii** emptied often enough, and **iv** used by the people in the community?
  b Describe the state of the pavements **i** in the early morning, and **ii** in the late afternoon. Are there any 'black spots' – perhaps outside a cinema, a fast-food shop, or a school? If so, give reasons why.
  c Design a poster to encourage the use of street bins. When are the streets swept, and is this often enough?
  d Find out whether there are recycling schemes in your area.
2 David Attenborough has said, 'The world's resources are limited. It actually offends me morally to see vast quantities of a resource like paper just thrown away.'
  a What does 'offend morally' mean?
  b Do you waste natural resources, and why?
  c If everyone chose the same answer to **b** as you, what would be the consequences of this choice?
  d Are you prepared to accept these consequences?

Investigating household refuse

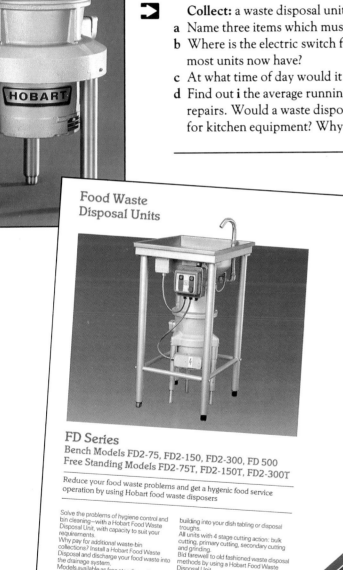

▶ **Collect:** metal and plastic dustbins, disposable plastic and paper sacks, and old books.
  a Half fill each container with books, and lift. Which was the easiest? the most difficult? the noisiest? the quietest?
  b If the containers had a heavier load, which might have burst? Why? How could you test this?

▶ **Collect:** damp refuse, and place it unwrapped in each container.
  a Cover containers and leave for two days. Which container is not suitable for damp refuse? Why? Safely dispose of the contaminated sacks.
  b Wearing a mask, scrub the dustbins with disinfectant. Was the task pleasant? What should be done with damp refuse? Why?

▶ **Collect:** a pile of old newspapers.
Devise a task to show that lining a dustbin also cuts down the need for scrubbing it out.

▶ **Collect:** a waste disposal unit, and its information sheet.
  a Name three items which must not be put in the unit. Why?
  b Where is the electric switch for the power? Why? What other safety factor do most units now have?
  c At what time of day would it be thoughtless to use the unit? Why?
  d Find out **i** the average running costs, and **ii** the cost of installation and service repairs. Would a waste disposal unit come high or low on your list of priorities for kitchen equipment? Why?

Food Waste Disposal Units

FD Series
Bench Models FD2-75, FD2-150, FD2-300, FD 500
Free Standing Models FD2-75T, FD2-150T, FD2-300T

Reduce your food waste problems and get a hygenic food service operation by using Hobart food waste disposers

Solve the problems of hygiene control and bin cleaning—with a Hobart Food Waste Disposal Unit, with capacity to suit your requirements.
Why pay for additional waste-bin collections? Install a Hobart Food Waste Disposal and discharge your food waste into the drainage system.
Models available as free standing units or for building into your dish tabling or disposal troughs.
All units with 4 stage cutting action: bulk cutting, primary cutting, secondary cutting and grinding.
Bid farewell to old fashioned waste disposal methods by using a Hobart Food Waste Disposal Unit.

▶
1 Examine a variety of other bins for use in the home. Keeping fitness of purpose in mind, choose one for the bathroom and one for the sitting room, giving reasons for your choice. Resources: shop, magazines.
2 Sharmin chose a wicker basket for the kitchen sink because she admired the weave. State your opinion of her choice.
3 How often is your household refuse collected? Is this frequent enough? If not, whom could you contact to make a complaint? Find out the correct way to dispose of an old settee.
4 You value the concept of recycling. State how you would hygienically sort and store household waste before taking it to the skip.
5 Monitor the contents of your household waste for a week, and answer the following exam question: Name four kinds of household waste. State, with reasons, how you could deal with each type.

(Southern Examining Group)

Pets, not pests

A house fly, a head louse, and a human flea

Flies spray food with saliva to soften it. Then they suck up the liquid food through their mouth tubes. They are attracted by the smell of decay, crawling around dirty toilets, dustbins, and refuse tips to lay their eggs. They fly from these highly infectious areas on to uncovered food in cafés, shops and homes.

Fleas and lice are blood suckers. They pierce the skin and inject saliva into the blood stream. This stops blood clotting, so it can be sucked up through their mouth tubes. Any disease the pest carries is injected straight into the blood stream. They live on rodents (rats and mice), domestic pets, and people.

Collect: various pesticides for flies, cockroaches, and mice.
a Study the label for instructions. Are they easy to understand?
b If using in the kitchen, what should you first do?
c What other health precautions would you take? Why?
d Why is it important to destroy the eggs of insect pests as well?
e How will you dispose of the empty containers? Why?

Many health studies show that having a pet is good for people's health. Fondling the dog, stroking the cat, or chatting to the canary is soothing. It reduces feelings of tension, stress, and loneliness. However, people with breathing problems may be allergic to feathers or fur – the family doctor can advise on this. In what way is taking the dog for a walk good for health?

Do you agree with the findings of the studies quoted above? Observe and record the behaviour of one person you know while he or she interacts with his or her pet. What disadvantages might there be in keeping a pet?

1 Give three reasons why food should always be kept covered.
2 Investigate the habits and life cycle of one pest. State how you would try to get rid of it at each stage of its life cycle. Resource: the pest control officer.

3 Some housing authorities do not allow tenants to keep pets. State your opinion of this ruling, and be prepared to discuss it in class.

Clean food

Food hygiene regulations control the preparation, packing, storage, and sale of food and drink. All premises involved in preparing food and drink are regularly inspected by public health officers. Food poisoning is a **notifiable** disease – doctors must report all cases to the local health authority to prevent an outbreak in the community.

Salmonella bacteria breed in the human gut and bowel. They pass out in the faeces. They are on the unwashed hands of people who have just used the toilet. What do you think happens to the germs when those people sell, cook, or serve food? What hygiene rule must be kept after using the toilet?

Staphylococcus bacteria live in the breathing passages, and in the openings of the skin. Normally they are harmless, but a cold or a small cut causes the bacteria to multiply and become infectious. Why must all cuts be protected by dressings? Why must handlers of food wear masks?

---

1 List six ways in which food can be contaminated in the picture above.
2 List six things you would do to improve the hygiene of the toilet in the picture.
3 Redraw the picture, showing how you would store the refuse.
4 You suffer an attack of food poisoning after eating a pork pie. Would you **a** think it was just bad luck, **b** report the shop for breaking the food hygiene regulations, **c** warn the shop you will complain to the authorities if they do not return your money, or **d** just warn your friends about the shop? Why?

5 It is people themselves that are the main source of food pollution.

Discuss.

Investigating noise

Noise intensity is measured in decibels, and the maximum safety level is 87 decibels. Any noise over this can damage the hearing. The delicate hair cells of the inner ear become less acute at picking up sound vibrations. Over the years, this causes deafness. But people with a high sensitivity to noise can become partially deaf while they are young.

Collect: a vacuum cleaner.

a Switch it on and try speaking above the noise. What happens to the level of your voice? Does noise create more noise? Why?

b Cover your ears. Does this give you much protection?

Collect: various manufactured ear plugs, and cotton wool.

a Working in pairs, devise, plan, and carry out a task to find out which of these noise protectors you would recommend.

b Role-play speaking to a partially deaf person while there is background noise. In turn, observe how both the speaker and the person spoken to change the expressions on their faces. Discuss your findings.

Collect: information on sign language.

a Create and send a message in question form to your partner.

b Evaluate your success by having your partner send a reply.

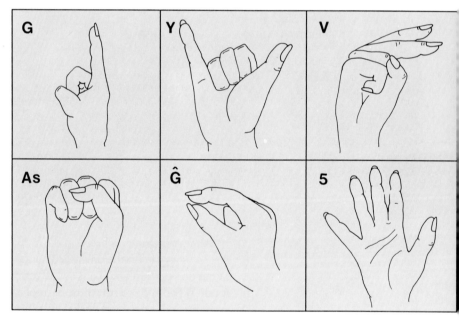

Noise is a pollutant, as it is a serious health risk. **Relentless** and **impulse** noise cause the most damage – use resources to give two examples of each. Both can cause mental and/or emotional pain. They make people anxious, tense, and upset as they try to resist the sounds.

1 List the machines in a home which produce noise. Devise a task to find out their order of decreasing sound.

   ● Changes in home technology are responsible for a huge increase in noise.

   Comment on this statement.

2 Do you think there is a human need for **a** noise, and **b** quiet? Why? Suggest one way in which people living close together can resolve these conflicting needs.

Investigating town planning

Before town planning, towns and cities just grew higgledy-piggledy. The plan of Oldville shows the kind of health mistakes that were made. The study of town planning is very recent. Many people still live near railway stations, factories, and busy roads. These can all cause serious pollution. The arrow showing the direction of the prevailing wind is important – why? As well as unpleasant odours, name two other pollutants which are carried by moving air.

Study the plan of Oldville and answer the following:

1 Small children lack road sense. Name the special danger at the site of the nursery school.
2 Sick people find noise particularly painful. Comment on the site of the hospital.
3 School children are especially vulnerable to infectious diseases. What serious health risk is near the school?
4 Name the problems which could arise from the school being sited between the river, the railway station, and the railway lines. If you could resite the school, where would you put it? Why?
5 Name two sources of pollution near the old people's home. Comment on its distance from the housing estate. Describe the journey an elderly person who needs daily hospital care must take. What is your opinion of this site?
6 Describe the view from the housing estate. Why do you think the people here find their homes difficult to keep clean? In what ways do you think a depressing view might affect health?

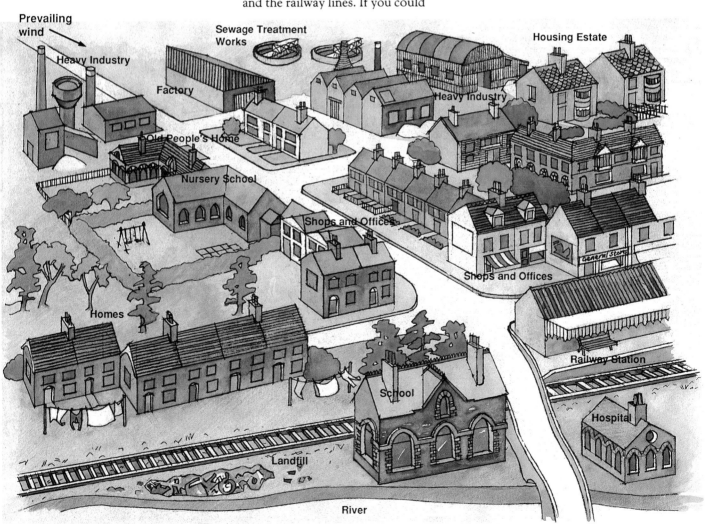

After town planning

Ideally, town planners develop new towns and housing estates around a neighbourhood scheme. They choose pleasant environments free from the risk of pollution. The sites for houses, factories, offices, shops, schools, health centres, parks, and playing fields should be within easy reach. Most should be within walking distance, and not crossed by railways or roads, which are dangerous and cause an unnatural divide in a community.

🗨 Study the two photos on the left. Do you think town planners always get things right? Be prepared to discuss your answer in class.

1 Newville has plans for a bus station, a nursery school, and a sheltered housing block. At which of the vacant sites, A, B, or C, would you locate each? Why?

2 Compare the plan of Oldville with that of Newville. Which of these two towns would you choose to live in? Why?

3 Invite a town planner to discuss his or her role in the community.

Newville

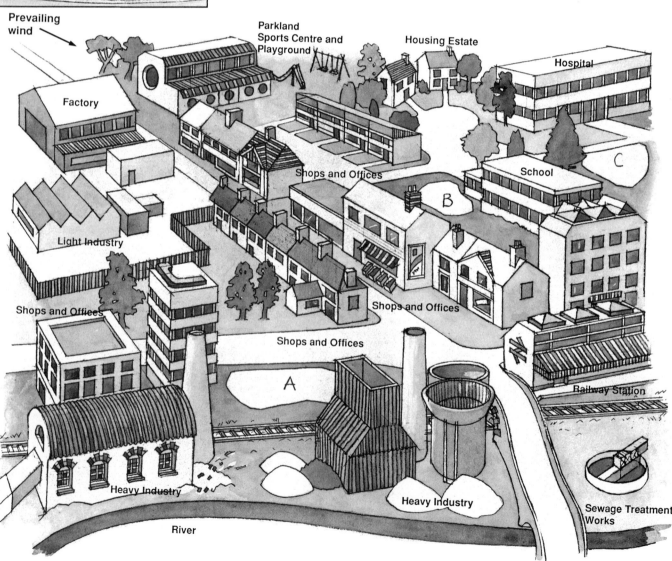

Further work on Chapter 5

1 Define the word 'biology'. Define the word 'technology'. **Biotechnology** is the study of how to use living things in place of other natural resources. For example, useful microbes digest (break down) decaying refuse. As they do this, they produce methane – a **biogas**, which can be used as fuel. Interesting experiments are being carried out with **gasahol** – an alternative to petrol, made from sugar cane and other food crops.
In what ways will the use of biogas help to **i** save precious land, **ii** reduce smoke pollution, and **iii** cut down the amount of sludge dumped in the sea?

2 Find out about the work of the Countryside Commission. Design and make silk screen posters or car stickers to publicize one of their activities.

3 Visit a recycling plant and write about the various methods of conservation.

4 Invite a speaker from the Water Board or one of the other public utilities to discuss their work. Ask the speaker about particular problems concerned with waste of the resources he or she works with.

5 Observe and make a rough estimate of the amount of food thrown away each day at your school. Find out what happens to it. Suggest ways in which it could be recycled.

6 Investigate the misuse of electricity in your school. Suggest ways to help both staff and students become more aware of conservation issues.

7 Explain why cooked and raw meat should be stored separately.

(Midland Examining Group)

8 Explain briefly why keeping a warm, ready-mixed feed in a vacuum flask for the night feed may be harmful to a baby. *(Northern Examining Association)*

9 State *two* ways in which technological change can affect the lives of individuals.

(London and East Anglian Group)

Now look again at the objectives at the beginning of the chapter, and check that you have achieved them.

Biotechnology: experimental edible mushroom cultivation; numerous cultures of fungi growing on wood shavings in conical flasks.

6 *A*bout money

By the end of this chapter, you should be able to:

- read a bank statement and balance an account.
- understand how interest is earned on savings.
- work out the full interest (APR) charged on credit.

- interpret a credit agreement before signing.
- analyse the advantages and risks of credit.
- understand more about your money-related values.

What is money?

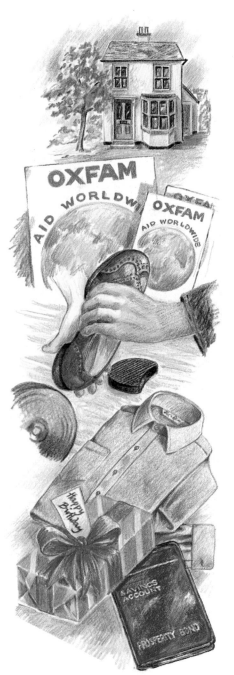

Money is a material resource. It can be exchanged for many things, such as:

- goods and services.
- overseas aid.
- presents at birthdays.

- more money in savings.
- a home of your own.
- financial independence.

Collect: items for a class 'swap shop'.

a Plan a class 'swap shop'. You may bring more than one item but the total amount must not be above the limit your teacher sets.

b Clean and, as far as possible, repair and restore the item.

c Students who do not wish to swap goods can offer a service instead, such as coaching for study or sport, cutting or setting hair, etc. Write a card describing your skills in very attractive terms.

1 Listen to a radio programme running a swap shop. Identify those items most frequently offered. Do they have anything in common? Are they: practical, or for pleasure? things people grow out of, or become bored with?

2 Name some items you would expect to be swapped **a** after Christmas, **b** in late spring, and **c** in autumn. Why?

3 It is a fact of life that the majority of young people, whether in paid employment or on unemployment benefit, are chronically short of money!

Do you agree? Discuss this statement in class.

4 Money is a resource which helps people achieve some of their goals.

Analyse this statement.

Money and you

Some people do not value money: it comes very low down on their list of priorities. Some people prize it above all else. Find out more about your money-related values by analysing the following statements in class. You may prefer to work out the appropriate column for your replies at home. Copy this chart and fill it in.

Statement	Agree	Disagree	Likely to agree in ten years
I want a good job, and a nice family, home, and community life.			
Everyone should study for a career.			
Most people should get married.			
Children use up a lot of your resources.			
People should not have children before they can afford to raise them.			
Children bring love, so money is not that important.			
I know I can control my own future.			
I am good at managing money.			
I keep to a plan of regular saving.			
Saving for a home makes me feel secure.			
All homes should be insured.			
I worry about money a lot.			
Hard work almost always pays off.			
Unemployment is dreadful for most people.			
Most people on social security are lazy.			
I take good care of my health.			
When I am sick, it is usually due to my careless health habits.			
I know I have a great deal of control over my health.			
The ideal man does not want his partner in life to work.			
Women who are economically inactive are usually lazy.			
I would share a bank account with my partner.			
Each person is responsible for the choices he or she makes in life.			

Would you value a career as a thief? The most usual crimes are theft from shops and people, burglary from homes, and handling stolen goods. The peak age for convictions under the age of 21 is 15 for boys and 14 for girls – the rate for boys is over four times higher than for girls. Do you think stealing helps a person to become **a** financially independent, and **b** mentally and emotionally secure?

1 What is meant by 'money-related values'?
2 Do your replies to the questions above help you understand more about yourself? Which, if any, of your original replies would you like to change now, rather than wait until you are ten years older? Why?
3 What is your opinion of these questions? Would you like to add, or subtract, some? If so, state which.

Investigating the world of work

Collect: the situations vacant page in your local newspaper(s).

a If you had to start work today, which job would you choose?
b What education do you already have that you could use?
c What kind of personality would you need for the job?
d Which skills do you have to help you find and hold the job?
e Who would give you a testimonial, or act as your referee?
f How much money would you be earning?
g Is this amount satisfactory for now? for the rest of your life?
h Is this a job you would like for the rest of your life?

Now choose any job you would really like, and answer the following:

a What level of education is required for the job?
b How long is the training likely to take?
c What kind of personality is most suitable for the work?
d What is the future outlook for the job?
e Is there work in the community or will you have to move?
f How will the job affect your present family? your future family?
g Are you prepared to accept all the consequences of your choice?

A 1986 American survey asked school leavers to list the workplaces they thought most desirable. The results are on the left.

Workplace	Females (%)	Males (%)
Large corporation	26	28
Small business	19	18
Self-employed	34	50
Social services	21	4

Study the gender difference in these findings. Being self-employed involves planning, managing, controlling, and making a profit on your own business. Are the girls in the survey more reluctant to **a** take risks, **b** control staff, or **c** be in competition? Can you think of other explanations? Do the different sexes have different values or goals? If so, why?

Do a similar class survey and have a full class discussion on these issues.

The survey asked both sexes which work factors they valued (results on left). Make a similar list of your values when seeking a job.

Factor	%
Interesting to do	87
Use skills and abilities	72
Good chance for promotion	67
Predictable, secure future	64
Chance to earn good money	58
Chance to make friends	53
Worthwhile to society	41
Chance to help in decision making	33
High status or prestige	32

1 Plan a visit to your local Jobcentre. List those jobs which might be suitable for you. Then list the jobs most in demand. How many are to do with the social services? Note which jobs state 'equal opportunities employer' (see p. 41).

2 Identify all the factors affecting choice of career.

About income

Income is any money which comes in from the following:

- student grant.
- unemployment benefit.
- wage packet.
- pension.
- tips.
- business profit.
- rent from lodgers.
- odd jobs.
- interest on savings.
- overtime.
- bonuses.
- inheritance.
- large gifts.

When you fill in your income tax form, you must state your gross income – that is, all the money you earn, receive, or get in any way.

Deductions from income may include:

- income tax.
- National Insurance contributions.
- union fees.
- pension plan.

Disposable income is the amount of money you have left after all the deductions have been made – your 'take-home' pay or net income.

a Your gross earnings are £98 per week. State your yearly income. Your total deductions amount to £27 weekly. State **i** your weekly take-home pay, and **ii** your annual disposable income.

b You borrow your total gross earnings and spend them before pay-day. What mistake have you made? Write about some of the problems this mistake could cause you.

In times when there is unemployment, only a percentage of people get earned incomes. As well as unemployment benefit, there may be other benefits you can claim:

training – on courses that include work experience.
further study – on courses for new work skills.
part-time work – you may not have to lose your benefits.

In 1985, the average gross weekly wage in Britain for all male workers was £192.40; for all female workers £126.40. The average for male manual workers was £163.30; for female manual workers £101.30. The average for male non-manual workers was £225.00; for female non-manual workers £138.80. Turn back to p. 41 and discuss these figures in relation to the Equal Pay Act. What conclusions can you draw about how well the Act is working?

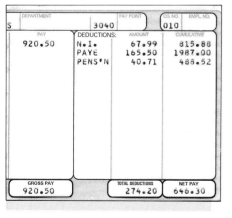

DEPARTMENT		PAY POINT	CO. NO.	EMPL. NO.
S	3040		010	

PAY	DEDUCTIONS:	AMOUNT	CUMULATIVE
920.50	N.I.	67.99	815.88
	PAYE	165.50	1987.00
	PENS'N	40.71	488.52

GROSS PAY	TOTAL DEDUCTIONS	NET PAY
920.50	274.20	646.30

1 In 1985, who earned more – manual or non-manual workers? What implications about preparation for the world of work can you draw from this?

2 Jane and Paul plan to marry and start a family immediately. They decide Jane should not study for further qualifications as she intends to be a full-time homemaker. What are the likely consequences of this decision **a** to Jane if the couple are infertile, **b** to Jane if the marriage does not work and there are children to support, and **c** to the whole family if Paul becomes disabled or unemployed?

3 Using *Social Trends*, find the latest average weekly earnings:
   a for all male and then all female employees.
   b for male and then female manual employees.
   c for male and then female non-manual employees.
   Compare your data with those in 1985. Comment on your findings.

4 There are different schemes to help women who have raised a family and want to return to work. Investigate one.

Do you need an account?

Money in a savings account earns interest. Jim deposits £100 at 5 per cent interest (0.05 times the total sum) for one year, and earns £5 interest.

Principal	× Rate	× Time	=	Interest
£100	0.05	1 year		£5.00
£150	0.05	2 years	=	?
£200	0.75	1 year	=	?
£50	0.25	1 year	=	?
£500	0.75	2 years	=	?

(To convert a percentage to a decimal, move the decimal point two places to the left and drop the percentage sign or the words 'per cent'.)

Work out the following:

£500 for 1 year at 6 per cent   £35 for 1 year at 5 per cent
£60 for 2 years at 4 per cent   £960 for 1 year at 11 per cent
£450 for 1 year at 7 per cent

Method	1976 (%)	1984 (%)
Cash	59	39
Bank/building society	27	43
Cheque (including giro)	12	16
Other non-cash	2	2

The table on the left shows how people were paid in Britain in 1976 and 1984.

Study the trend for the methods of job payment. By how much did the percentage change for cash payments, and over how many years? If the trend continued at the same rate, what is the percentage of people being paid in cash now? What conclusions can you draw about the need for an account?

High Street Bank

Current account   Mortgage
Savings account   Safe deposit
Personal loan   Cheque card
Travellers cheques

Building Society

Current account
Savings account
Mortgage
Cheque card
Travellers cheques

Girobank

Personal loan
Current account
Cheque card
Travellers cheques

1 Copy and complete the following sentences:
   a Money for daily spending can be kept in a . . .
   b Money for long-terms bills can be kept in a . . .
   c Money for savings should be kept in a . . .

2 Investigate your banking options. Working in pairs, plan a visit to a finance company of your choice. Identify such factors as days and hours of opening; speed of service; frequency of statements; helpfulness of staff; cashpoints in your area; closeness to home/public transport; rates of interest on savings; 'free' offers to students; and any other. On your return, compare the class findings. Select, with reasons, a finance company which might best suit your needs.

3 Write a brief essay stating the reasons why you think having an account is necessary or unnecessary.

A current account

Collect: a blank cheque, and a paying-in slip.

a Make copies of each.

b Pay a gas bill of £48 by filling in the date, the name of the Gas Board, the amount of money in words, the same amount in figures, your signature, and the record of your cheque.

c Withdraw £20 in cash by filling in another cheque, putting 'cash' beside 'pay'.

d What is your account number? What is the cheque number of your cash withdrawal?

e Put your wages of £102.49 into your account by filling in the paying-in slip.

A **bank statement** is a list of your transactions – money **credited to** or **debited from** your account. The final amount may not be exact, as it takes time to clear cheques sent by post. When you check your monthly statement, remember a few cheques may be uncleared, and money paid in may not yet be credited to you.

Details	Payments	Receipts	Date	Balance
				196.06 c
balance forward			1 FEB	146.06 c
Counter Credit:		50.00	7 FEB	96.06 c
	549303	50.00	7 FEB	198.55 c
	549304	102.49	16 FEB	152.15 c
		46.40	16 FEB	15.93 c
	549302	136.22	17 FEB	11.68 d
	549297	27.61	21 FEB	90.81 c
	549305	102.49	24 FEB	57.82 c
	549306	32.99		

Using a cash card with your PIN (personal identity number)

a Assuming there are no amounts uncredited and no uncleared cheques, how much is in the account on 16 February and on 24 February?

b What happened to the account on 17 February?

c Add your wages (£102.49 plus £17.00 earned at a part-time job) to the statement, and deduct the Water Board's uncleared cheque of £52.53. What is the final total?

Cash dispensing machines save time, and let you have cash outside banking hours. Do not keep your cash card and PIN (personal identity number) together – if they are stolen, cash can be drawn on your account, so you should phone your bank immediately to make sure that payments are stopped at once. In 1987, two out of five people in Britain used a cash card each week.

Explain the meaning of the following: current account, withdrawal, credit, debit, statement, transaction, uncleared, uncredited.

More about savings

After school each day, you buy a 40p ice-cream cornet. Then you decide to buy a smaller 20p one instead, as you are watching your weight.

a How much money do you save over a school term of twelve weeks?

b How much do you save in a year – three school terms of twelve weeks?

c You invest those savings at 5 per cent for one year. Work out the interest and then your total savings.

d You reinvest your total savings at 5 per cent for another year. How much interest do you earn? What are your total savings?

e Did you earn more interest in the first or second year, and by how much? Why did this happen?

When the interest you make is added to the **principal**, the amount of the principal is larger. This is **compound interest**.

You dislike school lunches, so you buy hamburger and chips at a local take-away.
Collect: ingredients for a packed lunch.

a Cost them, and work out how much you save in a year – three terms of twelve weeks – by having the packed lunch instead of the take-away.

b Repeat the above exercise from c to e.

Advertisements for savings plans can be confusing. Try to work through the following:

Maturity time	Interest rate	Minimum	Compounded
18–24 months	10.8%	500	Daily
12 months	9.6%	500	Daily
6 months	9.2%	1000	Daily

Savings Account – No maturity restrictions			
	Minimum balance	Interest rate	Effective annual yield 5.39%
Christmas Club	£5	5%	
Holiday Club			

– 5 FREE DAYS' INTEREST!! Deposits paid by the 5th earn from 1st.
– Interest is compounded daily, paid quarterly, and must be left for 1 year to earn effective annual yield. Principal withdrawn before maturity loses 90 days' interest.

a How often does the bank compound interest?

b How often does the bank pay interest?

c How long must you keep your money in the bank to earn 10.8 per cent interest?

d What penalty do you pay if you take your money out before one year?

e How many days' interest do you get if you deposit £5 in a Savings Club on 5 May and withdraw it on 31 May?

f How many days' interest do you get if you deposit £5 in a Savings Club on 11 May and withdraw it on 31 May?

➤ Collect advertisements for savings plans from the financial section of a newspaper. Work through as many as you can.

About credit

Credit is a way of buying goods or services with an agreement to pay at a later date. You are borrowing money, so there are interest charges to pay. In a way, credit is 'buying' money – which means you are the consumer. You should shop around for a good credit deal as you would for other consumer goods. Page 82 explains some of the terms used in credit deals, and the risks credit can involve.

Compare the cost of one credit deal with another by using the **APR** – the Annual Percentage Rate. This is the extra money which is charged for arranging the credit deal. It is added on to the interest you already owe. The APR makes clear exactly how much the debt will be and when you must repay it.

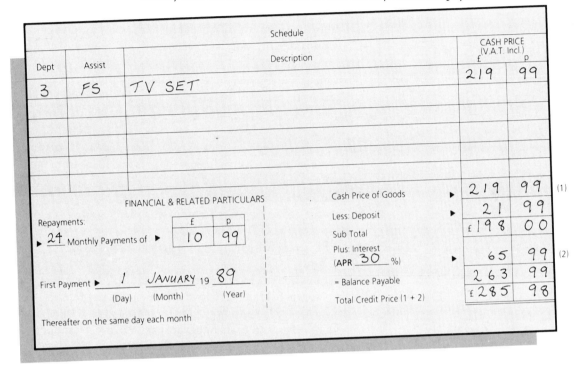

Look at the department store credit agreement shown here.

a How much is the deposit? What percentage of the original cash price is it?

b What is the APR?

c How much is the interest?
   This is the difference between the total credit price and the cash price – the cost to you of 'buying' credit.

d How much is the monthly repayment? Over how long a period are the repayments to be made?

e The same department store offers a credit card (see p. 81) with a current APR of 29.8 per cent. What percentage interest is that per month?

Always ask for the APR or 'true' rate of interest on any loan. The lower the APR, the better the credit deal. Sometimes, interest-free credit is offered. This means the total repayments must not add up to more than the cash price.

---

1 Your fares to work cost £30 per week. You buy a bicycle on credit with an APR of £12.99 per week. Has using credit actually helped save you money?

2 Role-play a persuasive salesperson successfully selling a TV set on credit to a customer.

3 Collect advertisements for goods with details of the APR. Find **a** a good credit deal, and **b** a poor one. Stick them in your book or file, and next to them work out the arithmetic of the deal.

Types of credit

➤

Collect: samples of two completed hire-purchase agreement forms.
a When can you take the goods home?
b When do they actually belong to you?
c What might happen if you fall behind with payments **i** before, and **ii** after a third of the payments are made?
d Buying goods on hire-purchase is sometimes called a 'conditional' sale. Why?

➤

Collect: two mail-order catalogues.
a Choose one item from each and fill in the sales forms. Is interest added to the credit loan? Work out the total costs.
b Compare the price and range of items with those in your local shops. State two advantages and disadvantages of home shopping.
c Name, with reasons, two groups of people who benefit from shopping by post.
d Explain what happens if the goods do not meet with your approval.

➤

Collect: two press advertisements for personal loans from finance companies other than banks.
a What kind of security is requested?
b Do you need to have a guarantor (see p. 82)?
c Is the interest/APR stated clearly?
d Is it higher than the interest on a personal bank loan?

Pawnshops operate by arranging for you to leave something valuable with them as security (see p. 82) for a cash loan on which you pay interest. You get a 'notice to debtor' which tells you **a** how to redeem the goods, **b** whether they are insured by the pawnbroker, and **c** when they may be sold if you cannot repay the debt. If you do not want your goods sold, you must continue to pay interest. If there is no insurance and your article is damaged or lost, you must keep repaying what you owe as well as putting up with the loss.

Moneylenders lend cash at a very high rate of interest. People have spent their lives just trying to pay the interest. It is a criminal offence for anyone to stop you in the street or call at your home to offer a cash loan. Beware loan sharks!
  Before you agree to any credit deal, ask yourself these questions:
a Do I really need the goods, or loan?
b What is the cash price of the goods?
c How much do I need to borrow?
d What is the best credit deal I can get?
e Can I really afford the payments?

● Live now, pay later.

Analyse this statement.

Credit cards

Credit cards allow you to buy goods and services without a cheque or cash. The money is charged to a credit company, such as Access, or Visa. You receive a monthly statement of how much you owe. If you pay within a certain time, there is no charge – you get free credit during that time! If you do not pay then, you are charged interest at a fairly high rate.

There is a top limit of spending on most cards. The amount depends on the state of your finances. If you buy expensive goods, the salesperson may telephone the credit company to check you are within your limit. Sales staff may also telephone to check that the card really belongs to you – up to 900 cards are lost or stolen every day. In 1985, 4200 thieves were sent to prison for offences involving Barclaycard alone. Sales staff are trained to watch for suspicious behaviour, and to keep back any cards which may have been stolen.

In 1986, 150 million credit cards were printed. They are so convenient it seems likely that cheques will soon be outdated. But there is a danger with 'plastic money': it has been called the quickest way to get into debt. Some people spend far more than they can afford; others forget to pay their accounts monthly, and the interest on the debt grows at an alarming rate. In 1986, the credit companies estimated that the average debt on all cards worked out at £1000 per cardholder.

1 Moira boasts that she cannot resist spending money. Would you advise her to become a cardholder? Why?

2 Do a survey of shops and services in your community which accept credit cards. Which card appears to be most popular?

3 Contact a card company and find out **a** at what age you can first apply for a card, and **b** the current rate of interest.

Explain the meaning of these signs.

The risks of credit

Before a credit deal is made you are asked to sign an **agreement**. This sets out your rights and obligations. Once you have signed the agreement you are totally responsible for the debt. If you buy on credit at home, you can cancel the deal by written letter within three days.

A **creditor** is the person or company to whom you owe money.
A **default notice** states you have failed to keep the agreement.
Security against a loan is something you have which the creditor may take if you default. It must be as valuable as the amount you want to borrow.
A **guarantor** promises (guarantees) to pay the debt if you default.
A **debt collector** is hired by the creditor to visit the defaulter's home. If the debtor cannot pay, the item can be repossessed and/or other goods taken in lieu.

Yvonne's parent refuses to act as guarantor for a second-hand car. Yvonne asks her friend, Marge, promising there is no risk involved. Marge agrees and, three months later, receives a default notice. Marge tells Yvonne to sort out her own debt – and forgets all about it. Next month, a debt collector arrives and tells Marge, 'You signed as guarantor. You are responsible.' Marge writes a cheque for £300, all the money she has. The debt collector takes her new music centre and a leather chair to make up the difference in what is owed.

  Why do you think Yvonne's parent refused? Role-play the above situation.
  Being in debt is a serious social problem which is not often talked about. This is because the debtor feels too worried or ashamed. The golden rules about debt are:
a Never take out another loan to pay off a debt. Discuss why.
b Never hand over a benefit book as security. This is illegal.
c Never ignore bills. The interest keeps rising; creditors do not go away.
d Offer to pay the creditor a small amount weekly till your finances improve.
e Go at once for free advice to a Money Advice Centre, a law centre, a Consumer Advice Centre, or a CAB (Citizens Advice Bureau).

---

1 Explain the meaning of the following: debtor, guarantor, security, creditor, default notice.
2 You do not want the salesperson to think you are ignorant, so you sign a credit agreement without really understanding it. Later, you find you cannot meet the payments. Investigate what you can do by contacting one of the above agencies. Write about your findings.

Further work on Chapter 6

The gift that could win a fortune!

Why not give your friends and relations the present that could be worth as much as £250,000? Premium Bond Gift Tokens come in a choice of three attractive greetings cards and you can buy them at your post office in multiples of £5 up to £60. It's the present that puts excitement into a money gift!

Haywain

PREMIUM BONDS

Your chance to win a quarter of a million!

NATIONAL SAVINGS

1 Plan a trip to the post office and do a full investigation of Premium Savings Bonds.

2 Using the phone directory as a resource, contact a football pools company and investigate some costs, enterainment value, and chances of a win.

3 Compare your financial position over a year if you spend £5 a month on Premium Savings Bonds or the football pools without winning either.

4 ERNIE comes up trumps, and you win £500. Plan what you would do with the money, and state why.

5 Plan, with reasons, what you think an elderly person might do with the £500.

6 Plan, with reasons, how you think a newly married couple might use it.

7 Plan how a nuclear family with two children might spend it.

8 Money is used for very different things at the different stages of the life cycle. Analyse this statement in essay form.

9 Investigate the services of your local post office. Choose one of the following options, and collect the necessary leaflets or application forms: free postal service for blind people; the correct way to wrap and address a parcel; how to register and insure letters; buying a television licence or stamps; collecting welfare benefits; applying for a driving licence; sending a money order through the post; applying for a passport; buying National Insurance stamps.

Practise filling in the application forms, write about your findings, then pool all the information in class.

10 a Suggest **four** methods of saving that would provide interest.

b Comment on the suitability of **one** of these methods when saving for a piece of furniture.

c Study these figures:

Dining table and chairs
Cash	£210.99
Deposit	£20.99
20 weeks at	£12.35
	APR 30%

i What is the total cost of the item using the credit arrangement?

ii What is meant by APR? *(Welsh Joint Education Committee)*

Now look again at the objectives at the beginning of the chapter, and check that you have achieved them.

Money management

By the end of this chapter, you should be able to:

- distinguish between wants and needs.
- set goals and priorities for use of money.
- identify some choices in spending.
- create and balance a budget.
- analyse the function of insurance.
- know the effect of inflation on fixed incomes and savings.
- analyse decisions about savings.
- know how the job market, individual and community spending, and advances in technology are interdependent.

Wants and needs

HAVE YOU GOT A SPARE COAT?

You are marooned in the Arctic. List your immediate needs.

What could you do to provide **a** shelter, **b** food, and **c** warmth? Which human resources would you use to wrest these things from the material resources around you? Would money be of use? Why?

In the home, list the material resources essential to maintain life. Include public utilities. What resource is needed to acquire these things? Where does the resource come from for **a** retired people, **b** employed people, **c** unemployed single parents, **d** economically inactive homemakers, and **e** students? Which groups are likely to have least of these resources? Why?

You long for new boots. Is this a **need**, or a **want**? Divide the following reasons into needs and wants – there are no 'right' answers:

a to help you look smart
b to participate in a walking tour for the disabled
c for protection on the muddy paths near your home
d to save on fares for public transport
e because almost all your friends are wearing them
f to be the first person with the latest fashion
g for a job interview to work in a warehouse

Compare your answers in class, and discuss how values affect whether items are considered needs or wants.

---

1 Copy and complete the following sentences:
   a Needs are the goods or services . . .
   b Wants are the goods or services . . .
2 Select any item you long for, and repeat the above task.
3 List some goods and resources which might improve your quality of life. How would this list differ for **a** an elderly person, and **b** a new parent?

Choices about spending

Sam and Jas each have £10 to spend. The following is a list of the immediate goods and services they could spend it on, and their reasons for spending it on each:

- jacket to be dry cleaned
- library books overdue
- hair due for a cut
- interested in latest film
- wanting new sketch pad and etching pen
- saving for new bus pass
- treating friend to birthday meal
- tempted by advertisement for hairdryer
- adding to holiday fund
- crazy over the latest pop cassette
- liking to give new spot lotion a try
- should order new slimming diet
- owing £3.10 to parent from last month!
- wanting snacks to keep energy level up
- time to add to savings account
- wanting an art poster to brighten up room
- new shoes must last – get heel tips
- old address book falling apart
- clothes . . . clothes . . . clothes!

Collect: £10 in Monopoly money.

a Working as a group, make a rough estimate of the costs of each of the above.
b On your own, rearrange the above list in the order of priority for you.
c Now spend your Monopoly money on whatever items you wish.
d Record which amounts are for short-term and which for long-term satisfactions.
e Compare your choices of spending with the rest of the class.
f Discuss why different people choose to spend their money in different ways.
g Turn back to p. 22 and re-read your list of personal goals.
h Check it with your above list of priorities.
i Do you wish to change any of your spending? If so, why?
j What do you think is the function of checking your goals before you allot your resources?

---

1 Sam forgot his list. He bought the new cassette, a magazine for weight-lifters, a packet of incense sticks, the art poster, a pen with a funny gadget, some sweets, and a fizzy drink. On his return, he asked his parent for money to pay the library fine.

   Discuss Sam's choices and his priorities.

2 Sam's parent refused to lend the money. The £3.10 Sam owed was meant for the electricity bill. What might be the consequence of not being able to pay this bill? If you were Sam's parent and affluent (well-off), would you lend the money? Why?

3 Do you think needs or wants should have priority when spending limited resources? Why?

4 You are in a wheelchair. Allot the £10.

Planning a budget

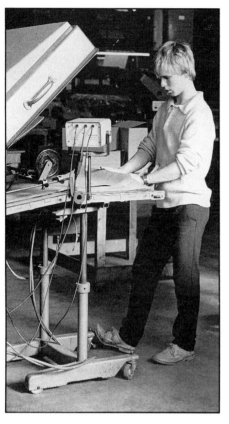

A **budget** is a personal plan to help people manage their finances. It is a way of keeping control of money so you know how much is coming in – **income** – and how much is going out – **expenditure.** Below are two budgets.

Working teenager	£87 per week	Widowed pensioner	£70 per week
Board and lodging	35.00	Rent and community charges	25.50
Lunch at work	9.00	Fuel and lighting	8.50
Fares	18.50	Food and drink	24.25
Clothes	10.00	Clothes and launderette	3.75
Leisure	7.00	Leisure	2.00
Savings	4.50	Telephone	5.00
Extras	3.00	Extras	1.00

Sam, the working teenager, lives at home with his parents. Mr Green, the widowed pensioner, lives alone. Sam would like to spend more on leisure but is saving up for a motor bike. Mr Green keeps his room well-heated – why? His leisure activity is a game of darts at the pub.

a List the expenses Mr Green has which Sam does not. Who pays for these expenses in Sam's home? Do you think Sam is getting a good deal from his board and lodging? Why?

b Why does Sam need to spend more on clothes than Mr Green?

c How could Sam economize on lunches at work?

d Why has Mr Green not included fares in his budget?

e Give two reasons why Mr Green does not budget for savings.

f Sam gets a £4 reduction in his take-home pay. Which expenses do you think he might economize on, and by how much?

g Mr Green could choose to do without a telephone and have more money for leisure. Would you recommend this? Why?

h What kind of a life style does Mr Green have – affluent or penny-pinching? Do you consider this to be more painful **i** after a lifetime of work, or **ii** at Sam's stage of life? Why?

The motor bike Sam wants costs £560. It is available on credit at an APR of £6 per week over a period of two years. How much is the total cost of the bike on credit? Sam is waiting until he has £100 in savings before he buys the bike. How long will this take to save? How much will he spend during this time in fares? What alternative does he have (see p. 79)? Would you advise Sam to buy the bike now? Why? Work out the figures, and write out your workings.

1 Which items of **a** Sam's and **b** Mr Green's expenditures are fixed (the items do not vary)?

2 Are these fixed expenditures needs or wants? What priority would you give them in a budget? Why?

3 Which items in both people's budgets are fixed, but cost variable amounts? Do you think all fixed expenses must have priority? Why?

4 Mr Green pays his community charge and telephone bill in instalments. He budgets these costs weekly (see p. 87) and puts aside this long-term money in a tin. At times, he gets so weary with watching the pennies that he takes the money out of the tin and treats his friends to a round of drinks. What non-material need is he allowing himself to satisfy? Find out and comment on today's pension rate for a retired widower.

Budgeting for large bills

Public services include British Rail, clean water, the safe disposal of sewage, gas, electricity, post, and telephone services. They are sometimes called **public utilities.** Mr Green budgets weekly for these in the following way:

Week	Date	Meter reading	Units used	×	Price per unit		Cost
1	2/1/88	72479					
2	9/1/88	72562	83	×	6.4p	=	£5.31
3	16/1/88	72663	101	×	6.4p	=	£6.46
4	23/1/88	72758	95	×	6.4p	=	£6.08
5	30/1/88						
6							
13							

Total cost of units for the quarter	=	
Add standing charge of £6.98	+	£6.98
Total bill for the quarter (13 weeks)	=	
Divide by 13 to find one week's cost	=	

Make a copy of the above chart.
a On week 2, where did the figure 83 come from?
b Why was it multiplied by 6.4?
c Work out the correct dates for weeks 6 to 13.
d Make up the meter readings for weeks 5 to 13.
e Work out the units used and complete the chart.

Other ways to budget for long-term bills include the following easy payment schemes:

● savings stamps – bought from fuel showrooms and post office.
● slot meter – get one installed to pay for fuel as you use it.
● monthly budget – ten or twelve months with a giro, bank, or savings account.
● showroom payments – pay what you can, when you can, towards your next bill.

Work out the weekly gas or electricity bill at home or school by reading the meter and filling in a record chart. Why should you read the meter at the same time on the same day of each week? Would you expect the units used to be higher or lower in the summer months? Why?

---

1 Investigate costs by planning a visit to your gas or electricity showroom. Find out the cost of having a slot meter installed, the extra charges in using the meter, the kind of homes most likely to have them, and the amount of profit a landlord or landlady may take. Discuss the advantages and disadvantages of a slot meter. Find out what 'standing charges' mean, and what the utility company spends them on. Most public utilities have a code of practice (see p. 106) to assist people in genuine hardship. Obtain details and comment on this.

2 Find out whether there are standing charges on the telephone and water board bills. Do you consider this fair? Why?

A household budget

People on salaries with heavy financial commitments need to plan their budget over a full year. The advantage of an annual budget is that you do not suddenly find yourself swamped with bills. You know what bills you have to pay, when you have to pay them, and how much they are likely to be. Banks and building societies provide a budget account service to help householders spread their bills over a year. They charge a small fee for this service.

The Smith family's net income (see p. 75) is £11 080 per year. Together with the bank manager, they have made a list of the larger household bills. The list is added up to find their annual expenditure. The total is divided by twelve. This amount is moved from the Smith's current account into their budget account at the beginning of each month.

Estimated costs	£
Mortgage or rent	3500
Community and water charges	800
Fuel and lighting	700
Insurance premiums	350
Credit repayments	300
Fares and car expenses	500
Telephone	325
Television licence	63
Holidays	300
Clothing	1550
Christmas and birthdays	200
Savings	420
Charge for service	50
Estimated total	9258
Money moved monthly to budget account	771.05

Consumer expenditure in Britain Percentage of total expenditure	1976	1986
Food	18.4	13.8
Alcoholic drink	7.6	7.0
Tobacco	4.1	3.2
Clothing/footwear	7.7	7.0
Housing	13.4	14.9
Fuel and power	4.7	4.8
Household goods and services	7.6	6.6
Transport and communication	14.9	16.7
Recreation, education, and entertainment	9.1	9.4
Other goods and services	12.6	16.8

1 Why is the Smith's annual expenditure divided by twelve?
2 How much money do the Smiths have left over each year? Name some items you think they might need it for.
3 How much are the Smiths charged for their budget account service? Do you think it is money well spent? Why?
4 Name one monthly, one quarterly, one half-yearly, and one annual bill.

1 From the table above, what are the trends for spending on **a** food, **b** alcohol, and **c** tobacco? Discuss them, and try to work out some reasons for these trends.
2 Which two items of consumer expenditure interest you most? Why?
3 Women are more budget-conscious and less likely to get into debt than men.

Comment on this statement.

About insurance

Insurance is protection against loss. You agree to pay a certain sum – a **premium**. The insurance company guarantees to **compensate** (pay) you for a specific (particular) loss by fire, theft, or accident. The contract you sign is a **policy**. It is a legal document, so read it carefully first! Look for the **exclusion clauses** – losses you are not covered for. An 'all risks' policy can be misleading, as things like coins, jewellery, and stamps still have to be separately insured.

Do you need insurance? Imagine you have started work and rent a small flat. What are the consequences if:
- you injure your back and become disabled for life?
- you catch glandular fever and are off work for 10 months?
- you leave a tap running and it overflows into the flat below?
- a friend trips over a rug in your home and breaks a leg?
- a small fire damages the wall furnishings in your flat?
- the camera you are buying on credit, and the television you rent, are stolen from your flat?
- a parent becomes ill and you stop work to be a full-time carer?
- your freezer breaks down the day after the guarantee expires?
- you are fired from your job?

Which of these unpredicted events will completely change your life style? Discuss them in class.

National Insurance contributions (NIC – see pp. 48 and 75) are money you pay into the welfare state fund throughout your working life. This money acts as an insurance and savings to protect you in times of financial need. Which of the above unpredicted events are you insured against by your NIC? Find out and name the social security benefits you can claim.

You are liable for any damage you cause to other people or their goods. Name the events in the list above for which you are personally liable. Discuss whether you might want to insure yourself against personal liability. Why?

Choose any room at home and list the contents. Include floor coverings, lighting fixtures, shelf brackets, and nails. Work out a rough estimate of the costs of the items on your list. Things such as heating systems, electrical wiring, and plaster and paint for the walls are difficult to cost. But if the room were destroyed, they would all have to be replaced. Discuss whether you think you might want a household goods insurance, and why.

1 Make a list of all the items you possess. Work out how much it would cost to replace them. Collect leaflets and application forms from different insurance companies, and compare **a** the cost of their premiums, **b** the items you must specify, and **c** the exclusion clauses. Fill in an application form. Find out about **a** life insurance, and **b** insurance fraud.

2 Choosing to have insurance is about weighing the risks of unpredicted events against the cost of the premiums.

Discuss this statement.

Budgeting on a limited income

Fixed expenses	Fixed but variable expenses	Flexible expenses
Shelter	Food and drink	Clothing
Community charge	Utilities	Personal
Savings	Fares	Leisure
Credit repayments	Laundry	

a Work out your disposable income.

b List the expenses for each item in the 'fixed' column above, total them, and deduct them from your income.

c List the expenses for the 'fixed but variable' column, total them, and deduct.

d Divide the items in the 'flexible' column into long-term or short-term needs, and small or large expenditure.

e Decide which, if any, short-term needs you must get from the flexible budget, such as toothpaste, cinema ticket, and dry cleaning, and deduct them.

f Decide which, if any, long-term needs, such as a winter coat, or new curtains, might be bought on credit. Budget for the deposit and the fact that you must add the weekly instalments to the fixed budget list.

g At this point, there may be no money left. Work through the flexible list again and cross off those items you must do without.

Debbie and Sam are on unemployment benefit. Find out how much this is for a single person aged 17. Working with this figure and the information below, draw up a budget for a Debbie, and b Sam.

Debbie's flat share is £10 weekly and her share of utilities £4. She has no savings, but makes credit repayments of £3 weekly. Sam lives at home and pays £12 for board and lodging, and saves £2 per week. They both spend time, money, and effort applying for jobs. List the costs this is likely to involve. Should these costs be fixed or flexible? Why?

Sandra, age 17, is a single parent of a 5-month-old baby. She receives a total of £56 in IS and FC (p. 50). The rent of her damp bed-sit is £22 per week. She spends £12.50 a week on heating – why? Work out a budget for her, keeping in mind the items she needs for the baby. Describe the kind of life style Sandra is likely to have.

At the weekend, Debbie has £3 left. She cannot decide whether to invest it in a small party for her flatmates, or get her shoes mended, her jacket cleaned, or her hair cut for the job interview on Monday. Debbie decides to invest in the party as it will cheer her up. Which would you choose in Debbie's place? Why? What do you think is meant by 'invest in yourself'?

Investigating second-hand goods

What is **VAT**? These letters stand for Value Added Tax. VAT is added on to most of the goods you buy and the services you pay for. It is a tax on spending – the more goods and services people use, the more VAT they pay. It is another way in which the government raises money from its citizens.

Do you pay VAT on everything? Plan a visit to a department store and compare the prices of the same shirt (or a similar one) in children's and adult's sizes. Apart from the extra cloth needed for the larger sizes, how can you account for the steep increase in price?

Repeat this task in a shoe shop.

Plan a visit to a book shop and find out the average price of **a** a hardback, and **b** a paperback book. Note the design, the lighting, and the furnishings of the store. Is the atmosphere bright, cheerful, attractive? Now visit a book stall and note your surroundings. How do they compare with the book shop? Now compare the prices of both hardback and paperback books in the shop and on the stall. State two reasons for the steep decrease in their respective prices.

Plan a visit to an Oxfam shop, an auction room, a jumble sale, or any second-hand store. Note the range of items sold in these places. Examine the condition of some items – look for things like a frayed edge on a rug, a broken handle on a saucepan, or a missing zip on jeans. Could you repair them? If so, what would the costs be? Estimate the life style of the other shoppers. Are they **a** bargain hunters, **b** on social security, or **c** the average mix of people you see in any store?

In the long run, who do you think pays for the furnishings of a shop? How could you **a** furnish a bed-sit, and **b** clothe yourself without paying VAT? What other costs would you also be avoiding?

---

1 Complete this sentence: 'I do/do not like the idea of recycling second-hand goods, as my priorities are . . .'.

2 Food is also exempt from VAT. Have a class discussion on why food and children's clothing are exempt from VAT.

The consumer and the community

What are the benefits of home computers to **a** the individual, **b** the family, and **c** the community? Consider some negative points to the individual – the cost of the home computer, the cost of additional packages, the money you lost in interest on savings to buy it, other items you could have bought instead, the time spent in learning skills, and any others. What are the disadvantages of home computers to the family, and to the community?

Draw a similar circle with a hair dryer in the centre and repeat the above task. Fill in as many spokes of the wheel as you can. Write about the benefits to the individual, the family, and the community. Prepare a class discussion on some of its drawbacks and advantages.

Draw a similar circle with a microwave oven in the centre, and repeat the above task.

Find out how many people in the class have **a** a home computer, **b** a hair dryer, and **c** a microwave oven. Are these numbers likely to increase or decrease in the future? Why?

---

1 List as many new products and services caused by changes in technology as you can. Analyse the effects, both positive and negative, on the individual and on the community.

2 Advances in technology affect the economy of the whole community.

Analyse this statement.

Supply and demand

The cost-of-living index shows how much you can buy with your money – its **purchasing power.** The index varies, because it is based on the price of things such as food, clothing, and mortgage rates. If prices go down, can you purchase more or fewer goods with your money? The cost-of-living index is called the **Retail Price Index** (RPI) – 'retail' refers to the price of goods in the shops.

Do a musical parcel activity with your teacher. The aim of the activity is to buy as many goods as you can – you may need a trial run first.

Collect: £10 Monopoly money, swap shop goods to act as 'parcels', and music.

a   Select one person to be in charge of the music.

b   Each swap shop item costs £1. You may bid more or less for it.

c   Pass the 'parcel'. When the music stops, the person holding the 'parcel' (unless it is the teacher) bids for the item. Any student may then put in a higher bid. You are only allowed 30 seconds to decide on your bid. The item goes to the highest bidder and is removed.

d   If the teacher is holding an item when the music stops, it is removed from the stock.

e   Continue until all the goods are sold.

Was it easy or difficult to bid in competition? In what way did the supply of goods affect the demand for them? How did you feel when you were outbid? Did the scarcity of goods affect the prices they fetched? Did this get worse, or better, as the supply of goods decreased? What happened to the purchasing power of your money towards the end of the activity?

Complete the following:

a   When goods are in short supply, their value . . .

b   When goods are in short supply, the purchasing power of your money . . .

c   Inflation is a long-term upward movement in prices – too much money chasing too few . . .

d   In times of high inflation, the purchasing power of your money . . .

If your earnings do not go up at the same rate as inflation, your real standard of living goes down. If the rate of interest on your savings is lower than the rate of inflation, then your savings are not worth as much. The disadvantage of saving during high inflation is that when you withdraw your money, even with the interest added, its purchasing power has dropped.

1   In what way does inflation affect a person living on a fixed income (income which does not increase)? Name two groups of people inflation is likely to harm.

2   When choosing a savings plan, what should you check against the rate of interest your money will earn? Why?

3   Explain some ways in which the consumer and the community are financially interdependent.

Savings for a home?

A 1986 survey by the Building Societies Association found that 65 per cent of people aged 16–19, and 82 per cent of people aged 20–30, hoped to buy a home within two years.

You can borrow money to buy a home from a bank, a building society, a housing association, or a local authority. How much you can borrow depends on what you can afford. The guideline in 1988 was three times your main income plus one times any second income; or two times a couple's joint income. Find out what the guideline is now. It helps if you already have a savings account – can you work out why?

You can usually borrow up to 95 per cent of the price of a new home. The rest you find for yourself, and put down as a **deposit.** If a home costs £40 000 and the loan is 95 per cent, you borrow £38 000 and pay a deposit of £2000. When you borrow over 80 per cent, the loan company takes out an insurance guarantee policy which covers it against any risk. The cost is passed on to you in a lump sum paid with the deposit.

A **mortgage** is the deed you sign as security for the loan until the money is repaid. You agree to pay a certain amount monthly, usually spread over 25 years. You do not legally own the home until the last payment is made.

You borrow £25 000 for a 30-year mortgage with a fixed interest rate of 11 per cent. Work out your total repayments. Is this correct (p. 79)?

In fact, repayment costs cannot be worked out this way. On the left is a table of repayment costs on a loan of £25 000 with APR included.

Years	APR%	Total
20	12.0%	£63 004
25	11.9%	£74 413
30	11.8%	£86 446

1970 – £12, 000

1990 – £135, 000?

How can a £25 000 home end up costing £86 446? Is this not a very expensive way to 'save' money?

Think, very carefully, about inflation. What happens to money during the time you are buying? And, as even a low rate of inflation reduces the purchasing power of the pound, the money you repay after the first few years is worth far less than when you first signed the agreement – the mortgage deed.

Now think, very carefully, about supply and demand. In most urban areas, there is always a shortage of housing (p. 110), and in Britain, land for building new homes is scarce. What happens to the price of goods – and housing – when there is scarcity? In fact, in 30 years' time, the same home is likely to be worth several times the £86 446.

---

1 Why is it usually worthwhile to invest your savings in property? Answer in as much detail as you can.

2 What other reasons might there be for so many young people hoping to own a home of their own? What drawbacks might there be?

3 Find out about **MIRAS** – Mortgage Interest Relief at Source – and comment on this government subsidy for home owners.

Further work on Chapter 7

Leah, married with three children, buys everything on credit and gets into debt.
Noah, married with three children, saves every penny and lives like a pauper.

1 Discuss some likely effects of Leah's money management on **a** herself, **b** her family, and **c** the community.
2 Repeat the above task for Noah.
3 What would happen if everyone managed their money in the same way as Leah?
4 Repeat the above task for Noah.
5 You have inherited £500 from a great aunt with the proviso that you invest it – £250 in some form of savings, and the remaining £250 to improve your status in life. Plan both your investments, giving reasons for your choices. Work out the figures in as much detail as possible for your teacher to see. Be prepared to discuss one of your plans in class. If necessary, change or modify your choices after you have evaluated the discussions in class.
6 People have unlimited wants and limited resources.
It is scarcity of resources which creates the need for choices.

Discuss these statements.

7 Name *two* financial problems that might occur when a person suffers a temporary loss of income.
Critically assess the factors that need to be considered before using credit.

(Welsh Joint Education Committee)

8 Bringing up a child takes a large part of a family's budget. Investigate any suitable ways of feeding and clothing a child to achieve maximum value at minimum cost. *(Southern Examining Group)*

Now look again at the objectives at the beginning of the chapter, and check that you have achieved them.

8 Consumer issues

By the end of this chapter, you should be able to:

- identify various marketing skills.
- analyse the effects of advertising on the consumer.
- study product information on packaging and labelling.
- know the role of promotional material in marketing.
- understand your rights as a consumer.
- know the various consumer protection agencies.
- develop shopping skills for goods and services.

What is a consumer?

Count the number of articles you are wearing. Count the material resources you are using for this lesson. Now try to list all the things you have consumed during the last three hours. Have you included services in your list?

Create your own definition of a consumer.

What kind of a consumer are you?

a Turn back to p. 21 and discuss Mark's shopping problem. Have you been in a similar situation?

b Has a salesperson persuaded you to buy something you do not **i** really like, or **ii** actually want? What is the salesperson's job?

c Do you think it is easy to be intimidated (overwhelmed) by an expert salesperson? What resistant skills do you need to develop?

d Are you an impulse buyer? Has this been successful for you?

e Are you influenced by advertising? If so, in what way?

f Does the place where you shop affect the choices you make?

g Do you study labels, ask how to maintain articles, and check whether there is a guarantee?

h Find out how many people in the class have taken faulty articles back to a shop.

i Write about and be prepared to discuss one disastrous shopping experience you (or someone you know) has suffered.

j Discuss how a consumer feels after a disastrous shopping experience.

Create and role-play small scenes which demonstrate each of the above.

How do you rate your skills as a consumer? Write your answer in as much detail as possible.

Marketing

Manufacturers make new products, or improve old ones. These products have to be **marketed** – sold. Services such as building societies, car hire, home plumbing, or shoe repairs also need to market their wares. Marketing is a set of skills used to sell a product or service to get the best profit possible for the manufacturer or service industry. Marketing skills include market research, product testing, packaging and labelling, management of sales force, 'point-of-sale' displays, promotions, pricing the product and advertising it through the media, direct mail, and sponsorship.

What effect do you think point-of-sale displays like this have?

It is expensive to make a new product or service. To cut down the risk, market researchers are hired to find out such things as whether there is a gap in the market, what the **competition** is and what the consumer likes or dislikes about similar products. Researchers do **comparison shopping** – are other brands cheaper? longer lasting? better quality or design? more cost effective? Trained interviewers using special questionnaires find out exactly what the public want, or do not want. The answers are carefully analysed, and conclusions are drawn about the new product or service. Market research is also used after a product is launched to test the public's response.

Collect: advertisements from the local newspaper(s) for services.
a You are starting a local service of your own: window cleaning, manicuring – anything you choose. Practise advertising your service by filling in the classified ads box in the local press. Was the task easy? How much did it cost?
b Discuss your results and evaluate them in class.
c Compare the price of your local paper with a glossy magazine. What conclusions can you draw about advertising costs in magazines? on local radio? on national television? How could you check your conclusions?

Working in pairs, choose any one product and 'market research' it. Plan your questions carefully, making sure they are not leading to an answer – for example, ask 'Do you like the colour?', rather than 'Don't you think the colour is attractive?'. Role-play your market research in class, and evaluate your work.

Have you been interviewed for market research?

97

Advertising

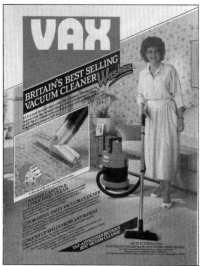

The main function of advertising is to sell goods and services. If the words, sounds, and visual images used in the advertisement are appealing enough, a **demand** is created – people want to buy what is being offered. Advertising agencies work for companies, and have to get results.

➲

Collect: advertisements for a wide variety of goods and services.

a Sort the advertisements into the age groups you think they're intended for: children, teenagers, young adults, families, the elderly, etc. Discuss and write about the different words and images used to attract each group.

b Pick out some stereotypes: the serenely smiling mother and babe, the cheeky but lovable child, the houseproud mum, the sporty type, and so on. Find and list as many other stereotypes as you can.

c Pick out some anxieties: the girl with spots, the boy with bad breath, the mother with the wrong washing powder, the home without insurance, etc. In what ways do you think using fear encourages people to buy the product?

d Pick out advertisements directed at young men. Sort them into those which flatter and those which hint at social failure. Discuss and write about the images and words used to appeal to young men.

e Repeat the above for young women. Then study the sex stereotyping. How obvious is it? Try to rewrite the copy so that the advertisements you looked at in both **d** and **e** appeal to both sexes.

f Pick out phrases such as 'dare to be wicked', 'full of nature's goodness', 'made with you in mind', and 'lasts up to three times as long'. Discuss what these phrases actually mean.

g Find advertisements which use humour to sell a product or service. Write about those which amuse you, and give reasons why.

h Study advertisements for credit cards. Describe the kind of life style which seems to be promised if you become a cardholder.

i Find advertisements which use 'hard' information only. Are there any hidden messages? Do you think they are succesful, and why?

j Many advertisements are highly imaginative, beautifully designed, and full of glamour and style. Choose a few and discuss their appeal.

k Not all advertisements work. A few deeply offend. Describe, with reasons, one you dislike.

Most people have powerful fantasy lives about the superhumans we dream we could be. Advertisers study our dreams and fears. Do you think they can use our emotions to persuade us to buy a product we may not really want or need?

💬

1 Discuss the different emotions the advertisements here might arouse.

2 Describe four ways, with examples, in which advertisers use family situations to promote their products.

(Southern Examining Group)

💬

3 The less confident people are about themselves, the more vulnerable they are to the 'hidden persuaders'.

Discuss and write about this statement.

4 Advertising is an entertaining form of brainwashing, which the consumer can easily control.

Analyse this statement.

More about advertising

Product promotion

Some food manufacturers **sponsor** (pay for) their own advisory bodies. Their function is to give advice to the consumer on all aspects of their product. Some well-known agencies include the Milk Marketing Board, the Sugar Bureau, the Flour Advisory Bureau, and the Butter Information Council. They produce leaflets full of interesting and useful information, including original ideas for recipes. Schools benefit from these leaflets as they are 'free promotion material', and can give far more in-depth information than a textbook.

⮕

Collect: leaflets from the Sugar Bureau and other food advisory groups.

a Why are they called 'free promotions'? Name the food each is promoting.
b Pick out some information which you think is useful and important.
c Study the pictures and wording for unnecessary promotion of the product, and state, with reasons, whether you consider this is advertising.
d Compare the amount of useful information with the amount of promotion.
e Do you think this is a good way for food manufacturers to advise consumers about their products? Why?

The Health Education Authority, funded by government, warns people of the health risks of too much milk, sugar, butter, and white flour in the diet (see Chapter 16).

⮕

Collect: its leaflets on nutrition.

a Compare the contents with those from the milk, sugar, butter, and flour advisory bodies.
b Write about your findings.

Sports sponsorship

Sports sponsorship is popular with manufacturers, as most sports get wide television coverage. Professional sports people such as tennis stars sometimes wear advertising labels on their clothing. In what way do they benefit from this? The advertisements are usually to do with sports products, but not always. What is your opinion of this?

In fact, many sports rely on the money from sponsors to help pay for young people's training.

1 Who, in the final analysis, actually pays for all advertising?
2 Watch a sports programme and notice the number of hoardings carrying different advertisements. Are any for harmful products such as alcohol or tobacco? What is your opinion of this?
3 Hoover and Singer are well-known brand names. What products do they make? Name three other well-known household products, and name their makers. What do you think is meant by 'brand loyalty'?

⮕

4 The Advertising Standards Authority (ASA) has a code of practice (p. 106) which states that advertisements must be legal, decent, honest, and truthful, and must not exploit fear, violence, or supersition. Can you find an advertisement which you think breaks this code? Practise writing a letter to the ASA stating your complaint in clear, simple terms.
5 Do an individual study of **promotional** or **prestige advertising**. This can be sports sponsorship, a magazine competition, or an educational promotion.

Packaging and labelling

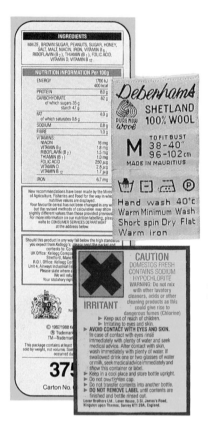

The main functions of packaging and labelling are:

- to hold the contents.
- to protect the contents.
- to keep the contents fresh.
- to show the contents.
- to state the contents.
- to state their safe and correct use.
- to make the contents look appealing.

Which of the packagings below can be recycled (p. 64)? Which do you consider necessary and which unnecessary? Why?

Packaging technology for preserving food has made great advances, and foods which used to spoil quickly can now be kept fresh for a much longer time.

In Third World countries that use less packaging, food spoilage is high. The World Health Organization estimated 30 per cent of much-needed food was lost world-wide in this way in 1986.

But packaging is expensive and is said to waste the earth's energy resources. Making and disposing of packaging uses about 5 per cent of the UK's energy.

a Food packaging adds about 7p to the cost of a £1 grocery bill. State, with reasons, whether you think food packaging is cost-efficient.

b Explain the purpose of date-stamping on food packaging.

c How could you test the idea that frozen foods need moisture-proof packaging?

Collect: deodorants – in sticks, in aerosol cans, and in roll-on packaging.

a Discuss which looks most **i** attractive, **ii** hygienic, **iii** convenient, and **iv** accessible.

b Read the labelling, then write down any health or safety warnings.

c Roll-on deodorant can reinfect spots caused by underarm shaving. Sprays may damage the ozone layer, which protects us from harmful radiation from the sun. Sticks tend to be messy, and less easy to use. Is getting the packaging just right as simple as it might appear?

d Which of the deodorants would you choose? Why?

Collect: a wide variety of labels from food and other household products.

1 Choose ten different labels and compare the amount of 'hard' information.

2 Make notes on how simple or confusing this information is.

3 Record all the information from the labels under the following headings: size, weight, content, health, safety, and instructions for use. Discuss what kind of information is missing from the labels. Comment on your findings.

4 Describe some ways in which packaging and labelling are used as another form of advertising.

5 Find out what the Food Labelling Act requires to be shown on food labels.

Supermarkets

Visit your local supermarket and draw a plan of its layout. Study the different displays and note where each one is. A great deal of marketing skill is used to tempt shoppers to buy on impulse. These skills are nearly always successful! Copy out the following list of questions before your visit, and take the list with you to check your work.

➤ a Where are milk and other dairy products stored? Does the display cabinet have a thermometer showing the temperature of the shelves? If so, what is it?

b Why do you think basic foods, such as bread, tea, sugar, and flour, are displayed in different parts of the store instead of being all together in one convenient place?

c Does the fresh fruit look attractive? Does it give an impression of 'goodness' and 'health'? Where are the fresh fruit and vegetables displayed? Try to work out the reason why.

d Prepared foods such as biscuits, cakes, sauces, and meals make high profits. Are they hidden away, or at eye level? Why do you think this is?

e Study the foods under refrigeration. Do they look tempting? Is there a focal point – a special arrangement to catch the eye? Which of these foods might you buy on impulse? Why?

f Is there usually a queue at the checkout? List all the goods for sale nearby. State, with reasons, why you think these particular goods are chosen to be displayed there.

The **unit cost** is the actual price per kg (or per pound) of an item.

a Which is the cheaper stewing steak, and by how much?

b To feed a large family, would you buy A or B? Why?

c Explain the reason for checking unit cost against weight and consumer cost.

d If A is 'fresh', does that imply B is old? Why do you think the word 'fresh' is used?

➤ **Collect:** frozen chicken, a moisture-proof ham pack, and kitchen scales.

a Weigh the frozen chicken. Defrost it, and weigh it again. Record both weights and compare them with the labelling weight. Discuss your findings.

b Weigh the ham pack. Remove the slices and spread them on absorbent paper. Weigh the slices again. Record and compare weights, and discuss your findings.

The bands and figures of the stock control code in the photograph are a computer code number. When an item is sold, a light passes over the code. It automatically registers the sale and feeds the information into the store's computer. The computer reduces the number of items in stock by one. The store has an up-to-date record of each item in stock.

---

1 Write briefly about your visit. Mention any other marketing skills you noticed.

2 In what ways does a stock control code help a store to be more efficient?

Where to shop

Working in groups, visit one of the places shown. Discuss your findings in class.

a Was the atmosphere exciting? soothing? boring? intimidating? In what ways might the 'right' atmosphere encourage people to spend more?

b Did you consider the sales staff polite? rude? informative? bored? Was there any pressure to buy? In what ways might the attitude of sales staff affect people's spending?

c Make notes on the prices, quality of goods, hours of trading, and ease of access (whether it was near home, a bus stop, or car parking facilities).

d Discuss the following statements:

● A good way to save money is to shop around for bargains.

● Shopping around is inconvenient; it wastes energy and time.

Where you decide to shop depends on your priorities. People with more time than money may prefer the bleakness of discount stores to soft carpets, piped music, stylish layout, and lavish window-dressing. People in a hurry may use speciality shops where they can get exactly what they want, or corner shops with late trading hours. People with little time or money may shop once a week at large stores with lower prices than speciality or corner shops.

1 Some people really enjoy shopping; others loathe it. What do you think might be the priority for **a** a parent with a hungry baby, **b** a friend assisting a person in a wheelchair, and **c** a coach party on a spending spree?

2 Pick one well-known brand of food and one household article. Compare the quality and price of the two items in three different kinds of shop.

3 Find out about bulk buying, telephone sales, and discount stores.

4 Housebound people may appreciate shopping by post. Explain how they could take part in a bulk buying scheme.

5 Discuss the advantages and disadvantages of different kinds of shop, and of other places where household shopping can take place. Suggest various ways in which a person confined to the home could cope with shopping for all aspects of his or her personal and household needs. Briefly evaluate one of the ways you have suggested, in the light of course work. *(London and East Anglian Group)*

Consumer advice

There are so many similar goods for sale it can be difficult to choose between them. And there are so many different advertisements that the consumer can become confused. When money is short, it is especially important for people to get impartial (unbiased) advice on how to buy wisely. Consumer Advice Centres (CAC), funded by government, give free and impartial advice.

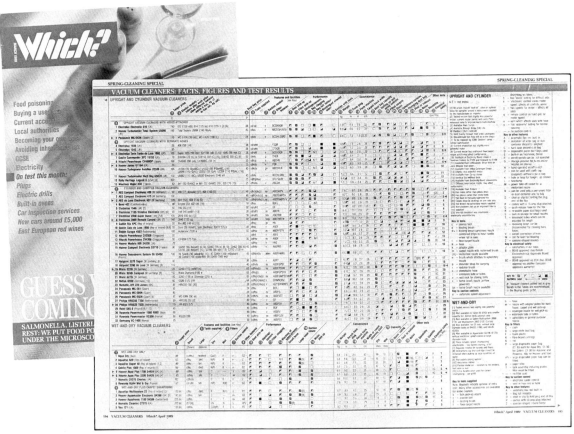

BEAB Approved via CCA

The Consumers' Association is funded by sales of the magazine *Which?* This shows the results of impartial tests on goods and services. Copies of *Which?* can be found in libraries and CAC.

The BSI (British Standards Institution) tests a wide variety of goods sent to it by the manufacturers. Only those products which pass strict tests for quality, durability, and safety may have the Kitemark attached to them.

The BEAB (British Electrotechnical Approvals Board) attaches or engraves this safety mark to or on electrical goods which pass their strict safety tests.

Other sources of advice include kin, friends, sales staff, sales leaflets, magazines articles, and CAB.

---

1 Choose, with reasons, a suitable vacuum cleaner for **a** an extended family, and **b** a one-person household.

2 You want to buy an iron, a tennis racket, and a toy. Name the people or places you could go to for advice. What difference might there be in advice from a sponsored agency (p. 99) and from an independent source?

3 Your friend has decided to purchase a stereo. What advice would you give him or her about finding information and selecting the method of payment? Briefly explain why the advice you give is important. *(London and East Anglian Group)*

Choosing a product

Look in your wardrobe and cupboards. Is there an article you have bought on impulse only to find it unsuitable when you got home? To cut down on **impulse buying**, think about your needs before you go shopping. Ask yourself the questions in the table – look at the sample answers given there:

Question	A shirt	An electric kettle
Why do I want it?	To match a new outfit	For my bed-sit
Do I really need it?	No, but I want it.	Yes, to save time.
Will it get much use?	Every weekend	Every day
What special features do I want?	Crease-resistant fabric	Automatic switch-off, good design
How long should it last?	About two years	A long time – five years?
Does it cost much to use?	Soap and warm water wash	240W – low electricity bill
Where can I get more product information?	Friends, sales staff, fashion magazines	Consumer Advice Centre, sales staff, leaflets
What happens if something is wrong?	Return it to the shop and get a cash refund	Depends on the guarantee
What else should I know?	—	After-sales service
How do I want to pay?	Cash	Credit loan
How much do I want to pay?	Up to £15	With APR, up to £23

For large or expensive items, your questions need to be more detailed:
a **Performance** Is it comfortable? easy to clean? easy to operate?
b **Aesthetics** Is it attractive? Does it suit the style of the room?
c **Size** Is it too big? too small? Does it fit into the available space?
d **Mobility** Is it on wheels? easy to move for cleaning purposes?
e **Protection** Is it a fire hazard? Are there any health or safety features?

1 You want to buy a gift for an elderly relative. Draw up a list of questions and answers to help in your decision making. Choose your priorities. Select a gift and write about the reasons for your choice.

2 You have overspent your budget and can afford either the shirt or the kettle, not both. List the priorities important for your choice.

3 You have £200 to purchase a sofabed. Turn to p. 167 for the size of the room. Repeat question 1 above, including questions for large items. Select a suitable sofabed. Describe its advantages and disadvantages. Evaluate your choice.

Consumer protection

The law has three basic rules for consumer protection. Goods or services must be:

- **of merchantable quality**. A new bag must not be damaged. It must work properly.
- **as described**. If the bag is described as leather, it must not be plastic.
- **fit for its purpose**. If the bag is meant to close to keep your books dry, then it must.

When you buy goods or services, you and the seller make a contract. The seller, not the manufacturer, is responsible if something is wrong. Your rights under the Sale of Goods and Trade Description Acts entitle you in this case to:

- a replacement bag or free repair; or
- your money back – you need not accept a credit note; or
- a cash payment of the difference in cost between a new bag and the faulty one.

You are not entitled to anything if you:

- were told about or saw the fault.
- change your mind about wanting it.
- did the damage yourself.
- got it as a present – the buyer must make the claim.

When something goes wrong, stop using the faulty goods. If possible, take the receipt and the faulty goods back to the seller at once. You can still complain if you have lost the receipt, or if the guarantee is out of date but the fault is due to poor manufacturing. If you cannot get to the seller, telephone or write a letter: keep a copy of what you said or wrote.

Some people find it difficult to make complaints: others really enjoy a battle. It is best to be polite, but firm. You have more chance of success if you interact with the seller in a calm and businesslike manner. If the seller disagrees with your complaint, ask CAC or CAB for further help.

1 Visit the enquiry desk at a large chain store with no fitting room, and ask about their policy for returning a garment which does not fit.
2 Role-play making a complaint about an umbrella which fails to open.
3 Role-play returning a carton of milk on which the date stamp is overdue to a seller who says you should have noticed the date.
4 The gift you bought a member of your family has proved faulty. Describe the steps you would take to put matters right.

More about consumer protection

What is a guarantee?

A guarantee is another kind of insurance.

Collect: a selection of guarantees for goods and services.

a Choose two for similar items and study the contents.

b Is one guarantee better? If so, in what ways?

c Study the exclusion clauses. Are they reasonable? fair?

d Where would you keep a guarantee? Why?

e If you lost the guarantee, would the sales receipt cover you?

What is a code of practice?

The Office of Fair Trading is funded by government. One of its functions is to protect the rights of the consumer. Working together with Trade Associations, the Office of Fair Trading produces codes of practice. These are guidelines about **a** the quality of goods, and **b** the standards of service you can expect.

Collect: a variety of code of practice leaflets.

a What is the meaning of the word 'reputable'?

b Is a disreputable company likely to have a code of practice?

c Does the code of practice mean consumers are likely to pay more or less? Why?

d Does it stop goods or services going wrong?

e What are the advantages, if any, of using companies which offer a code of practice?

1 Find out what the symbol on the left means.

2 Do you only buy goods or services from companies which have a code of practice? Why?

3 Public utilities have their own code of practice. Find out what happens in cases of genuine hardship when consumers cannot pay their bills.

4 A guarantee is consumer insurance.

Analyse this statement.

Further work on Chapter 8

1 Answer the following:
- What was the last item of clothing you bought?
- Where did you buy it?
- How did you pay for it?
- Do you still like it?
- How often do you wear it?
- What is its present condition?
- Were you influenced by an advertisement?
- Would you buy a similar item again?
- What will you do with it when you no longer use it?
- Do you consider it was money well spent?

2 Analyse all the factors which influenced your buying – interest in fashion, limited resources, advertising, marketing skills, ease of maintenance, time available for shopping, time and energy available for comparative shopping, etc.

3 Turn back to p. 96 and study the work you did there. Do you think you might now change some of your shopping habits? Why?

4 Select a small electrical appliance and demonstrate your consumer skills by writing a full description of all the factors you would consider before making your choice.

5 Your shopping skills depend upon a number of factors. Most of them are to do with you – your personality, your values, and your long- or short-term goals. To be an effective consumer, you need to recognize these factors.

Discuss.

6 Suggest *two* ways in which advertisements persuade us to buy goods.

(Midland Examining Group)

7 List *two* benefits to the consumer of advertising.

8 Briefly explain the *three* most important points you would consider in order to make an informed choice when buying bed linen. *(London and East Anglian Group)*

9 List *two* points to consider when buying nightwear for a young child.

(Welsh Joint Education Committee)

10 Informed choices and decisions reduce the risk of disappointment.
Say what would influence your choice when buying an outfit to wear to your cousin's wedding in Manchester in January. The wedding ceremony will be unfamiliar to you. Briefly explain your reasons.
Discuss the advantages and disadvantages of different types of shops and places where household shopping takes place.
Suggest various ways in which a person confined to the home could cope with shopping for all aspects of his/her personal and household needs.
Briefly evaluate one of the ways you have suggested, in the light of course work.

(London and East Anglian Group)

Now look again at the objectives at the beginning of the chapter, and check that you have achieved them.

9 Housing

By the end of this chapter, you should know:

- the psychological value of a home.
- the effects of density of population, and the housing shortage.
- the problem of homelessness.
- the government's role in housing.
- the importance of architects and housing design.
- factors about renting a home.
- how to choose an appropriate home.

What is a home?

Imagine you are opening the door of your own first home. Which of the following might you feel, and why?

- a little scared
- delighted
- free
- private
- lonely
- safe
- grown-up
- other

In the first minutes, would you want to:

- examine everything?
- bounce on the bed?
- make a hot drink?
- talk to neighbours?
- move the furniture?
- throw a party?
- plan to redecorate?
- unpack immediately?
- check door and window locks?
- find a safe place for the key?
- What else would you want to do?

- Having a place of their own helps people to feel independent, satisfied, responsible, and effective at managing their lives.

Analyse this view by matching your feelings and actions to these words.

1 What percentage of the elderly live in their own homes (p. 32)? Why do you think they choose to do so even when they are almost too frail to look after themselves? Answer in as much depth as you can. State some ways in which **a** individuals, **b** families, and **c** community services can help elderly people stay in their homes.

2 Homes are of psychological value – good for mental health and happiness.

Discuss.

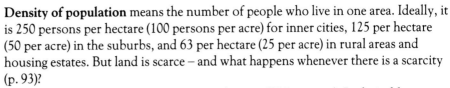

Land and housing

Density of population means the number of people who live in one area. Ideally, it is 250 persons per hectare (100 persons per acre) for inner cities, 125 per hectare (50 per acre) in the suburbs, and 63 per hectare (25 per acre) in rural areas and housing estates. But land is scarce – and what happens whenever there is a scarcity (p. 93)?

High rise blocks have 500 persons per hectare (200 per acre). In desirable parts of London, density in bed-sits is much greater. High density of itself does not cause stress – individuals can adapt to most environments. But they cannot adapt successfully to lack of provision for their mental and emotional needs. If they feel ineffective (not in control of their lives), then being forced to live in unsuitable housing can cause unbearable stress.

Some causes of stress from poor housing conditions include:

a poor town planning (p. 69).
b architecture which is insensitive to a family's needs.
c shoddy building materials, and poor workmanship.
d lack of amenities in older houses.
e noisy or dirty neighbours in high density areas.

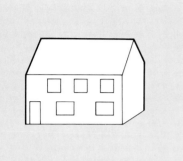

Detached
1 unit = 4 people

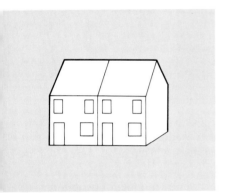

Semi detached
2 units = 8 people

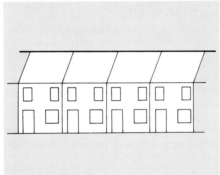
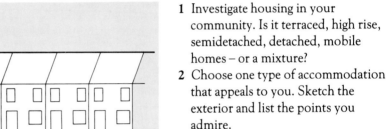

Terraced
4 units = 16 people

High rise
30 flats (units) = 120 people

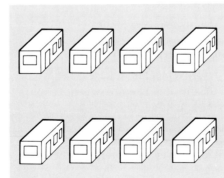

Mobile home
8 units = 32 people

1 Investigate housing in your community. Is it terraced, high rise, semidetached, detached, mobile homes – or a mixture?

2 Choose one type of accommodation that appeals to you. Sketch the exterior and list the points you admire.

3 Ask from two to four local residents in different types of housing if you may interview them for your school project. Find out how long they have lived there, the advantages of that type of accommodation, and the main drawbacks. Is there friendly interaction with neighbours? Are the local amenities good, average, poor? If they could change one thing about their home, what would it be?

4 Connect any negative comments to the above five causes of stress. Compare your findings with the accommodation you originally chose and sketched. Has your opinion altered in any way? Why?

109

Investigating housing shortage

Housing belongs to either the **private** or the **public sector**. The private sector includes individuals and families who buy their homes as dwellings; and landlords or companies buying property as an investment. The housing department of a local authority is responsible for the public sector – council homes.

A five-person household

A one-person household

A one-person household

People aged	1973	1985
16–24	1.5	3.6
25–44	2.4	5.3
45–64	8.1	10.6
65–74	25.7	28.9
75+	40.0	47.0
Total	9.1	12.3

The government controls the number of homes available in the public sector. This is called **public housing stock**. Between 1979 and 1986, one million council homes were removed from the public housing stock when tenants were given 'the right to buy' their homes.

Define a household unit (p. 36). In 1961, the average number of people in a household unit was 3.09. In 1985, it was 2.56. What was the trend for the numbers of people choosing to live together? Can you think of any reasons for this trend?

The table on the left shows the percentage of people in private households in the UK who live alone.

Which of the following do you think may have caused the increase in one-person households, and why?

a general rise in living standards
b the single-parent family
c the desire for privacy
d advances in technology
e improvement in welfare benefits
f the threat of unemployment
g the Equal Pay Act

h improved community services
i the numbers of homeless
j general changes in life style
k the increased divorce rate
l job opportunities
m changes in the elderly population

---

1 Do a survey of household unit size of the class.
2 Is family life going out of fashion? What was the total percentage of households with more than one person in 1973? 1985?

3 State the two major reasons for the housing shortage.
4 Social policy made by various governments is largely responsible for the shortage of homes.

Analyse this statement.

Being homeless

Temporary accommodation provided by a housing department

The housing department of a local authority is responsible for the distribution of housing stock. It rents council homes to people who **a** cannot or do not want to buy their homes, and **b** cannot or do not want to pay the high rents in the private sector. A points system based on the Housing (Homeless Persons) Act of 1977 gives priority to these vulnerable groups in the community:

- households with dependent children.
- pregnant women.
- the elderly.
- the disabled.
- the mentally ill.
- key workers.

The housing department has a statutory duty to help people who are homeless, or about to become homeless, and who are in **priority need**. Temporary accommodation is offered in small hotels or bed and breakfast lodgings until a council home can be found. Conditions for being homeless and in priority need include:

a being truly homeless – having no family or friends to take you in.

b not having made yourself homeless on purpose.

c being connected with the local community – through work, through close family ties, or by having long residence there.

In 1986, 109 000 households were found to be in priority need. The total number of households asking for help was 233 000. Of households not in the top priority groups, 14 per cent had been on the housing waiting list for nine or more years.

1 Find out what is meant by 'key workers'. Do you think they should have housing priority? Why?

2 Trudy, Tim and their 18-month-old baby have been given accommodation in a bed and breakfast hotel. Tim's gross pay is £108 weekly, his total deductions are £21 and his fares to work £16. The cost of the family's lodgings is £35. There are no cooking facilities. Trudy and the baby must vacate the room from 9 a.m. till 5 p.m.

  a Who do you think has the most stressful weekday, Tim or Trudy? Why?

  b Find out and comment on some amenities in your local community which Trudy and her baby could use during the day.

  c Create a weekly budget for the family. Comment on the life style they must adopt if they are to keep to this budget.

3 Keith cannot bear living at home. He goads his parents into such a row that they turn him out. Is he entitled to be housed by the local authority? Why?

4 Amanda leaves home because her husband is violent. There is no Women's Refuge in her community. Find out whether she is entitled to help from the housing department.

5 Should there be conditions for homelessness? Why?

6 Do an individual study on homelessness. Contact: Shelter, and SHAC.

Some design problems

Over the last forty years, and especially in the 1960s, local authorities have often replaced houses on streets with blocks on estates. Architects have designed fixed, inflexible house plans. They worked to fixed, inflexible budgets. Do people lead fixed, or flexible, lives? From your investigations, should plans be fixed or flexible? Why?

In high rise blocks:

a are the lifts always reliable?

b can the elderly manage the stairs?

c what happens to a person in a wheelchair?

d if you were a parent with young children, would you be keen to face this climb every day?

e when the lift is working, how does it feel to share it with a stranger who might be violent?

f how does it feel to enter a lift which has been vandalized – defaced with graffiti, litter, or human sewage?

People in high rise blocks may suffer a sense of isolation – of being cut off from families, friends, and community life. Why is this?

Multi-storey maisonettes were built on low rise estates. This caused a high child density – lots of children in one place. If play is not supervised, too many children together will run wild. It is difficult and unpleasant for parents to patrol communal gardens, and the elderly and disabled fear being knocked down. Instead of enjoying community spirit and neighbourly interaction, families can become locked in feuds.

When those children reach their teens, they can turn into gangs and terrorize the estate.

How might each of the following improve life in a flat?

a A block should consist of no more than twelve homes.

b It should be no more than three storeys high.

c High child density maisonettes should be on the ground floor.

d The other two storeys should be ordinary flats.

e There should be only one staircase and no lift.

f There should be no communal play areas. The ground should be divided up among the tenants, who are responsible for their plots.

g The site should contain only one block, which must be freestanding and not linked by walkways.

Some exterior problems

On some housing estates, there has been a huge increase in burglary. Study the picture and the following text to work out why:

- ground floor windows should be clear glass.
- doors, porches, meter sheds, etc. should not jut forward.
- the facade should be clearly seen from homes across the street.
- the frontage should be 3 to 5 metres (10 to 15 feet) deep and end at a waist-high wall or fence with a front gate.
- there should be waist-high side fences between adjacent homes.
- the house should face the road, not the back of the next row of houses.
- back gardens should face other back gardens and the only access be from the front; for example, through the garage or down a side path.
- corner houses should have gardens facing both streets.

Architects and planners have been blamed for being insensitive to the needs of individuals and families. In 1979 their spokesperson said, 'Children are our hope for the future. Their welfare is, or ought to be, among architects' and planners' closest concerns.' One study of children in high rise blocks found many were understimulated. They had lost their natural curiosity and eagerness to explore life. Their parents, especially their mothers, were depressed, and suffered **isolation stress.** What were the housing problems causing this?

1 It now seems families do better in streets of terraced or semidetached homes. State, with reasons, why.
2 Name some satisfactions in having an individual garden.
3 Families with young children are no longer housed above the fifth floor. Describe three ways in which living in a third floor flat can affect the parent of a 2-year-old child. Suggest, with reasons, ways of dealing with this situation. *(Southern Examining Group)*
4 You are choosing a home in **a** a high rise, and **b** a low rise estate. List the design mistakes you would hope to avoid.

Leaving home

Before leaving home, think about yourself and your needs:

a Are you fiercely independent? happy on your own? fond of company? good at sharing? shy and awkward with people you do not know?

b Can you shop, cook, clean, mend, and generally look after yourself? Do you want to do these chores at first? Will you have the time?

c Can you prepare nourishing meals? Can you afford the materials and labour costs of eating out or buying take-away food?

d Can you organize your life style, keep to a budget, and plan a daily routine?

e Are you good at making choices? Do you wait for others to make the decisions and then go along with their plans, whether they suit you or not?

---

1 Why do you think it might help to learn more about your needs before leaving home? Which questions have the greater priority for you? Relate your answers to the kind of home and life style you are likely to need. It might be helpful to discuss some of the issues in class.

2 Susan, age 19, is unemployed and living at home. She gives her parents one third of her benefit – find out how much that is at today's unemployment rate. She does not help with the homemaking. Do you think Susan is good at sharing? Discuss some of the things she could do to help at sharing home life.

3 Investigate the laundry options and costs you are likely to have when you leave home. Make a complete list of the laundry you produce in one week – bed linen, towels, clothes to be washed, and garments to be dry cleaned. Visit a launderette and find out the cost of a laundry bag, the amount of laundry a washing cycle will hold, and the total costs of a weekly wash, including travel fares, if any. Visit a dry cleaning service and ask for a list of their prices. Imagine you have no washing machine, so laundry at home must be done by hand. Compare the costs of home laundry with **a** those of the launderette, and **b** sending the total wash to the dry cleaners. Which option is the cheapest? the easiest? the most time efficient? If there were no facilities for laundry in your new home, which option would you choose? Why?

4 Plan, carry out, and evaluate the above investigation as a practical assignment.

A place of your own

Divide the class into five groups. Plan, carry out, and evaluate a full investigation into the accommodation below. Compare all the class findings on the blackboard under separate headings: rent, other costs, meals provided, privacy factor, communal facilities, house rules, standard of furnishings, loneliness factor, value for money, and any other.

Problems can arise over sharing facilities.

1 In a flat share, Brenda makes long-distance telephone calls without putting money in the box. Role-play the scene when the telephone bill arrives, with suggestions on how you would solve the problem without too much upset.

2 Rajan annoys the other lodgers by spending too long in the bathroom. They want to complain to the landlord, but you do not believe in direct confrontation. Devise a practical plan to show Rajan he is being insensitive to the needs of others.

3 Your plan does not work. Rajan acts more selfishly than before. From what you have learned on consumer complaints (p. 105), write down and be prepared to discuss how you would
a approach Rajan directly, and
b complain to the landlord.

4 Which type of accommodation do you think most suitable for a a girl aged 19, attending college in a town where she knows few people, and b a boy aged 16 on a 3-month training course? Give reasons to justify both your choices, commenting under the headings: social life, independence, cost involved, amount of work involved in the day-to-day chores. In which type of accommodation would a person be most likely to feel lonely?

(Scottish Examination Board)

5 Unless each person accepts the concept of interdependence, the sharing of accommodation does not work.

Analyse this statement.

BANBURY, recently refurbished 2 bedroom flat, close town centre, one year let, £320 p.c.m. inclusive. — Tel. (0280) 70520 9-5.30 p.m. Friday. [1]

BANBURY. Unfurnished 3 bedroom semi, full gas central heating, large garden, garage, carpets and curtains, £350 p.c.m. inclusive rates. — Banbury after 5 p.m. [1]

COMFORTABLE and clean room in shared house, all modern conveniences. — Banbury 5983 [1](p4637)

FULLY FURNISHED flat to let, two bedrooms, lounge, kitchen, bathroom, village location. — Telephone 0926 8120 [2]

RATLEY, a most appealing characterful cottage property, benefiting from charming cottage features, fully furnished, 3 bedrooms, solid fuel central heating to radiators, rent, £375 p.c.m. inc. — Apply to Bigwood (0295) 27119 [1]

ROOMS to let, £30. — Banbury 3059, anytime. [1](p488)

SINGLE BEDSIT, near Horton hospital, £40 p.w., inclusive heating. — Banbury 6530 [1](p217)

SMALL wage, negotiable, plus free accommodation in farmhouse near Edge Hill to single person (no work involved) in return for keeping an eye on elderly active lady who needs company in house at night (own transport essential). — Apply Edge Hill 029587

£700 PCM   CHIPPING NORTON   1st CLASS GRADE
A 4 bedroom (master en-suite) semi-detached period town House with 2 reception rooms, large kitchen. Secluded garden. Available for 1 year.

£600 PCM   HEADINGTON   1st CLASS GRADE
A 3 bedroom semi-detached House with extended living/dining room in quiet area. Ideal for a family. Available now for 6 to 12 months.

£350 PCM   BLADON   BUDGET GRADE
A 1 bedroom 1st floor Flat in grounds of country House. Suit single/couple.

£550 PCM   WITNEY   1st CLASS GRADE
A 3 bedroom, master en-suite, detached House in a quiet Close, close to town centre. Fully furnished and equipped. Ideal for a family.

£450 PCM   BLACKBIRD LEYS   BUDGET GRADE
A 3 double bedroom Maisonette fully furnished and equipped. Suit professional sharers.

£850 PCM   CHARNEY BASSETT   1st CLASS GRADE
A 4 bedroom detached period House with large lounge and open fire, 2 further reception rooms and 2 bathrooms. Large garden. Overlooking village green. Available July for family.

£750 PCM   LONG WITTENHAM   1st CLASS GRADE
A large 4 bedroom thatched Property with 2 bathrooms, study and sitting room. Available for six months. Family only.

£650 PCM   DIDCOT   1st CLASS GRADE
A 4 bedroom, 2 reception room detached House. Fully furnished and equipped with gas central heating. Fully enclosed garden and double garage. Available mid June for 1 year. Family only.

£350 PCM   DIDCOT   1st CLASS GRADE
Recently built 1 bedroom ground floor Flat fully equipped and furnished. Located near to station. Available from May.

About renting

As a **tenant**, you pay **rent** to live in a home which is not your own. The **landlord** or **landlady** may be a private citizen, the local authority, or a housing association. You are not responsible for maintenance (repair, upkeep, and cleaning) of the outside.

You need to find out:

a How long is the agreement to rent for?
b Does the rent include the community charge, ground rent (if any), and water rates?
c Does the rent include hot water, heating, or lighting?
d Is 'full board', 'half board', or 'breakfast only' included in the rent?
e Is cooking in the room allowed? Is there a communal kitchen?
f Are there meters for electricity, gas, and the telephone?
g Are the bath and toilet facilities shared? If so, by how many people?
h Are there rules about children, visitors, or pets? Can you redecorate, or put up pictures on the walls? Can you use the garden, or hang out washing?
i Who is responsible for the maintenance of shared bathrooms, landings, stairs, and hallways? Who is responsible for unplugging sinks or toilets, and for waste disposal?

▶

Collect: newspaper ads of board and lodgings, flat shares and bed-sits.
a Discuss and write out in full what the abbreviations in the ads mean.
b Compare the advantages and disadvantages of each type of accommodation.
c Choose one you think will be suitable and write a reply stating your age, occupation or study course, the length of time you expect to rent the premises, the name of your bank, and one person who will supply a character reference.
d Role-play **i** ringing the landlord or landlady to arrange to view the accommodation, and **ii** the discussion when you meet.

1 Four students are planning to share rented accommodation during their first year at college.
   a List six points the students should consider when looking for suitable accommodation.
   b What questions should the students ask the landlord or landlady about the use of the accommodation before deciding to rent it?
   c Explain ways in which the students can organize themselves in order to prevent problems caused by sharing accommodation.
   d Suggest a small piece of household equipment which the students might find useful. Give reasons for your choice.   *(Southern Examining Group)*

2 The light bulb in the communal bathroom keeps disappearing. You cannot afford to replace it any more. What can you do to solve this problem?

Renting and the law

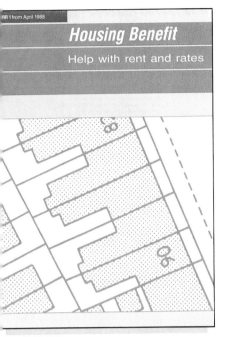

The landlord or landlady must provide tenants with a rent book stating his or her name and address, the amount of rent due each week or month, your rights to protection against **eviction** and **harrassment**, and the rights concerning **rent control**. If you think the rent is too high, you can apply to the **rent tribunal**, which has statutory powers to fix a **fair and reasonable rent** over a set period of time. The amount is not based on what you can afford: it depends upon what kind of property you are renting, the condition it is in, and where it is located. In a few cases, the rent tribunal has raised the rent instead of lowering it.

The rent tribunal also tries to sort out disagreements between the landlord or landlady and tenant. It protects you against unfair eviction and harrassment. Once the rent is controlled, neither landlord/landlady nor tenant can apply for a change until the set period of time is over. If you are in unfurnished accommodation, apply to the rent officer instead.

The Rent Act of 1977 gave tenants in private accommodation **security of tenure**. What do you think this means? (Council tenants were given the same in 1980.) In return, you are expected to behave in a 'tenant-like manner': paying your rent regularly, keeping the property in good order, not being noisy or a nuisance to your neighbours, and not damaging the furniture and fittings by ill-treatment or neglect. Any one of these things is called **objectionable behaviour**, and gives the landlord or landlady rights to repossess your home.

Notice to quit can be given by the landlord/landlady to tenants. It must be given in writing, four weeks before the date to quit. The following information must be included:

a No person can be evicted without a court order.
b A court order can only be applied for after the notice to quit expires.
c Advice is available from CAB, a housing advice centre, a rent officer, a rent tribunal, or a solicitor.
d Help with legal costs may be available under the Legal Aid scheme.

---

1 You need extra cash, so have rented your spare room to a friend. He buys new curtains and a vacuum cleaner, and says that is his contribution instead of rent for the next three months. He has no rent book. Analyse this problem.

2 Role-play a scene in which you have overspent and ask your landlord if you can be 'in rent arrears' until your next pay cheque in three weeks' time.

3 Study the wording in a rent book. What is meant by 'security of tenure'? List the conditions under which you might lose this right. Discuss whether you consider them fair.

4 You become unemployed, long-term sick, or disabled, and you can no longer pay the rent. List the sources of help available to you (p. 50).

Homes and life style

Before choosing a home, you need to consider your life style. A single person may need a modern bed-sit; a family with young children needs a larger home with space for play, prams, and bicycles; elderly or disabled people do not want stairs; keen DIY-ers look for old houses to renovate. At different stages of the life cycle, people choose different homes.

Some factors to consider before choosing a home include:

a **size**   How much space is needed? The guideline for space is 1.5 persons per room of an average house. Is there a garden? a garage? a place for drying clothes?

b **site**   How close are schools? workplace? shops? public transport? health centre? Do the main rooms face south to catch natural warmth and light from the sun?

c **amenities**   Are there the five basics: inside toilet, bath or shower, wash basin, kitchen sink, and a separate hot and cold water supply?

d **protection**   Is it healthy, with no rising damp, and no rooms without natural lighting and ventilation? Is it safe? Is it solidly built, with no faulty electrical wiring and/or gas pipes?

e **maintenance**   Is it easy to clean and look after? Is the kitchen well planned? Are costly repairs needed?

f **design**   Are there any design faults? If it is a high rise, what floor is it on? If it is a low rise, is there a high child density?

Choose, with reasons, a home for each of the below from the housing on p. 108.

Further work on Chapter 9

1 Would you prefer to rent or buy your home? Why? Discuss some advantages and disadvantages of each.

2 Working in groups, find out about the following:
   a a mortgage endowment policy.
   b a pension-linked loan.
   c ground rent on leasehold homes.
   d an estate agent's costs, and who pays.
   e the work and costs of a valuation officer.
   f the work and costs of a surveyor.
   g service charges in a block of flats.
   h average water board charges.
   i hiring a van, and removal costs.
   j connecting up telephone, gas, and electricity, and the costs involved.
   Pool all the information and discuss the 'hidden' costs of buying a home.

3 In 1985, 16 500 homes were **repossessed** – taken back by the loan company. In 1986, this rose to 21 000 homes. From January to June of 1987 alone, 11 600 homes were repossessed.
   The worry of heavy mortgage repayments can cause stress. Discuss the following:
   a People are so keen to buy a home they get into debt.
   b People forget about the extra expenses on top of the deposit.
   c It is too easy to get a mortgage – loan companies are to blame.

4 Safe as houses, or mortgaged up to the hilt?

   Discuss.

5 a Name *two* sources from which the money can be borrowed to buy a home.
   b Comment briefly on *one* of the sources named in **a**.
   c Apart from the deposit, what other expenses might be encountered when buying a home?
   d Suggest *four* different points to be considered before deciding to buy a home.
   e Evaluate the benefits of owning your own home. *(Welsh Joint Education Committee)*

6 Imagine you have moved into a flat with two friends. Look at the list below.
   a Which expenses should be shared by all and which are personal?

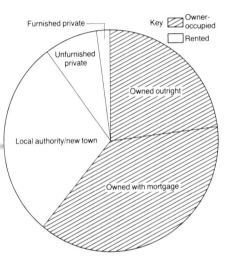

Households owned and rented by their occupiers, 1985

	Shared expenses	Personal expenses
electricity bill		
rent		
food		
clothes		
magazines		
bus fares		
entertainment		
birthday presents		
telephone bill		

   b Your weekly wages are enough to pay your expenses. Some of the shared expenses will have to be paid monthly. How can you make sure you have enough money for these monthly expenses? *(Scottish Examination Board)*

Now look again at the objectives at the beginning of the chapter, and check that you have achieved them.

10 Building materials for a home

By the end of this chapter, you should be able to:

- identify some examples of what you consider to be fine architecture.
- interpret some building plans and housing design.
- have a working knowledge of various building materials.
- understand the effects of weathering on a home.
- analyse the properties of different paints.

Styles of architecture

Study these homes, and the photographs on p. 112. Do you think that architects design homes to:

- look beautiful?
- last a long time?
- be cheap and cheeful?
- withstand the weather?
- be functional?

1 Which of these homes most appeals to you? Why?
2 Which home might be a fire hazard? Why?
3 List all the building materials you can find. **Masonry** is the covering name for stone, brick or concrete. Find out the basic ingredient in masonry.
4 What does 'weathering' mean? Describe the climate these homes are designed for. Collect pictures of homes for two very different climates. Why is housing often referred to as 'shelter'?

Planning a home 1

1 Study these designer plans. Find out and learn the meaning of the symbols used here.
2 Jean, her mother, and their Alsatian dog had to leave their council home – why (p. 66)? Jean works in a supermarket, and her mother is a mail order agent. Both like the outdoor life, neither enjoys household chores. Jean is a keen dressmaker. Her mother visits the library twice a week. They love their mobile home, but are sad they cannot afford a car. They especially budget for good lighting – why?
   List their priorities in choosing a mobile home and state in what ways it suits their life style. What drawbacks might there be, and why?
3 Describe the life style of the people for whom the terraced home (plan shown below) would be suitable.

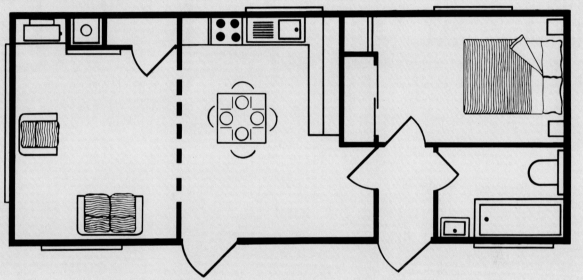

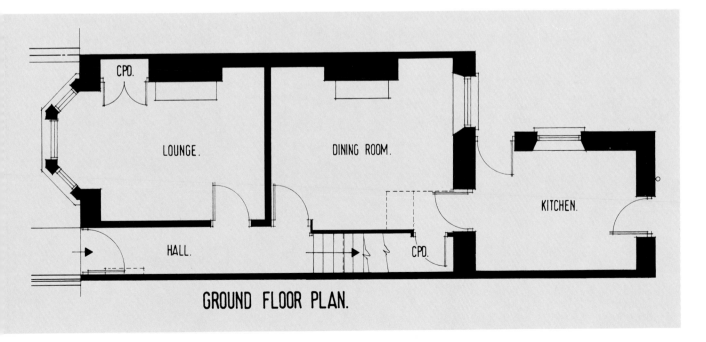

GROUND FLOOR PLAN.

More planning

1 Choose and describe the life style of one group of people for whom each of these homes might be suitable, giving reasons for your choice.
2 State all the community services and the local amenities both groups of people are likely to use.

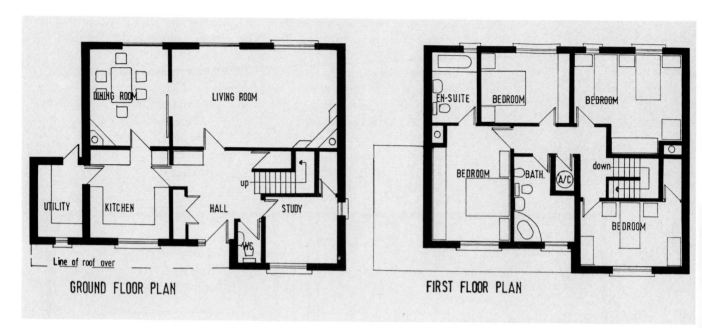

GROUND FLOOR PLAN

FIRST FLOOR PLAN

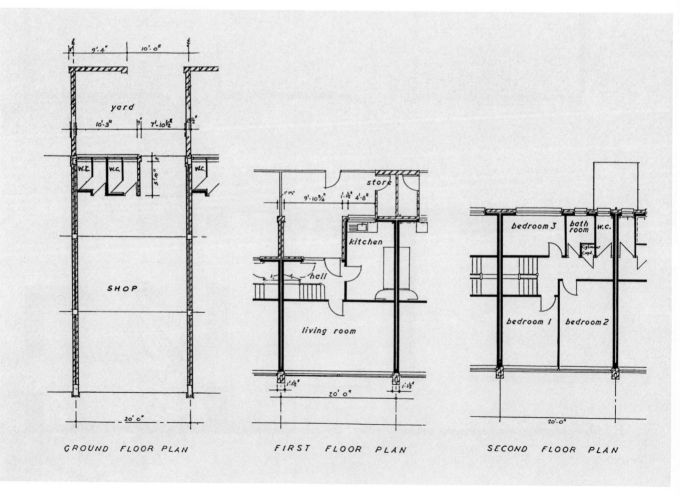

GROUND FLOOR PLAN

FIRST FLOOR PLAN

SECOND FLOOR PLAN

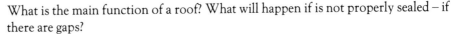

The roof

What is the main function of a roof? What will happen if is not properly sealed – if there are gaps?

Collect: roof tiles, diagonal props, and a stream of water.

Devise a simple task to find out why tiles are laid in an overlap rather than edge to edge.

Roof tiles are now usually made of concrete, as slate (the traditional material) is becoming scarce. They are less brittle than slates, quicker to lay, and easier to replace if they fall off. The tiled roof on the left in the picture is sloped so that snow and rain cannot settle. Why does it jut out over the walls? Find a gutter and a downpipe. What is their function?

It is more practical to build high rise homes with flat roofs (centre of picture) so that air vents, water tanks, and heating systems can be easily maintained. The roofing material used is felt matted into tough sheets by rolling, pressure, and heat. **Bitumen** (tarry pitch) is added to make the material waterproof. A slight **camber** (arch) allows the rain to drain into gutters and flow away into downpipes. Find a camber in a road near your home.

Tiled roofs are supported by thick frameworks of wood (right of picture). Damage to the framework will make the roof ripple or sag. Why is it essential the wood is kept dry?

Layers of felt roofing are placed under the tiles for protection against the weather and for insulation (p. 140). Some roofs have attic windows, chimneys, or pipes built into them. Patches of metal called **flashing** seal out the rain.

Skylines can look mysterious or beautiful. Do a survey of the roofs in your area. Sketch or photograph three different types of roof which you think both attractive and functional. Find and draw some flashing, and explain how it functions.

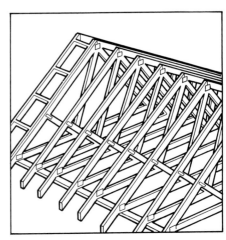

The outside walls

Many outside walls are built of bricks. Bricks are made from clay moulded into oblong blocks and heated in kilns; they are long-lasting, and cheap to produce. All outside and some inside walls are **load-bearing** – they support the weight of the floors and roof (see p. 130). Where gaps are left for windows and doors, strong supports called **lintels** must be built into the walls. Find the lintel in the diagram of cavity walls below.

Collect: blocks of wood, concrete, plastic, and brick; rolls of fibreglass and foam; and white anhydrous copper sulphate, which turns blue when wet.
a Stand the blocks and rolls on end in 2 cm of water, so the tops are dry. Put a small amount of the copper sulphate on each top and observe at 10-minute intervals.
b In what order did the materials absorb moisture? Record your findings.

If bricks are porous, why are they used to build walls which should be dry?
Collect: a bag of cement, water, three bricks, and a trowel or large knife.
a Mix the cement and water according to the instructions to make **mortar.**
b Dampen the three bricks slightly to increase their absorbency. Spread the mortar 1 cm thick on the top sides of two of the bricks. Stick the three bricks together and leave to dry overnight. Try to pull them apart. Now answer the question above.

Half-built cavity brick walls with butterfly wire ties

Two outside walls are built, with a **cavity** (air space) between them. The cavity stops damp passing to the inner wall, and stops heat passing out. For better insulation, the cavity can be filled with foam or fibreglass. **Wire ties**, bonded into the mortar at regular intervals, keep the two walls together.

1 Explain the functions of the following: load-bearing walls, lintels, mortar, fibreglass, and wire ties.
2 What would happen to a load-bearing wall if a lintel were not installed?
3 Homes built 50 years ago may not have cavity walls. Devise a simple task to show the function of a cavity wall.

4 Find out how concrete is made. What is reinforced concrete? What advantages, if any, does concrete have which brick lacks?

Foundations and floors

The foundations of a home must be deep and strong enough to support its weight. Trenches are dug and concrete poured into **footings**. The spaces are filled with crushed rock and sand. A plastic sheet is laid over the top to stop damp rising up from the ground. All outside and any inside walls which are load-bearing are built up from the footings to give them extra strength.

Concrete floors are called **solid**. They are made by pouring concrete over the plastic sheet and leaving it to set. They lack the slight bounce of wood. They can be cold, noisy, and tiring to walk on, but they can take the full weight of heavy floor tiles such as marble, brick, parquet blocks, or slate.

A **joist** is a thick beam of wood used for floor, ceiling, and roof supports. Wooden floors – **suspended** floors – are made of timber planks or chipboard (p. 126) nailed across joists. Joists are always horizontal and load bearing – they support the weight of all the structures above them. On the ground floor, **air bricks** or **grids** allow air to circulate under the floor to keep the wood dry and free of mould. The air holes are very small to prevent rats and mice getting in. It is best not to choose very heavy tiles on suspended floors, especially upstairs.

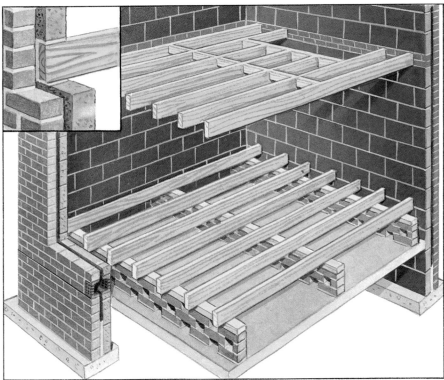

Collect: a small plank, bricks, and a stone floor.
Devise a simple task to find the differences in effect in standing on a stone floor and a wooden (suspended) floor.

1 Watch the work at a building site. Find out what is being built. Notice the depth and extent of the foundations. Try to name some of the materials used.
2 What are air bricks? Explain why they are not needed for solid floors.

3 How can you tell whether a floor is solid or suspended? Which is more likely to be used upstairs, and why? Devise a task to find out which is more tiring on the feet. From your findings, discuss the implications for the choice of floor in a gymnasium or discotheque.

Wood as a building material

In a **timber frame** home (see the photo on p. 120), thick beams called **studs** are spaced at regular intervals. Like joists, studs are load-bearing. To make up the outside walls, **weatherboard** or **clapboard** is fixed across the studs. The cavity walls have a waterproof membrane that must not be punctured. Timber homes look attractive, but are less permanent and need more maintenance than masonry homes. Which of the two is more likely to be a fire risk?

Collect: samples of woods – weatherboard, clapboard, chipboard, plywood, etc. Many building materials are **composites** – made of a mixture of things. Composite woods are made from wood chippings or pulp, treated with different chemicals, glued together, and compressed into boards. Feel the different textures for their strengths and weaknesses. Which do you think unsuitable for outside walls, and why? Try to identify some different woods inside the home.

Collect: strips of painted and unpainted wood.
Devise a simple outdoor task to find out which of the above has more protection against weathering.

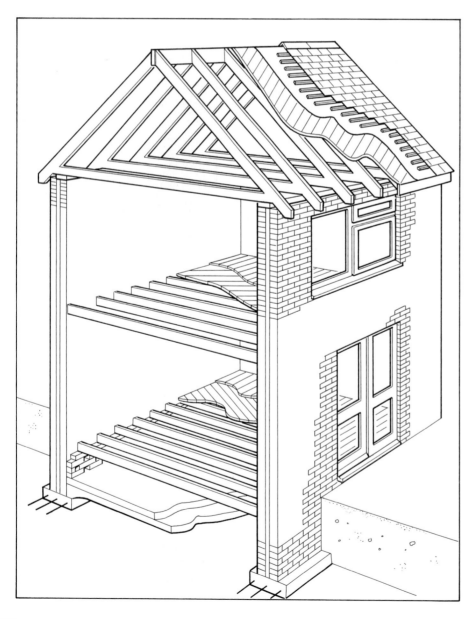

1 Outside walls can be built of masonry or wood. Discuss some advantages and disadvantages of each.

2 There are many different kinds of wood – beautiful, functional, plain, etc. Increase your wood awareness by trying to name the various kinds around you. Contact: suppliers of wood varnishes, preservatives, polishes, waxes, and paints.

A great deal of wood is used as a building material in both timber frame and masonry houses.

Metals and plastics

Modern gutters and downpipes are made of **ribbed PVC** – polyvinyl chloride. This is a composite plastic, made into hard sheets of material. The ribbing stops debris (bits of leaves, silt, etc.) from blocking the flow of water. PVC gutters need no maintenance except checks for blockages by birds' nests, tennis balls, and so on. Older pipes of cast iron can crack, leaking water into the walls.

Collect: a wood block, a hammer, and long nails made of steel, copper, galvanized metal, and aluminium.

a Hammer the nails halfway into the block. Leave the block outdoors where it will be exposed to weathering for several weeks.

b Record your findings and write about the weathering properties of the four materials.

c Why does a householder need this information? Where are metals used on the outside of a house? Look for: door hinges, locks, latches, garage doors, garden gates, etc.

Rust is a corrosive which forms on iron or steel as a result of exposure to oxygen and moisture in the air. **Galvanized metals** are metals coated with **zinc** to make them rust-proof. Plastics do not rust – how could you test this?

Modern window frames are made of aluminium. It is weatherproof, does not rot, rust or warp, is lighter to use, is more permanent, and is easy to maintain.

Outside walls are protected from weathering by **render** (stucco). Render is thick plaster made from cement, lime, and sand. It gives a smooth surface which is easy to maintain, and can be painted for further protection, or to add an individual touch. In hot countries, **whitewash** reflects back the sun's glare and keeps the home cool.

1 Return to your investigation work into housing on p. 120. Choose any one building and check for metal and plastic materials used on the outside. Notice any signs of weathering and describe them. What suggestions could you make to prevent further damage?

2 Draw a rough sketch of the outside of your home, and complete the above task.

Damp, rot, and woodworm

Fungus is a mould which grows on damp wood. It causes **dry rot** – the wood starts to crumble. It also causes **wet rot** – the wood is so soaked it splinters off. A damp home smells musty. Wallpaper peels and plaster flakes away from the walls and ceilings. The air is unhealthy. People get coughs, colds, sore throats, and chest infections. The young, sick, and disabled are particularly vulnerable – and old bones ache painfully in a damp room.

Collect: eight bricks, and a strip of polythene sheeting or some bitumen (tarry pitch).

Stand two piles of four bricks in 2 cm of water. On one pile, lay the polythene sheeting or bitumen between the third brick and the top one. Leave overnight. Record your findings.

This is a **damp proof course** (DPC). What is its function? Why must it be between bricks 15 to 20 cm above the ground?

The main reasons for damp are:
a rain coming through roof or outer walls.
b blocked gutters, pipes, air bricks, or drains.
c rising damp from a faulty DPC.
d drying out of moisture in a new house.
e an older home without cavity walls.
f condensation (p. 141).

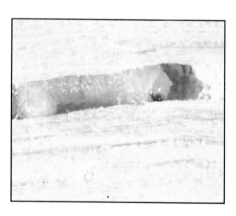

A damp house is expensive to treat. The cause of the trouble must first be found, and then put right. All rotting wood must be torn out and replaced. Waterproof chemicals can be forced between bricks in old houses with no DPC.

Woodworm is a covering name for various kinds of beetle. They lay eggs inside wood. The grubs feed on it, develop into insects, and bore their way out, causing the typical holes of woodworm. By then, the wood you cannot see may be almost eaten away. Joists, studs, floors, and roof timbers infested by woodworm can be very unsafe. The eggs and grubs of woodworm beetles must be destroyed with special insecticides.

1 Sketch the outside of a home. Mark in the danger areas for damp, and name the checks you would do to find out the cause.

2 Specialists are needed to treat serious woodworm, but if you have a small item of furniture at home which needs treating, you might like to choose this as a practical assignment. Contact: any specialist firm in the phone book.

Investigating paint

Collect: tins of metal and wood primer; tins of metal, wood, and stone paint; white spirit and water; paint brushes; newspaper, rags, and protective clothing.

Plan a visit to a builder's yard, a scrap yard, a demolition site, or a skip. You need to collect pieces of used metal such as lamp holders, shelf brackets, chairs, or a water pipe; breezeblock or rough concrete; and strips or blocks of wood and plasterboard. If any items are painted, examine them for the effects of weathering, and try to work out if this happened because the paint was badly applied. Remove the paint with an appropriate paint stripper.

Working in pairs, devise, plan, and carry out tests for the following statements:

Too much paint on a brush results in a dripping mess.
Insufficient paint lets the surface show through.
Brushing up and down and then across spreads paint evenly.
Paint sticks to hands and anything it lands upon.
Different kinds of paint are removed by different methods.

Metal primer acts as a seal and protects against corrosion.
It is difficult to cover bare metal with one coat of paint.
A coat of primer helps paint stick to metal.
If too much paint is applied, it spoils the finish.

Paint soaks into bare wood and the finish is rough.
Wood that is sealed with primer needs less paint.
An undercoat reduces the amount of top coat needed.
It is not cost efficient to use top coat on bare wood.

If paint is brushed on breezeblock, the result is unsatisfactory.
Paint on breezeblock must be forced inwards with the top end of the brush.
If paint is not forced inwards, rain will cause it to flake off breezeblock.
Stone paint acts as a thick, hard-wearing surface on breezeblock.

1 Evaluate the smooth finish of your paint-work by its visual and tactile appeal. For a tougher evaluation, leave the items outdoors to weather for several weeks.

2 Record your findings and write about **a** the importance of correctly applying paint, and **b** the sealing and protective characteristics of paint.

The inside walls

Inside walls are called **partition** walls. They divide a home into rooms. They can be made of bricks, or concrete blocks, or plasterboard nailed firmly to studs. Plasterboard is thin, easily damaged, and less soundproof and fireproof than brick or concrete walls. Ceilings of plasterboard are fixed to the underside of joists. Plaster is a pasty mix of lime, sand, and water, used for coating ceilings and walls. As plasterboard is easily damaged, you need to take care with your work.

Collect: a sheet of plasterboard, ready made plaster, and a trowel.
a Cover the board with a thin coat of plaster. Leave till next lesson.
b Add a second coat for a smooth, waterproof finish. Does your board need a third coat?

In high-cost housing, a third coat is added and then the whole wall is painted. In low-cost housing, the plaster may be omitted and paint put directly onto the plasterboard. Tape is put over the joins to stop them showing through.

All homes have outside walls, inside partitions, floors, and a roof. The roof rests on the outside walls. These, with some inside walls, support the weight of the floors. In turn, all this load is supported on the foundations (p. 125). The roof, outside walls, and upper floors are part of the **structure**. They are built in such a way as to support one another and to spread the load evenly.

Some inside walls are also **structural** – they are load-bearing. Others only have to support their own weight. Plasterboard walls nailed to studs are usually non-load-bearing, but not always. It can be difficult to tell which inside walls are part of the structure. As a general guide, any wall supporting the joists of the floor above will be load-bearing.

 1 Study some inside walls at school and at home. Some will be concrete or brick; others will be plasterboard. Try to work out which.

2 Set up a simple test to show that plasterboard is not as soundproof as a brick or concrete wall.

Further work on Chapter 10

1 a Find out who is responsible for the structural maintenance of a council home.

  b Mary, a keen driver, is a single parent of a 5-year-old. She lives with her friend Vanessa, who is keen on DIY. The family have been offered a council flat in a run-down area of town. They have £500 in a joint savings account. Mary wants to use it as a deposit for a car, but Vanessa wants to buy a dilapidated cottage going cheap. Discuss their different priorities. Which person's goals do you think are long- or short-term, and why?

  c What advantages and drawbacks might there be for Mary's child in either home? Which housing option do you think the family should choose, and why? (As in most problem solving, there is no right or wrong answer to this.)

  d What other alternatives might be open to the family about i housing options, and ii the money in their joint savings account?

2 Cut-price homes can mean cut-price materials and shoddy building work. The National House Building Council runs an insurance scheme for people buying new homes. Find out about it. If possible, ask a spokesperson to give a talk on changes in building materials resulting from the new technology, and/or the various skills of builders, from bricklayer to site manager.

3 Find out about the statutory improvement grants for homes without the basic amenities. What percentage of the grants are taken up by householders? Where does the rest go? Contact: the housing department of your local authority.

4 Draw a sketch of the outside of your home. Mark in all the places which could be trouble spots. From your findings, which repairs and/or maintenance would you suggest, if there were sufficient funds and other resources available? Which jobs could you undertake yourself?

5 Find out about and do an individual study on housing associations.

6 No choice of home is likely to be perfect in every way.

  Discuss.

7 If you could have only *one* item of measuring equipment in the house which one would be the best to choose:
  a metre stick?
  a 30-cm ruler?
  a 5-m retractable tape measure?
  a 1.5-m measuring tape?
  Give *one* reason for your choice. *(Scottish Examination Board)*

8 Briefly describe how you would try out your choice of a new household cleaning liquid cream on light-coloured paint work at home. *(London and East Anglian Group)*

Now look again at the objectives at the beginning of the chapter, and check that you have achieved them.

11 *About heat*

By the end of this chapter, you should be able to:

- apply your knowledge of the three methods of heat transference to problems of heat in the home, family, food, and textiles.

- identify the main issues of energy conservation, and apply them in the home situation.

Heat energy

Body temperature in °C	Body health
43.0+	Death likely
43.0–41.0	Loss of consciousness
37.7	Sweating begins
37.0	Just right
36.0	Shivering begins
35.0–34.0	Weak, mentally dulled
34.0–32.0	Breathing and heart rate weak
32.0–30.0	Loss of consciousness
28.0	Death likely

Heat is a form of energy. All energy originally comes from the sun. The sun's rays heat the earth and the things on the earth, but not the air in between. This is **radiated heat**. Materials on the earth absorb the heat and radiate it back into the air, which then warms up.

Energy can be converted – it can change from one form to another.

The world's store of energy is being used up more quickly than it can be replaced. The less the store of energy, the more expensive it becomes. There are many ways to conserve heat in the home while making sure people stay healthy. **Heat conservation** is the most efficient way to use heat with as little waste as possible.

People have a **constant core temperature** – a constant heat inside the body. Heat energy is vital for life, and extremes of core temperature will cause death. The chart shows what happens if people become too hot or too cold.

Energy stored in plants provides kiloJoules in food.

Energy stored in coal, gas, and oil provides heat in the home.

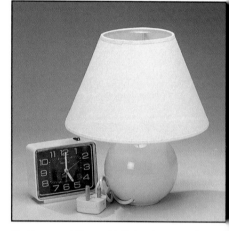

Electric power stations and batteries store energy to power light, heat, and sound systems, and household appliances.

Having a constant body temperature means people can live in very hot or very cold conditions; but they must adapt their life style to suit their environment. The factors to consider in adapting to hot or cold weather include:

a how heat travels.

b heat gain and loss in the body.

c the age and health of the person.

d the importance of clothing and food.

e the temperature in the home.

1 Write out the definition of 'heat conservation'.
2 What is the optimum (best) body temperature for health?

How heat travels

Temperatures naturally tend to **equalize** – to become the same. Heat travels mainly from hot places to cold. **Heat transfer** happens in three ways.

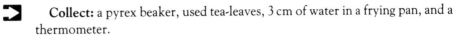

➡ **Collect:** a pyrex beaker, used tea-leaves, 3 cm of water in a frying pan, and a thermometer.
a Half fill the beaker with water. Add the tea-leaves. Stand the beaker in the frying pan.
b Heat slowly for two minutes. Observe and record what happens.
c Turn up the heat until the water boils. Record your observations.
d Turn the heat off. Measure and record the water temperature when the tea-leaves stop moving. Discuss your findings.

This is **convection**. When cold, molecules are densely packed together, but when heated, they expand and become lighter, and so they rise. Cold molecules are pulled in underneath to replace the rising ones. This sets up currents of water which circulate the heat. **Convection currents** of air transfer heat in the same way.

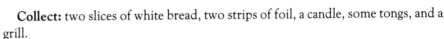

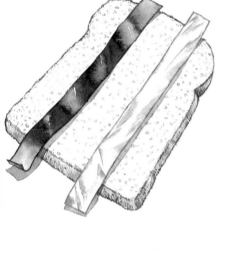

➡ **Collect:** two slices of white bread, two strips of foil, a candle, some tongs, and a grill.
a Blacken one strip of foil by using tongs to hold it in the candle flame.
b Toast one slice of bread on one side only. Record how the untoasted side feels.
c Toast the other slice with the two strips of foil on top. Record your findings.
d Why was white bread used rather than brown? Try to work out why the untoasted sides felt damp.

This is **radiation**. A grill (and a microwave oven) emit energy waves which heat the object they fall upon, but not the air between. All materials, including people, radiate some heat. Silver foil reflects back energy waves. Blackened foil absorbs them, gets hot, and sends out its own waves. Why do you think the second slice was slightly toasted under the blackened foil?

In an oven, food is cooked mainly by convection currents. But some **conduction** (heat from the baking dish) and radiation (heat reflected back from the oven walls) also helps. Conducted heat passes by direct contact – by touch. One molecule transfers heat energy to the next, and so on. Some materials are better conductors of heat than others. Devise and plan a task to find out which materials in a kitchen are good and which poor conductors of heat.

1 Feel your forehead. How does this show that people radiate heat? How was the radiated heat transferred to your hand?
2 Put on a pair of well-fitting shoes when you are hot. How does this show that when things are heated they expand?
3 Name two ways in which the above information could be used by a dressmaker.

Gaining body heat

Collect: a Celsius thermometer, antiseptic lotion, cotton wool, and a stop watch. Hold the glass end of the thermometer, not the metal bulb. Turn it slowly till you find the bar of mercury and the markings for body temperature. If the mercury is above the first marking, shake it down with a few sharp flicks of the wrist. Hold the glass end tightly. Mercury is poisonous, and broken glass very dangerous.

a Wipe the metal bulb with antiseptic on cotton wool.
b Place the metal bulb under your tongue and close your mouth.
c Hold the thermometer with your lips, not your teeth. Do not try to speak.
d Leave it for a full three minutes before removing. Record your finding.
e Shake down the mercury. Clean the metal bulb, return the thermometer to its case and put it safely back in the First Aid box.

1 Work out the average body temperature of the class.
2 Why must the bar of mercury be shaken down both before and after use?
3 What is the health reason for wiping the metal bulb with antiseptic lotion?
4 Young children have their temperatures taken under the arm. They must not be left alone with a thermometer. Explain the reasons why.
5 Heat is measured in **therms.** What does the word 'thermometer' mean?
6 What does 'antiseptic' mean? Name three kinds of household antiseptic.

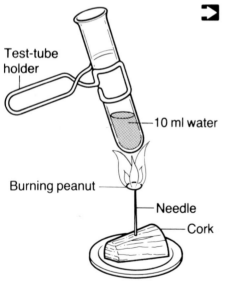

Test-tube holder

10 ml water

Burning peanut

Needle

Cork

Collect: a raw peanut, 10 ml (2 teaspoons) water, a cork, a needle, a test-tube, and a test-tube holder.

a Push the blunt end of the needle into the cork. Secure the peanut on the pointed end. Put the water into the test-tube, and heat the peanut until it starts to burn.
b Using the test-tube holder, heat the water from the flame of the burning peanut. Make sure you hold the mouth of the test-tube away from yourself and anyone else! Observe the burning peanut and the water in the test-tube. Record your findings.

Body heat comes from **cell respiration** – oxygen acts on digested (broken down) food, setting free the energy stored in it, and producing a great deal of heat. The energy is used for the body's **metabolism:** for growth, for fighting infection, for movement – even for sleep. It involves many chemical changes which also produce heat.

1 What happened to the water in the test-tube? Where do you think the energy came from to make this happen?
2 When oily food is heated, it sizzles. From your observation of the burning peanut, would you conclude peanuts contain oil? Why?
3 In your own words, explain how you proved that energy is stored in food.
4 What is meant by 'cell respiration' and 'metabolism'? How is heat produced in the body?

Losing body heat

Collect: ice cubes, a glass beaker, and a thermometer.

a Heat the solid ice until it becomes liquid water. At this moment, measure the temperature of the water. Record and discuss your finding.

b Now boil the water. Measure the temperature of the boiling water each minute till the water boils away. Record and discuss your findings.

Heat energy is needed to change a **solid** to a **liquid**, and a liquid to a **gas**. The boiling water stayed at 100°C. Heat above that temperature was used to change the liquid to a gas – the water **evaporated**. In the same way, sweating cools you down as heat is taken from the body to turn the water in sweat into a gas.

A man produces enough heat energy per hour to power a 100 watt electric light bulb; a woman 81 watts. If this heat were not removed, body temperature would rise to a dangerous level. Tiny drops of moisture constantly seep from the blood on to the skin, and body heat is used to evaporate them. This moisture is called **insensible perspiration** (you are not aware of it). At rest, a man loses 16 g of water an hour this way.

Vigorous exercise makes your metabolism speed up. You can produce about six times more body heat. You become breathless, your heart pounds, and you sweat. This is not the same as insensible perspiration. Sweat comes from the skin's sweat glands, and has traces of salt and body waste in it. The body gets rid of this excess heat by pouring sweat on to the skin, and a great deal more heat is lost in evaporation.

Collect: one other person, and a stop watch.

a Place your fingers inside your partner's wrist below the thumb. Move your fingers until a little beat can be felt. Press gently.

b Using the stop watch, time the beats for 15 seconds, then multiply the result by four to find the number per minute. Record your finding. (Heart beat can also be measured at the neck – find out how.)

c Measure your partner's breathing rate by watching the chest movements and timing each rise and fall with a stop watch. Record your finding.

Reading a thermometer and finding a pulse can be difficult at first. Practise on yourself. When using these skills on a sick person, you need to be calm, capable, and reassuring. People who are unwell can feel more upset if you are fussy or unsure. All these skills should be done when the person is at rest – you are measuring the **basal metabolic rate.**

---

1 Take a friend's temperature, pulse, and breathing rate. Describe your work and give a practical demonstration of your skills.

2 Investigate breathing and heart rate just before and just after 2 minutes' vigorous exercise. Show your findings on a graph.

3 Jumping about on a cold day will soon get you warm. Name two groups of people who may not be able to benefit from this information.

4 What does sweat contain which makes daily washing essential?

Problems of body heat

Overcooling

The heat of your skin varies, but the core temperature stays the same – within one degree of 37°C. **Hypothermia** is a serious condition in which the core temperature drops too low – 'hypo' means 'below'. A baby's ability to keep a constant core temperature is poor; and as people age, they produce less body heat, are less active, and are less aware of changes in temperature. The signs of hypothermia are mental confusion, loss of appetite, cold skin, and puffy hands or feet. Medical help is needed urgently, as the person must be warmed slowly, and with great skill.

In the home, the material factors to consider are lack of nutrients, draughty or unheated rooms, and thin, worn fabrics which do not conserve body heat.

An overhot baby should be cooled by sponging with tepid (not cold) water.

Overheating

A few babies are at risk of **hyperthermia** if they are kept too hot by over-anxious parents – 'hyper' means 'above'. The baby cannot lose heat by sweating, as moving air cannot get through the layers of clothes and blankets. Overheating mainly happens in hot climates, on holiday, when the air is very **humid** (full of water vapour), and sweat cannot evaporate because there is too much water already in the air. Moisture stays on the skin, no body heat is lost, and the core temperature begins to rise to a dangerous level.

---

1 Describe hypothermia. Which groups of people are most at risk? Why?

2 Imagine one of the radiators in your home or classroom has stopped working. Using DIY resources, find out which checks should be done to find out whether it could be an airlock.

3 Using the same resources, learn how to fix an airlock. State, with reasons, why the radiators of a wet heating system need to be bled twice a year.

4 Visit a local DIY shop, and investigate the different methods of draught-proofing a room. Choose, with reasons, one method of insulating the room on p. 167.

5 Babies, the disabled, and the elderly are particularly vulnerable to hypothermia.

Discuss.

Food and body heat

Nutritious food is always important for health, but climate can affect the quantity you need. In cold weather, cell respiration automatically speeds up, and more heat is produced to keep you warm. As food is the fuel used for cell respiration, you notice an increase in appetite. If you ignore this, you risk ill health through lowered resistance to disease and winter infections.

People have different basal (at rest) metabolic rates. Some are more efficient at converting food energy into energy for the body's needs. People with a lower metabolic rate tend to convert food energy into stored fat, which also keeps you warm. People with a high metabolic rate do not store fat. They may feel the cold intensely. If they do not increase their diet, they suffer constant coughs and colds in winter. People with extra weight problems should take vigorous exercise and adjust their diet – not reduce it.

Hot meals such as home-made soups, stews, and casseroles are welcome in cold weather. They can be based on meat, fish, eggs, or pulses, depending on family taste and dietary needs. Foods which are both nutritious and have high energy values, such as wholemeal bread, baked or steamed potatoes, brown rice, or pasta, can be served with these dishes. Care should be taken to include foods rich in Vitamins A and C (p. 192), as these help to protect against colds and chest infections. A hot drink will cause an immediate rise in body temperature. This is a 'false' rise and will soon drop if there is little nourishment in the drink.

In hot weather, people tend to feel less active. There may be a decrease in appetite. Foods with low energy values produce less body heat. Steamed fish or chicken can be served with raw vegetables and fruit. It is important to increase the amount of liquid intake, as a great deal more water is lost from the body in sweat, and must be replaced.

1 Curries, hot peppers, and richly-spiced foods are the popular diet in tropical countries. They produce instant sweating followed by rapid cooling. Create a dish to test this statement.

2 Body temperature should not be taken immediately after a hot meal or drink. Investigate this statement practically. Describe your work and give reasons for your findings. What happens after taking a cold drink?

3 Plan a menu for **a** an underweight young person in winter, and **b** a family in summer. Give reasons for your selection of dishes.

Clothing and body heat

Clothes/covering	Togs
Naked	0.0
Summer dress	0.75
Light trousers and top	0.90
Skirt, blouse, cardigan	1.20
Trousers, shirt, jumper	1.20
Suit and overcoat	2.25
Anorak	7.00
Good quality duvet	11.00

Thermal comfort happens when your skin is about 34°C. Without clothes, the air temperature needs to be 28–30°C. What are the main materials of the outer garments of the class? Relate this to the temperature outdoors. What conclusions can you draw about suitable materials **a** in warm weather, and **b** in cold weather?

Factors to consider when choosing winter clothing include: insulation properties, bulk, weight, special cleaning needs, and length of drying time. Recent tests on underwear show it is the thickness of the fabric rather than the fibre or weave which conserves heat. The flow of heat through fabrics is measured in **togs**.

Test the speed with which a fabric absorbs and releases moisture.

Collect: squares of cotton, wool, rayon, linen, silk, and synthetic mixes.
a Float each square on water, recording the time it takes to become soaked.
b Repeat the tests for speed of drying.

For hot weather, choose a '**breathable**' fabric – one low in togs. An **absorbent** fabric stops sweat building up on the skin, and keeps the person in thermal comfort. In warm weather, garments need to be loose fitting. Tight bands round the wrist, neck, or waist cut down **ventilation** (air flow), which slows down the speed of evaporation and prevents the loss of body heat.

1 Explain the meaning of the following: thermal comfort, insulation, synthetic fibre, thickness factor, togs, breathable, absorbent.
2 Explain why **a** a vest will keep you warmer than an outer jacket, **b** oven gloves are safer than tea towels for carrying hot dishes, **c** plastic chair seats are unpleasant to sit on in hot weather, and **d** light colours are cooler than dark colours for summer wear (p. 133).

3 Select a warm weather outfit for **a** a baby, **b** a young person on a motor-bike ride, **c** an adult preparing the evening meal, and **d** a disabled adult alone at home all day. Give reasons for your choices. These reasons should include such factors as comfort, cost, visual appeal, durability of fabric, ease of cleaning, and protection.

4 Do an individual study on thermal underwear.

Heat in the home

Survey the type of fuel used in students' homes, and present the data as a pie chart.

Using resources, find today's data and present them as a pie chart. What is the trend since 1985?

Collect: water, heating rings, pans, an electric kettle, thermometers, and a stop watch.

a Devise a task to find out which heating ring boils one litre of water most rapidly. Note also which appliance **i** heats up, and **ii** cools down most rapidly.

b Repeat with an electric kettle, and compare your findings.

c Devise a task to find out whether it is easier to make a delicate sauce on an electric or gas ring, and why.

Of the heat energy used in the home, 85 per cent is for space (room) and water heating. Much of this is provided by gas, which is widely used for cooking too. Electricity is used mainly for lighting and running appliances.

As a class, list all the home appliances powered by electricity.

On your own:

a List your twelve favourite electrical appliances.

b Divide your list into human needs and wants. State why the way you divided your list will not necessarily be the same as other people's (p. 84).

c Imagine you have to reduce the amount of electricity you use. Cross off three appliances you can really do without.

d From the remaining list, choose the three appliances you would most want to keep. Analyse the values which influence each of your choices.

e Imagine you are doing this task in 10 years' time. Are there likely to be some differences in your priorities? If so, list them and give reasons for the differences.

f Repeat this task from a retired person's point of view, giving reasons for your different priorities.

g There is a power failure in your area. State, with reasons, two groups who are likely to need most assistance.

h Devise a task to reduce one source of energy in your home. Record your **a** successes, and **b** failures.

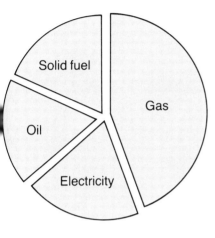

Fuel in the home, 1985

1 Find out the costs of **a** a unit of electricity, **b** a therm of gas, **c** a litre of paraffin, and **d** a kilogram of one type of solid fuel. How is each delivered to the home? Name any storage problems. (If you find this task easy, go on to learn how to calculate the sizes, quality, and quantity of these different fuels required to heat a specific area.)

2 Choose appropriate cooking appliances for **a** a student in a bed-sit, and **b** an extended family with no budget worries. Give reasons for your choices.

3 Some appliances are more 'power hungry' than others. Find out and discuss the meaning of this.

Heat loss in the home

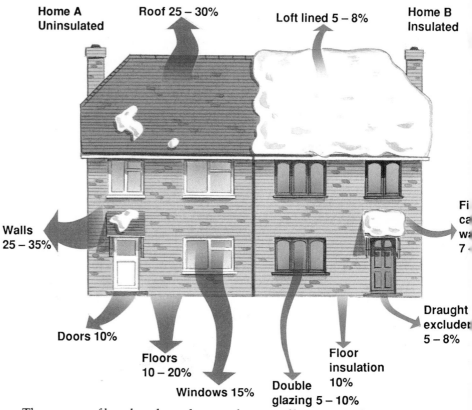

Home A Uninsulated — Roof 25 – 30%

Loft lined 5 – 8% — **Home B Insulated**

Walls 25 – 35%

Fi ca wa 7

Doors 10%

Floors 10 – 20%

Windows 15%

Double glazing 5 – 10%

Floor insulation 10%

Draught excluder 5 – 8%

The amount of heat lost depends upon the type of home. Test this as follows:

Collect: a thermometer, a wall radiator, a square of silver foil, and tape or pins.
a Measure and record the temperature of the wall behind a radiator.
b Measure a wall without a radiator and compare your findings.
c Where do you think some heat from the wall behind the radiator is likely to go? Test this by loosely attaching a square of silver foil behind the radiator. Measure the temperature. What conclusions can you draw from your findings?
d Padded foil blankets are now available to reduce heat loss through walls. If you were given one, would you attach it to an outer or inner wall? Why?
e What protection against heat loss does a flat have which a detached house lacks through **a** the roof, **b** the outside walls, and **c** the floor? Which wall of the home on the left is likely to be warm, and why?

In an old home, with no cavity walls (p. 124) and no proper roof insulation, about three-quarters of the heat produced is lost.

Room temperatures
People are less active at home and so produce less body heat. The guidelines for 'reasonable warmth' are: 21°C for the living room, 16°C for the hall, and 13–18°C for the bedrooms. In very cold weather, these temperatures may need a boost. People who are elderly or disabled usually need more heat – why? Newborn babies need rooms at 32–3°C. Active people may prefer to wear extra clothes and keep the heating low.

Visit a building site, builder's merchants, and DIY shops, and look at special provisions for insulation or safety factors in house design and building. Investigate the range of insulating materials used in the home in:

a the fabric of the building.
b household textiles.
c containers and equipment used for food preparation and storage.

(Southern Examining Group)

Condensation

Penetrating damp causes moisture on the underside *of the glass.*

Condensation causes moisture on the top *of the glass.*

Condensation occurs when water vapour in warm air lands on a cold surface and turns back to water. It is the opposite of evaporation (p. 135).

Collect: a metal spoon, a plastic one, and a wooden one, and ceramic, cork, and polystyrene tiles.
Breathe out on the spoons, then the tiles. Which materials have cold surfaces? Windows and other glass objects are cold – how could you test this?

The test shown in the photographs tells you whether a damp floor is caused by condensation or rising damp. Put a sheet of glass on a circle of plasticine over the damp area. Why is it important the plasticine circle is air-tight? How can you tell that the moisture on top of the glass came from condensation?

A patch of damp on the wall may be due to a fault in the brickwork or in the damp proof course. You can test this by removing a small area of plaster. If the wall underneath is dry, the problem is condensation.

Condensation on windows causes paint failure and rots wood. It can wet the insulation of the nearby walls (p. 124), which then does not work well. Bathrooms and kitchens have special problems, as new moist air is constantly being released.

How much does a man lose in a day from insensible perspiration (p. 135)?

Over-insulation is a modern cause of condensation. It happens when the home has been so tightly sealed against heat loss that the natural sweating of wood, fibres, and people builds up. A simple remedy is **ventilation** – moving currents of air which dry out the damp.

How do you feel in a very stuffy atmosphere? Some homes suffer the opposite of condensation. The air is so dried out by electric fires and central heating that it feels very uncomfortable.

Collect: two small house plants, one bell jar, and a humidifier.
a Stand the plants on a sunny window ledge. Cover one with the bell jar. Record your findings at the end of the lesson.
b Where did the moisture in the bell jar come from? How could you use this information to make a room with very dry air more comfortable?
c The humidifier also puts moisture back into dried out air. Devise, plan, and carry out a test to see how it works.
d Which do you consider more attractive, the humidifier or the plants? Why?

---

1 Investigate condensation. Which kinds of surface are often used in the bathroom and kitchen – hot or cold? In what ways can this add to the problems of condensation?
  a Run hot water into the hand basin. Record the state of the mirror and walls.
  b Run a little cold water into the basin before turning on the hot tap. What happens? What conclusions can you draw from this for cutting down condensation in the bathroom?
  c Name three things which give off water vapour in the home, and two rooms which have special problems.
  d An automatic cut-out electric kettle reduces fuel costs. Name one other advantage it has.
  e Find out what happens to wallpaper when regularly soaked with moisture.
  f Examine an old mirror to see the damage caused by condensation. You could choose to renew the backing as a practical assignment.
2 Do an individual study on ventilation. Include cooker hoods and extractors, and the safety characteristics of flues.

Conservation of heat

The Energy Efficiency Office states that Britain wastes £7 *billion each year* on its energy bills. In the USA energy conservation is taken so seriously that there are 'energy doctors' – specialists who visit the home to diagnose heat loss problems and prescribe cures. They use a **thermogram**, which gives high density charts of heat production and is mainly used in the UK by doctors to investigate tumours (lumps) in the body.

Activity	Litres
Washing hands	2
Cooking a meal	2
Washing up	6
Washing machine	120
Bath	91

Investigating heat loss in domestic hot water

One person uses about 50 000 litres of water each year. Hot water is used all year round. It can be the biggest consumer of energy, and it provides one of the easiest ways to cut energy costs. The table on the left shows the average amount of water used each time for a range of activities.

Do you leave the hot tap running while you **a** wash your hands, **b** prepare food, or **c** rinse glassware? Working in small groups:

a devise tasks to demonstrate some hygienic methods of avoiding the above waste.

b using a volunteer, a bath plug, and measuring jugs, devise a task to find out which uses least hot water – a shower or a bath.

c find out how much water is used in a dish washing machine, and suggest ways to conserve it.

d find out which modern detergents are effective in cold water, and suggest ways in which to apply this information.

e find out about the function of aerators and present your information in class.

f find out why regular draining of the hot water tank helps to reduce heat loss, and find out and demonstrate how to drain the tank.

g identify the insulating properties of immersion jackets and lagging, and find out and demonstrate how they are fitted.

h devise and demonstrate one household cleaning task for which you would always use hot water, and state why.

---

1 Invite speakers from the energy organizations to talk about their space and heating systems. Ask for details of **a** safety, and **b** pollution factors of the particular fuel.

2 As a practical assignment, design and make an attractive draught protector for a letter box from insulating materials of your choice. Record each stage of your work.

Further work on Chapter 11

1 Mr Green (p. 86) invests in an oil heater to save on fuel costs. He uses 7 litres a week. The company will not deliver this small amount so he must collect it himself.
   a Find out the cost of **i** the heater, **ii** the fuel, and **iii** a container to carry it in. What are his fuel costs for February?
   b Struggling home through the snow, he slipped and now will not go out again. State all the community services available to him.
   c What maintenance does the heater require to use the fuel efficiently? Discuss his choice of heater.

2 Choose a space heater for one of the following situations:
   ● Adrian, age 17, moves into an unheated bed-sit. He has just started work and there is not much spare cash.
   ● Baby Brown's parents dislike hot rooms, so keep the central heating low. They need a supplementary heater for the nursery.
   ● A working parent wants a heating appliance she can trust is safe, as her school age children arrive home before she does.
   ● Mr Green visits his grown up children, and constantly complains of the cold. An extra heater is needed for his room.

   Investigate all the heating options for your chosen situation. You need to visit different showrooms and be familiar with the full range of choices. Analyse the situation carefully in terms of 'your' particular life style and needs. The material factors to consider include:
   a choice and cost of fuel; its safety and pollution factors.
   b method of heat transfer, the amount of space requiring heat, and the efficiency of the appliance to meet that requirement.
   c cost of space heater, installation costs (if any), method of payment, and consumer protection and guarantee.
   d aesthetic appeal, maintenance, fuel delivery, and storage problems.
   e energy conservation and cost efficiency of your choice.

3 a Name a method of insulation which could be used in *each* of the following areas in a house:

Area	Method of insulation
i Windows	
ii Cavity walls	
iii Roof	

   b Name *two* benefits of a well-insulated home.
   c Suggest economies that might be made in relation to fuel consumption in the home. *(Welsh Joint Education Committee)*

4 a Suggest *two* ways in which you could insulate your loft.
   b Name *two* items that would keep an elderly person warm in a room with only a single bar electric heater. *(Midland Examining Group)*

5 The cost of using domestic appliances often depends on a number of points. Which of the following is likely to cost the least money in one week if used regularly by an average householder; a washing machine *or* a food mixer?
   (London and East Anglian Group)

Now look again at the objectives at the beginning of the chapter, and check that you have achieved them.

12 Plans for a home

By the end of this chapter, you should be able to:

- identify traffic flow in a room.
- interpret a room plan and begin furniture arrangement.
- identify the five work triangles.
- identify storage needs and systems.
- apply measurements of human shape to design.
- develop the details of a survey.
- attempt kitchen planning and design.

Planning a home 2

People interact with each other, and with their environment. They are affected by, and have an effect on, the things in the home. If you bang your head on a shelf, the environment is affecting you! If you alter the height of the shelf, you have affected it. Homes need to be planned so that people interact with their environment in safety. Are there other reasons for planning a home?

Ergonomics is the study of people at work – finding out the most efficient way of getting a job done. It used to be called 'time and motion' studies: what do you think this means? In the home, ergonomics is the study of the way people and household things interact – the effect they have on each other. Priorities to consider include comfort, appeal, safety, hygiene, economy, and efficiency. Different rooms have different functions so priorities are likely to change. In the living room, would you put efficiency before comfort? What would be your priorities in the kitchen?

Perhaps the most important factor to remember in planning a home for families is that small children need to be close to adults. They will not stay long in a room on their own. Nor should they be expected to. What other very important reason is there for not leaving a child alone?

1 List the factors to consider when planning a home. In which order of priority would you put them for **a** the bathroom, and **b** a bedroom? Why?

2 Name two ways in which applying the principle of ergonomics to the home can improve the quality of family life.

Putting up a room partition can give those using it more privacy.

A mirror adds depth and interest to this alcove.

Planning floor space

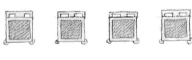

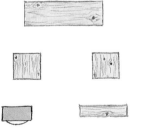

Net space is the area of one or more floors enclosed by walls. It includes space for a staircase, room partitions, bay windows, and fixed heaters. It is net as it does not include garage, balcony, or outside dustbin or fuel store. Work out the total net space of the living and dining area in the plan below.

Internal circulation means the way people move around inside a room – the flow of traffic. You need easy access to windows, doors, power points, shelves, telephone, storage space, television, and music centre. Most living rooms are full of life and activity. Perhaps the main priorities are comfortable seating, lighting, and storage space.

A home designer makes a plan of the room and a plan of the furniture – *all to the same scale*. This has been done in the example below. Copy the plan and make cutouts of the furniture. Arrange them on the plan, keeping in mind:

- the size of the room.
- the function of the room.
- the internal circulation.
- the function of the furniture.
- the overall appeal.

Keep moving the furniture until you are pleased with the effect. The shelves act as a partial room divider – move them if you wish. Does the result look cramped? comfortable? bare? Use less furniture, or add more. Does the room need a focal point – a centre of attraction which catches and pleases the eye? Choose small objects: candles, flowers, cushions, or pictures, to add personality and life to the room, but avoid a cluttered look.

---

1 Claire, age 2, and Simon, age 4, play in the room while their mother works in the kitchen. Is the swing door useful? Should it be jammed open or shut, and why? Arrange the furniture to encourage the children to stay in the dining area – why should you not block the toilet door? What would you do with the small objects, and why? What other protective factors do you need to consider?

2 Study the way furniture is arranged in magazine pictures of sitting rooms. Choose one you like and mark in the flow patterns.

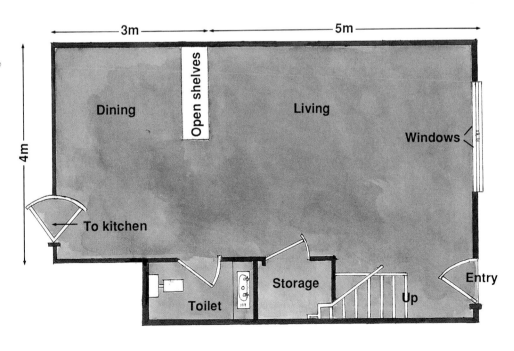

Kitchen layouts

The ideal kitchen floor plan is based on a triangle. Name the three work centres joined by each side of the triangle. The space inside the work triangle must not be a pathway through the room – why? Role-play taking a steaming pot from the hob to the sink as someone crosses the work triangle. Describe the kind of accident which could happen.

Working in pairs, stretch your arms out wide. Measure the distance between your fingertips. Ideally, no two work centres should be more than a double arm span apart. How far is this? Nor should the work centres be too close. It is awkward and can be dangerous if there is no room to work.

Make a copy of each of the kitchen layout plans shown here, and draw in the triangle which joins the work centres. Note the position of the sink in each plan – discuss why it is in the middle. Where are the **work surfaces**? Work centres and surfaces are not the same thing – explain their differences.

Architects used to design kitchens as work systems. These were small and easy to run, but they lacked comfort and appeal. Anyone working there was isolated from the rest of the home. What problems would this cause a parent and child? Modern kitchens are designed for people, not systems. Building regulations for new homes state there must be space for a table and two chairs, or a breakfast bar and stools. In what way might this regulation improve the quality of life for a person working in the kitchen?

1 On your copy of layouts C and D, mark in where you would put **a** a window, and **b** either a table and chairs or a breakfast bar. State why.

2 The single-line and galley are **corridor** kitchens. Name two households groups they might suit. State, with reasons, whether you consider them suitable for a large family home. Which kitchen layout do you **a** like the most, **b** like the least, and **c** think the most costly to plan and build?

3 Imagine you must convert your bedroom into a kitchen. Draw its floor plan. Decide on the kind of household group you are designing for. Choose a suitable kitchen layout and draw it in. Add some work surfaces. Are you satisfied with the result? What were your priorities in choosing that particular layout? Repeat the exercise for a different household group. Evaluate your results.

4 Comment on the kitchen layouts on pp. 121 and 122.

A   Single-line kitchen

B   Galley kitchen

C   L-shaped kitchen

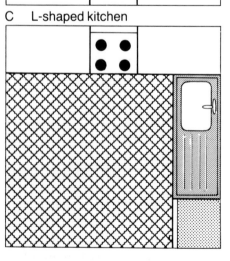

D   U-shaped kitchen

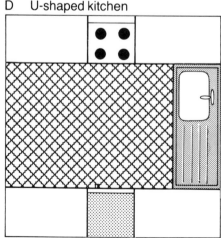

E   Island kitchen

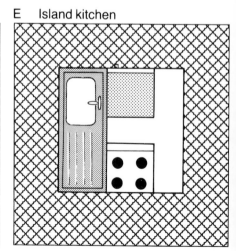

Kitchen layouts: five work triangles

Measuring human shape

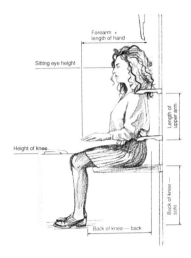

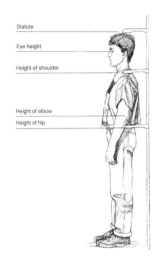

The word 'anthropoid' means human-like in shape. Gorillas and chimpanzees are anthropoids as their shape is more human than other mammals'.

Anthropometrics is the measurement of human shape. Architects and designers of furniture, clothes, shoes, and household appliances need anthropometric data. These are measurements of people's **stature** (height) and **reach** (arm and leg spans). They apply this information to their design plans to make a product which fits people. What might happen if you designed a turnstile without first checking anthropometric data?

Collect: a steel tape measure, a ruler, a pencil, and some people.
a Stand each person barefoot against a wall. Using the ruler, mark off height.
b Plot the data on graph paper. Does the curve resemble the one in the graph? If enough people are measured, the distribution of height is a bell-shaped curve. The majority of people are between the 5 and 95 mark. Where would you fix a shelf high enough on the wall so that people do not bump their heads – at the 5, 50, or 95 mark? The answer is not easy. Designers of mass production goods have to work for a range of people – those below 5 and above 95 are left out. Mass production fits the majority, not the individual.

Measure your reach and the other anthropometric data marked on these diagrams. Reach can be more important than height. Usually, the two interact. The shelf needs to be out of harm's way and still allow a short person to reach to the back of it. Designers have to find out in which direction the measurement is **critical** – most important. They cannot satisfy all the requirements of safety, ease of access, comfort, efficiency, convenience, and cost. Which of these factors must have priority if there are children in the home?

Plot the data on a graph. Does the curve resemble the one in the graph shown here? If enough people are measured, the distribution of height will always be a bell-shaped curve. Test this by measuring students from other classes and marking the findings on your graph. Or collect height sizes from home (not children) and mark in the findings.

From your graph, work out how many people would bump their heads if you fixed a jutting-out shelf at a height of 1 m 75 cm (5 ft 9 in). How many would it be at 1 m 68 cm (5 ft 6 in), and at 1 m 60 cm (5 ft 3 in)? At what height would the shelf have to be fixed so that nobody bumped their heads? Why are not all shelves fixed at this height? Where would you fix the shelf in your classroom? Why?

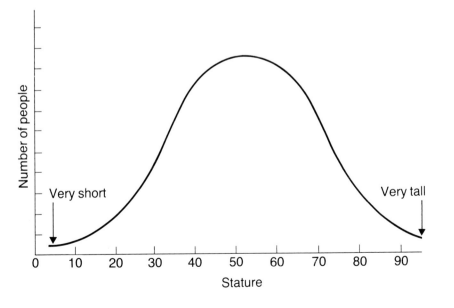

1 Designers of mass production goods have to work to an average range of people. Those at each end of the spectrum are usually left out. Mass production fits the majority, not the minority. Discuss the appeal of DIY home fixtures and fittings.

2 Visit a children's library, play-group, or toy shop. Make notes on the height of shelves, chairs, and display units.

3 Equate some problems of mass production to clothing, footwear, and food taste. What do you consider are the main advantages of mass production? Visit a specialist shop, such as Tall Girls, and comment on your findings.

Design for sitting

Work out how much time you spend sitting down each day. The average is 10 to 12 hours! A Consumers' Association survey found that half the population had back pain at some time, and 10 per cent almost all the time. The Office of Health Economics estimates the cost of treating back pain on the NHS is about £156 million per year. Do you think **a** we sit for too long? **b** there might be something wrong with the design of modern chairs? **c** technology in the home such as television, computers, and energy saving appliances is the cause? **d** none of these? **e** all of these?

A kneeling chair design

What health problem is avoided by this traditional Japanese way of sitting?

The human spine has a natural slight curve. A chair back should give good lumbar support. It should be high enough to support the upper part of the spine, with a slight tilt backwards for comfort when relaxing. A chair seat should be the correct height to allow the feet to rest flat on the floor. The width should allow for movement, and the edge should be rounded so as not to slow the blood supply. On long aeroplane flights, the flow of blood to the legs slows as the thighs are crushed on the seat. Blood fluids leak into the ankles and feet, making them tingle and swell up.

Collect: stools, and upright and easy chairs of different materials and designs.
a Sit on each in turn and comment on your findings.
b Tuck stools and uprights under your desk. Test for correct working heights.

1 How popular do you expect the kneeling chair to be? Why?
2 Do a class survey to find out which material is most often used on kitchen chairs and stools. Discuss the reasons for this.
3 Measure the height of shelves in the classroom and at home. Notice whether they jut out or are built in cabinet design. From both your height and reach findings, mark where you would place an extra wall shelf in **a** the living area, and **b** the dining area on your copy of the floor plan (p. 145).

Investigating chairs

'Who's been sitting in my chair?', asks each bear in the Goldilocks tale. Do people have favourite chairs in your home? If so, where do they face – and why? What is the connection, if any, between a favourite chair and the occupier? Do you think you will have a favourite chair in your own home, and why?

a Choose your favourite among these, and state why. Which room would it be in?

b List the other chairs in the order you prefer. Which rooms would you place each in, and why?

c Using resources, identify the style of each chair. Try to explain the feelings and mood each projects, such as luxury, comfort, efficiency, etc.

1 Plan a visit to a furniture store. Using the consumer check on p. 104 and other factors you may wish to include, choose, with reasons, a seating item for:

a a student spending long hours at a desk.

b a retired person who has difficulty with mobility.

c a very small kitchen.

d the bathroom.

e a large, smart hallway.

2 Using resources, find out and describe the design, materials, and construction of seating in a mobile home.

3 As a practical assignment, reconstruct or re-upholster a chair.

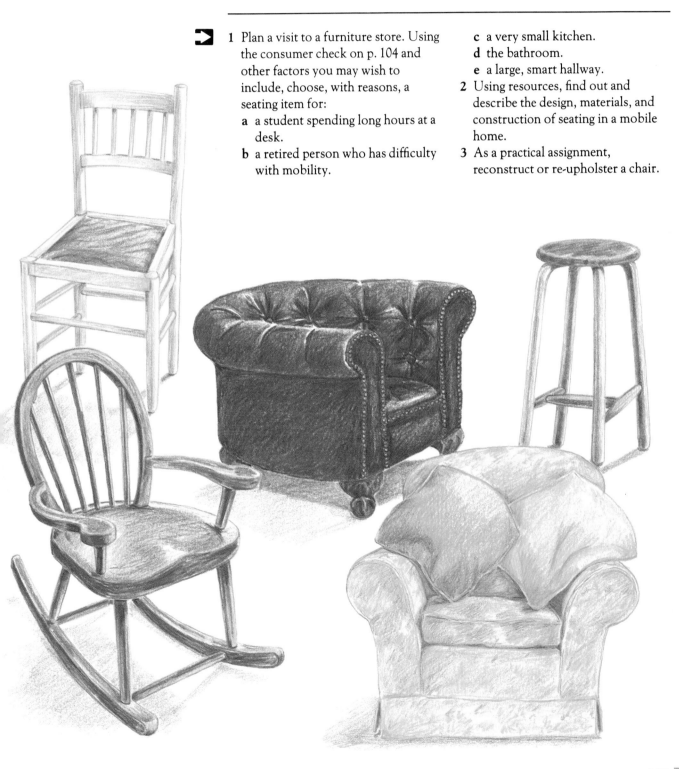

Design for standing

Surveys show that accidents happen more often when people feel hot, tired, and irritable. Are people likely to feel all of these things in a kitchen, and why? Using resources, find out how to lift weights in the correct manner. Why is this information important for working in the kitchen?

Collect: heavy pans, a 1-litre jug of water, high and low shelves, and a work surface.

a Reach up to the pans on the high shelf and lower them to the work surface.
b Bend down and lift pans from the low shelf to the work surface.
c Which was easier, and why?
d Repeat with the jug of water. Comment on your findings.

To avoid backache and accidents, where would you store the following, and why?
- rarely used, heavy items
- frequently used, large, or bulky items
- cutlery and utensils for cooking
- sharp kitchen knives

Name some items you would keep at chest height. Which rarely used items would you put on a high shelf, and why?

In your kitchen, standing upright without bending, test whether you can **a** touch the bottom of the sink, **b** place your palms flat on a work surface, and **c** reach both ends of the ironing board when standing at the centre. Stand on a brick or pastry boards, or bend slightly till you can. Mark and measure those heights and arm span. Compare the heights you find compatible with those other people in the classroom and at home find compatible.

Growth spurts in the teens are usually over by the age of 14 for girls, and 16 for boys. But some teenagers do not start growing till then. The ideal standing height for a work surface is between 875 mm (35 in) and 1 m (39 in).

---

1 You move into a flat share and find potential hazards, as in the above kitchens. You do not want to upset your new flatmates, but feel you should protect them (and yourself). Describe the potential risks and how they can be corrected. Write or role-play how you might solve this problem.

2 Ergonomics in the kitchen is good for a family's physical and mental health.

Discuss this.

Survey of cooking appliances

A large family may choose a solid fuel cooker which also heats the water. A microwave oven and electric kettle may be enough for a busy career person. Neither of these choices is necessarily so! Before deciding on a cooker, consider the life style of the people using it.

 1 Do a survey of the kind of cooker used by at least three people. Draw up a detailed questionnaire, and evaluate it in class. Create a neat and attractive list that you can show to the people you interview, and explain that doing a survey is part of your school work. You might feel more comfortable if you first role-play your approach in class.

Ask how many people use the cooker, but not its price, though this may be volunteered. Not everyone buys a new cooker. Name three other ways in which cookers may be obtained.

2 Study and comment on your findings. Combine them with the rest of the class to produce a fairly large survey. Discuss such things as choice of fuel, popular makes and colours, length of time cookers are expected to last, number of features required, faults found, use of guarantee, and general level of satisfaction. Draw, with detailed labelling, one popular cooker. State all the reasons for its appeal.

3 Plan a similar survey of freezers.

Storage systems

If your bedroom were photographed, would you be pleased with your storage system? Do you value a tidy room (p. 16), and why? Working in groups, create tasks to find out whether work is **a** more efficient, **b** quicker, **c** safer, and **d** more pleasing in a tidy or untidy room. Identify the principles of storage, and of keeping a work centre free of clutter.

Using resources, notice how belts, ties, and shoes are displayed in shops. Look at multiple skirt and shirt hangers, shoe racks, and hanging and revolving shelves. What special designs are used for the storage of awkward items such as ironing boards, vacuum cleaners, and garden equipment? What storage use, if any, is made of awkward corners?

Choose three different kitchen cabinets you like and study their design. List three hobbies and discuss their storage needs. Identify built-in and free-standing storage furniture. Name some advantages and disadvantages of each. Evaluate the storage space in the Home Economics room.

Analyse the storage needs in your bedroom. What are the likely costs? What about alternatives? Name an improvisation you could make. Draw up a plan to meet your storage needs.

1 As a practical assignment, make one of the following: padded hanger, shoe or laundry bag, covered shoe box for small items.

2 Find out about storage depositories in your area. Who is likely to use them? Why is renting storage space fairly costly?

Planning a kitchen

Priorities

When planning a kitchen, first draw up a list of your priorities. Who cooks – one person? the entire family? Does it include children? Are special safety factors needed for them? Is there room for a large family meal? Are there left-handed cooks in the household? Are there any elderly or disabled members of the household? Do guests help in the kitchen? What about hygiene and pets? Does everyone gather there for company as well as for food? Is the kitchen used for laundry? What else is it used for?

Each household will have a different list of priorities.

Planning your work

Decide on the household group you are planning the kitchen for. Keep to a simple group if you find the work difficult. As this is a large project, you may need special folders to keep your work in. You may also wish to work in pairs or in groups. Visit the Design Centre, or use manufacturers' catalogues and sales leaflets to choose your kitchen furniture. Check the height (p. 150) and draw models to scale of the equipment you think might be suitable (p. 145).

1 Think about your floor covering (p. 162). Consider the health and safety factors of adding an attractive rug and a door mat to the outside. Explain their hazards, how these can be avoided, and any special cleaning they will require.

2 Choose, with reasons, an appropriate lighting system (pp. 158–9).

3 Plan a choice of cabinets, giving reasons for your choice based on how to overcome storage problems.

4 Consider the kind of dining area you need: table with chairs, breakfast bar with stools, flap-top table with stacking chairs, baby's high chair, and so on.

Measuring up

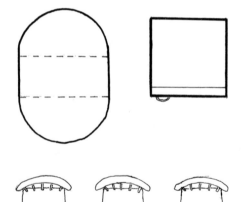
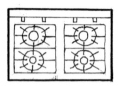
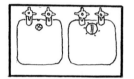

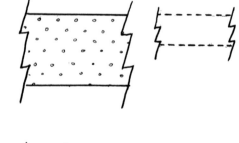

Copy this kitchen plan on to graph paper. Use a pencil and light pressure to do your first markings. Like all designers, you may change your mind many times! Notice the doors and whether they open inwards or outwards – why is this important? Lightly mark the flow of traffic through the room. Think about the work triangle and internal circulation inside it (p. 146). Think about the location and height of gas and electrical outlets (you do not have to use both). Choose the work triangle layout you think most compatible with your movements and needs. Lightly mark in where you want fixtures such as power outlets, lighting, hot water heaters, and gas pipes and flues if you choose to use gas.

Look at the distance from the window sill to the floor. As it is less then 105 cm (41 in), is there room for work surfaces underneath? Work out the measurements for curtains or a blind (p. 163). Choose and measure the cooker and refrigerator you wish to install. You may want to change these later. You cannot yet afford any other large appliances, but you optimistically leave a space near the sink for a washing machine to be plumbed in.

Designer tips include:

a the cooker should not be closer than 60 cm (24 in) or farther than 120 cm (48 in) from the sink. Why?

b burners or elements should not be under a window. Name two accident hazards from draughts.

c cabinets on both sides should have heat-resistant work surfaces. Why?

d try to place the sink under the window. This gives maximum use of daylight, saves wall space which might be wasted, and allows you to look at the view, or watch the pets or children at play.

---

1 Would you cover the walls with paint or wallpaper? Why? Which colours might be appropriate? Why?

2 What personal touches would you add to make your kitchen more attractive?

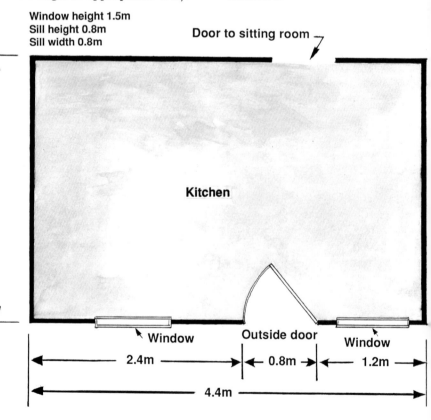

Window height 1.5m
Sill height 0.8m
Sill width 0.8m

Door to sitting room

Kitchen

2.8m

Window   Outside door   Window

2.4m   0.8m   1.2m

4.4m

Further work on Chapter 12

1 On your plan of the kitchen, is there an easy chair for the cook, and why? Would you like a television set, and why? Do you think it might distract attention from **a** interesting chat, **b** games and play, and **c** cooking times? How could you solve **c**? If you decide against television, what about a small stereo or radio? Where would you store your tapes, cassettes, or CDs?

2 State, with reasons, where you will site **a** waste disposal bin, **b** plastic bags, waxed paper, foil, and other kitchen wraps, **c** vacuum cleaner, brooms, brushes, and dustpan, and **d** ironing board and iron.

3 Where will you store washing powders, cleaners, polishes, and bleaches if there is a small child in the home? Why?

4 In most homes, the First Aid kit is kept either in the kitchen or in the bathroom. Where would you store it, and why? Find and describe a suitable storage container.

5 Terence Conran, founder of Habitat, once said, 'Kitchens seem to me to be the heart of any house. I'd suggest you spend your time and money making the kitchen a more pleasant place than anywhere else.'

   Discuss.

6 You wish to buy a set of kitchen knives. Give *two* points to consider when choosing them.   *(Midland Examining Group)*

7 Discuss the features which would be important when choosing an automatic washing machine for *each* of the following:
   a the owner of a small guest-house.
   b a single person in a small flat.

8 Many items of kitchen equipment are expensive. A young couple, earning an average income, are planning and equipping their kitchen. What advice would you offer to them? Give detailed reasons for this advice.   *(Scottish Examination Board)*

Now look again at the objectives at the beginning of the chapter, and check that you have achieved them.

13 Home design

By the end of this chapter, you should be able to:
- plan, design, and furnish your own bed-sit.

Colour

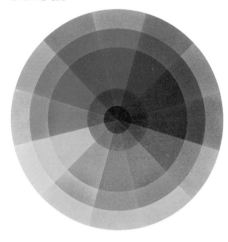

Think of a colour you like and one you dislike. Try to work out why. People's moods often interact with the colours around them. Some colours 'feel' cheerful; others 'feel' gloomy or have a stressful effect.

Make a colour wheel. List the colours under the headings: restful, cheerful, hard, soft, warm, and cold. Some colours will go in more than one list. Colours also interact with themselves. Those in **harmony** (adjacent on the colour wheel) give a co-ordinated effect. Those in **contrast** (opposite on the wheel) give a dramatic or highlighting effect.

Colour is powerful. It can affect the whole mood of a room. Some colours dominate others. Some interact by changing their **tones** (shades or tints). To make a **shade**, add black to darken. To make a **tint**, add white.

Collect: five 23-cm and five 8-cm square cards, and red, yellow, blue, pink, and grey paints.

a Paint each square a different colour. Place a small grey square inside a large red one. What happens? Repeat with other colours.

b Look at single colours in natural light (daylight) and artificial light. Record all the changes you observe.

Choice of colour is highly individual. There are no real rules, as the tone of a colour is affected by everything around it, especially light. Off-whites are a popular choice for walls. But an off-white on a paint chart can change from warm tones to cool, strong to muted, or bright to flat, on different materials. It can look greenish, reddish, or yellowish on a wall, a fabric, or a cup.

1 Study the paint chart. Find the same off-whites on fabrics and pottery. Do the tones of the colours change? Record what you observe.

2 A colour seen first under harsh shop lights can look different outdoors, and different again at home. How could you test this? When choosing colour, take any contrasting or co-ordinating fabrics with you. Why should you view both outside the shop?

3 List all the colours in your living room, and try to describe their effects.

4 Terence Conran once said, 'Off-whites can make you uncomfortable, pinks can be cold, blues can make you feel warm and content, while beige can damage your health!' Do you agree, or disagree, with him? Why? Relate your answers to food, home, family, and textiles. Discuss your opinion of beige.

More about colour

Colour and decoration

A **scheme** is a plan. Colour schemes need to be planned with the function of the room in mind. Strong colours such as black and red give a dramatic effect at night, but can be stressful first thing on a lovely spring day. Gold and white – gold and any colour – looks luxurious, elegant, and grand. Would you choose it for a bed-sit with furniture made up of old crates? What do you think might be the effect? Where does gold interact best: in a local authority office, or a hotel?

Complete the following:

Colour	Description	Effects
Reds	Warm and bright	Bold or exhausting
Greys	Cool and quiet	Elegant or depressing
White	Pure and clean	Dazzling or antiseptic
Black	Strong and bold	Dramatic or dreary
Blues	Cool and restful	
Yellows		
Greens		
Browns		

Colour and food

Collect: food colourings, and mashed potatoes.

a Devise, plan, and carry out a task to find out whether students have colour preferences in food.
b Repeat the above task with glasses of water.
c Record and discuss your findings.
d Describe the colour of mould on bread.
e List fresh, uncooked foods in separate colour columns.
f List your favourite prepared foods in separate colour columns.
g Name three popular colours of prepared foods.
h Which foods, if any, remind you of sunlight?
i Discuss some reasons for the colours food manufacturers choose to add to prepared foods.

Colour and clothing

Colour interacts with your skin tones. These vary according to your mood and state of health. Your favourite coloured shirt may flatter your skin one day, and clash with it the next. Colour for clothes can be high fashion one year, 'dead' the next. Do you think a colour that is in fashion for clothes is likely to be suitable for a room? Why?

1 Find food labels with colour additives. Are the foods fresh, frozen, or prepared? Why do you think colouring is added? What colours are used for **a** icing wedding cakes, **b** Father Christmas outfits, and **c** a newborn's clothes? Discuss their likely associations in people's minds.
2 As a practical assignment, you could choose to make jam or tomato soup, comparing the natural colour with the canned variety.

Lighting

Look at the classroom windows. Estimate what proportion of the walls they cover. Do you consider they let in enough light? Imagine the glass has been removed – name three other functions of windows. In what ways, if any, are school windows different from those at home?

Collect: a large, moveable mirror.

a Move the mirror to the wall opposite a window. Is there more light in the room? Why?

b Move it to the side of a window. Is the effect different, or much the same?

c Remove the mirror. Has the room lost some of its appeal?

d Darken the room. Move the mirror close to a lamp. Describe the effects.

e Mirrors increase the amount of light in a room by reflecting it back. They make space seem larger and more interesting. From your findings, analyse these statements.

f What implications can you draw from your findings about the use of mirrors in rooms other than the bathroom and bedroom?

Artificial lighting

Do you feel more, or less, cheerful when the sun is shining than on a dark, overcast day? Medical studies have shown that the number of people suffering from depression rises steeply in the winter months. When these patients were exposed to strong artificial light for a few hours each day, they reported feeling far less unhappy, and more in control of their lives. When they improved the artificial lighting at home, the majority recovered and became effective at managing their lives once again.

Special needs

Most children go through a stage of being afraid of the dark. Parents cannot prevent this, and trying to reason the fears away – 'See, there's nothing to be afraid of' – may not work. It may even make matters worse, because the child has the added terror of feeling abandoned by the beloved parent to the dark. Would you give a frightened child a night-light, and why?

By middle age, most people need spectacles for close work. Any person with even a mild sight impairment should pay extra attention to lighting needs. Elderly and disabled people need a strong bedside light, with easy access to the switch. Describe the kind of accident which could happen if the switch is on a distant wall.

---

1 Examine the lighting resources at school and at home. List the main differences. Do curtains affect the amount of natural light in any rooms? If so, would you want to avoid this, and why?

2 Study the effects of lamp shades on lighting. Sketch the designs you like. In what way might a close-fitting shade be a fire hazard? Find out how night-lights are protected from this risk.

More about lighting

Most homes are wired for a central light hanging from a **ceiling rose**. This gives **general lighting**, but has a dull, flattening effect. **Task lighting** is needed for close work. A combination of lamps brings a room alive, creating interesting focus, or a soothing atmosphere. Dimmers control light intensity, cut electricity costs, lengthen bulb life, and alter the whole mood of a room.

Collect: blue and green threads mixed together, black and white paper, 15 W, 60 W and 100 W lamps, a stop watch, a window shelf, and a work top. The tasks can be shared among the class. Work as quickly as you can. Time and record your speeds.

a Separate the threads into colour piles at the window on the black paper.
b Repeat at the work top in a darkened room under the 15 W, 60 W, and 100 W lamps.
c Repeat **a** and **b** on top of the sheet of white paper.
d Discuss all the results.

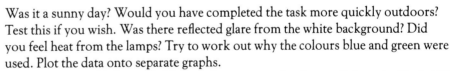

Was it a sunny day? Would you have completed the task more quickly outdoors? Test this if you wish. Was there reflected glare from the white background? Did you feel heat from the lamps? Try to work out why the colours blue and green were used. Plot the data onto separate graphs.

The amount of light needed for a task is measured in **lux**, or light units. Each 100 lux is equal to 35–40 W per square metre from a filament bulb, and 10–15 W per square metre from a fluorescent bulb. Guidelines for lux include 200 for background lighting, 400–600 for close work such as reading and sewing, and 900 for long hours at fine detail tasks. The ergonomics of lighting are complex but essential for safety in the workplace. In what ways can lighting help to prevent accidents in the home?

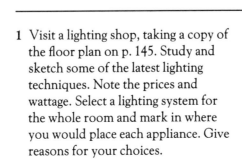

Lighting should not dazzle. What is wrong with the position of these lamps?

1 Visit a lighting shop, taking a copy of the floor plan on p. 145. Study and sketch some of the latest lighting techniques. Note the prices and wattage. Select a lighting system for the whole room and mark in where you would place each appliance. Give reasons for your choices.

2 An aunt with partial sight comes to visit. Discuss the things you could do to meet her lighting needs.
3 Spending money on attractive lighting is a cost and energy efficient way of adding to room design.

Analyse this statement.

Pattern

A pattern is a set of lines, shapes, or colours arranged to form a design. It provides interest and contrast. Sketch a pattern you like and one you dislike. Try to give reasons for your choice. Add colour to both. How has it affected your patterns? Do the pattern and colour interact to create harmony – are they co-ordinated? Or are they contrasted to create an interesting effect?

Some patterns are so familiar we associate them with a particular life style. Why are the designs so popular? Stripes and spots are examples of a simple pattern repeated over and over again. Look at patterned wallpaper. How often is the pattern repeated? Do you think the numbers of times a pattern is repeated affects the overall appeal? Bold stripes or spots can look smart on a shirt. What do you think they might look like on a wall?

Collect: striped, spotted, and plain fabric, an iron, and an ironing board.
a Iron the striped fabric for a full minute. Do the stripes dazzle, or seem to move?
b Repeat with spotted fabric, then with plain. Record your observations.
c How could you apply this information when choosing patterns for a room?

Pattern is as powerful as colour. It can affect the whole mood of a room. Large patterns and dark colours make a big room look smaller. Small patterns and light colours create an impression of space. Some people are extra-sensitive to pattern; a bold one dazzles their eyes. How could you test whether a small pattern has the opposite effect? Keep looking at rooms and the patterns used on floors, walls, curtains, cushions, and furniture fabrics. Ask yourself – will they irritate me after a while? are they calming? fussy? dramatic? stressful?

Terence Conran has said, 'A pattern drawn with warmth and coloured with harmony can give a room rhythm, drama, vigour, comfort, serenity, and a sense of life. A pattern drawn harshly and coloured insensitively will undermine you just as certain colours can.' How do you evaluate the patterns you drew? Where could they fit into a room? Would you like to change the design and try again?

Does tartan remind you of a particular place?

Where might you expect to see chintz?

Design and interaction

Texture

Feel your hair. Is it smooth or springy? Texture is the way a material feels to the touch. The main textures are warm and cold, and smooth and rough, but there are many shades in between. Touch your nails, skin, shoes, clothing, and five different objects near you. Describe their texture – silky, soft, harsh, gritty, and so on. Do textures, like pattern and colour, have a different effect on your mood? Do you think they affect the mood of a room?

The interaction of colour, pattern, and texture creates the total design, and states the mood of a room. The guideline for pattern is 'one bold one is enough'. What about colours? Do you think textures look better in contrast to one another? It does not matter if you get some answers wrong. Even skilled designers have to keep on trying different combinations until they get the effect they want. Keep the function of the fabric in mind. What happens to a zig-zag pattern on pleated curtains? Would you make a cushion cover from a coarse-woven fabric?

What kind of life style does this design suggest: calm? orderly? dramatic? chaotic? Co-ordinated products are useful if you are not sure of your taste. You lose individual style, and gain mass production appeal. However, some products wear out before others, and cannot always be replaced.

---

1 Design a pattern, perhaps using a computer, for one of the following: a bright summer shirt, wallpaper for a child's room, and a rug to disguise the sofabed in a small flat. Add colour. Evaluate the result, giving reasons for your choice.

2 What is meant by 'texture'? Choose five samples of different fabric texture and stick them in your book.

In what ways does texture affect the type of fabric chosen for **a** nightwear, **b** bed linen, **c** towels, and **d** sports clothes? Write down your favourite meal and list the textures of the various foods. State, with reasons, whether you consider texture an important factor in **a** shopping for fresh food, and **b** choosing the menu for an evening meal.

Choosing a floor covering

Does your floor need to be wear resistant? stain resistant? water resistant?

Collect: squares of floor coverings as illustrated, a block of carborundum (an abrasive mixture of carbon and silicon used for sharpening knives), oil, bleach, blackcurrant juice, coffee, squares of formica, recommended adhesive, and kitchen scales.

a Rub each square twenty times with the carborundum block. Compare the squares for wear resistance.

b Dab the liquids on to each corner of the squares. Leave for 15 minutes, clean thoroughly. Compare the squares for stain resistance.

c Stick each square to formica with the recommended adhesive. Weigh. Soak overnight in cold water. Wipe dry and weigh again. Compare the squares for water resistance.

Is the floor to be used for:

cooking?	laundry?	dancing?
eating?	playing?	sitting?
sleeping?	bathing?	

Is the floor solid or suspended (p. 125)? Does it lead directly to outdoors? Are prams or bicycles kept on it? Can pets shed hairs or make paw marks? Is it difficult to clean? to maintain?

Is the floor noisy or quiet to walk on? Does it feel warm, cool, or cold? Is it attractive? Does it fit in with the room design?

Will a baby, or an elderly or disabled person use it? If so, what health and safety factors need to be considered?

1 Find out the cost per square metre of the above floor coverings.

2 Choose, with reasons, a suitable floor covering for a kitchen.

3 Choose, with reasons, a covering for a nursery floor.

4 Large patterns, deep colours, and borders will make a room look smaller. Choose, with reasons, an attractive floor covering for a small sitting room.

5 Choose and cost a suitable floor covering for the young person's bed-sit on p. 167. Give reasons for your choice.

Curtains

Curtains can make a small window appear larger if they are hung outside the width of the window.

Do curtains have the opposite functions to those of a window (p. 158)? During the day, net curtains add privacy. At night, heavy curtains reduce noise from the street and shut off the outside world. Curtains can add greatly to the appeal of a room. They should usually be either sill or floor length; anything in between can upset the proportion of a room.

Headings allow the curtains to hang gracefully when closed. Pinch pleats suit heavy, floor-length curtains. Pencil pleats work better with net and lighter fabrics. Why must you always allow extra material for them?

Fix the curtain rail in place first. Then measure the length from the rail to the sill or floor. Add 15–25 cm (6–10 in) for headings and hems. Measure the width of the rail. Add 5 cm (2 in) each side for hems. Light fabrics need three times the width of the rail to look graceful. Heavy fabrics need one to two times the width. Before you choose a fabric, check:

a Is it suitable for the function of the room?
b Does it fit the life style of the people using the room?
c Is the fabric pre-shrunk? If not, allow extra for shrinkage.
d Is it patterned? Allow extra for pattern repeats both in length and width.
e Is it flame-resistant? Name two rooms in the home where this may be needed.
f What is the fibre content (for washing or cleaning)?

Blinds are particularly useful for kitchens and bathrooms – try to work out why. They look best in small rooms, or in large rooms on small windows. They are easy to clean, have simple modern lines, roll up out of fire's way, and let in all the light. They can be cut to the exact size of your window, and made up in the same fabric as your furniture – or you can design and make them yourself.

Choose, with reasons, curtain fabric for the windows in the plan on p. 167. Work out how much fabric you need for ceiling to floor curtains. Think about linings, and find out about milium fabric curtains. Would you consider them a suitable choice? Why? Compare the price of ready-made curtains with the cost of making them yourself.

Curtain rails, tracks, poles, and headings

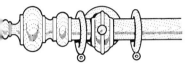
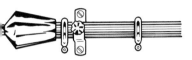

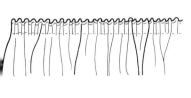
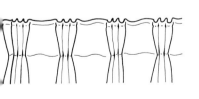
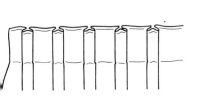

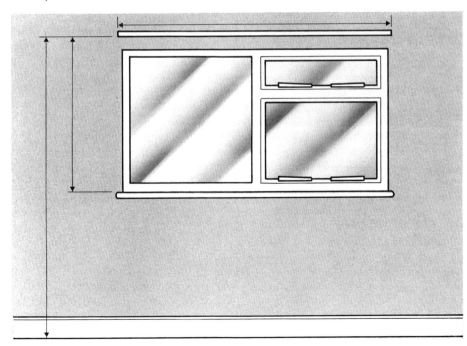

Wall coverings

You can brighten a drab room by changing the appearance of the walls. Fresh paint or paper has an immediate effect as the walls are two-thirds of a room's surface. What makes up the other third? Is the ceiling usually painted at the same time as the walls? Why? Before deciding on a covering, consider your options. New technology has made it possible to choose textures such as cork, straw, hessian, or wood; fabrics like silk, linen, velvet, or suede; vinyls, foils, and ceramic tiles. Within these options are further options – an almost endless choice of colours, patterns, textures, and designs.

Paint is the most popular wall covering throughout the world. Try to think of reasons for this. Again, choice is difficult as there are so many varieties. The two main types are **emulsion**, which is water-based, and **gloss**, which is oil-based. Emulsion is for walls and ceilings; gloss for wood and metal. Study the appeal of both on walls and doors. Why might a whole room painted in gloss feel tiring after a while?

Some gloss paints are **anti-condensation** – they feel cool, but not cold, to the touch. **Fire retardant** paint cannot stop a raging fire, but can help reduce the spread of flames from a small fire. **Fungus resistant** paints are used in humid climates. Where else could they be used, and why? **Anti-burglar** paints stay slippery when dry, to prevent outdoor walls being climbed. Others stick to the hands if heavy pressure is applied, and a permanent staining dye is released if the paint is removed with white spirit. **Bituminous** paints protect metals against rust corrosion. They are thick, usually black, and used in areas where extra weatherproofing is needed.

Why do you think the term wall 'covering' is now used?

1 State, with reasons, the type of paint you might choose for the following:
   a a slightly grubby ceiling.
   b a forgetful smoker's bedroom.
   c an inner wall with patches of damp.
   d a bathroom with no proper ventilation.
   e a metal cold-water tank in the roof.
   f a front or back door, garden gate, or wall.

2 Paint should be washable, with good adhesion and opacity.
   Interpret this statement. Name, with reasons, three rooms in which you might use washable paint.

Furniture and design

Plan and carry out visits to furniture stores, auction rooms, second-hand shops, and jumble sales, and look at magazines. Study the design of furniture – how it is constructed, the upholstery, the overall appeal.

1 Divide the class into three groups. Choose one of the plans on pp. 121 and 122 (not the caravan), and 'create' a family to live there. Develop their life style – number and ages of people in group, stage of life cycle, state of health, their values, goals, community support, and likely budget and heating needs. Working within 'your' appropriate budget and, where necessary, using credit schemes, cost and choose furniture for the bedroom and sitting room.

2 Using resources, design and make one piece of furniture yourself.

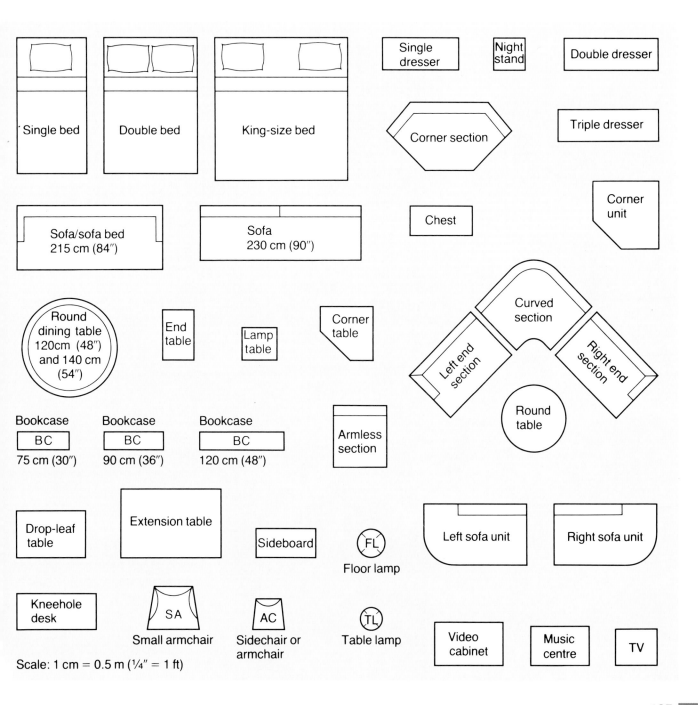

Scale: 1 cm = 0.5 m (¼″ = 1 ft)

Arranging furniture

A room plan must consider the main source of daylight, colours, patterns, textures, furniture, furnishings, floor coverings, artificial lighting, and accessories.

Some designer tips include:
- Plan on graph paper first and think the plan right through.
- Be flexible – changes can be made at any stage.
- Check for architectural features, such as a bay window, a fireplace, an arch, an alcove, or a sloping ceiling, and plan for them first.
- Choose one focal point and keep distractions away from it.
- Place large pieces at the wall opposite the focal point.
- Allow 90 cm (3 ft) between pieces for traffic flow.

Think about balance and the way the eye travels around different heights in a room. Each wall should be balanced from top to bottom – for example, a large picture above a small table makes the wall look heavy and the table frail. Think about what you might balance opposite a door. Keep good proportions by placing large pieces by large areas of wall, and small pieces by small walls. Pieces by walls should be parallel to them. Avoid using too much furniture.

Guidelines for space include:
45 cm (18 in) between low areas such as sofas and beds.
75 cm (30 in) at the sides of beds.
90 cm (3 ft) in front of cupboards, drawers, and wardrobes.
60 cm (2 ft) between wall and dining chair.
15 cm (6 in) between other furniture and walls.

Check the design gives:
a free access for door swing, window opening, cupboards and drawers, heat source, and electricity outlets.
b general and task lighting at appropriate heights.
c uneven spaces between furniture, for more interest.
d space in front of windows, pictures, and furniture.
e conversation areas within 2.5–3 m (8–10 ft) of each other.
f tables of suitable height near chairs and beds.
g television screen not facing the window.
h storage provided near point of use.
i some free space left in the room.

1 Repeat the graph work and making of furniture cut-outs you did on p. 145, and arrange the furniture. Compare your results with your first attempt, and comment on the difference, if any.

2 Beauty and good design are important in a room plan, but comfort and convenience should have top priority.

Discuss.

Further work on Chapter 13

1 Lack of money does not necessarily mean lack of style. In fact, it can bring out your creative talent. Choose colour, pattern, and texture before you choose the furniture. Fabrics with lovely, interesting, or lively designs will create the mood of a room far more than the style of the bed, table, or chairs. Most people buy furniture hoping it will last about 10 years. A bed-sit may well be a short-term investment – durability does not have to be a priority. Copy out the plan of your bed-sit shown here.

You have £1500 to spend. You can purchase the items you need at any place and by any method you wish. Not everything you need has to be bought, made, or acquired at once. Decide on your life style: a student on a grant? climbing the career ladder? a divorced person trying to build a new life? The hot water and central heating are adequate, but the room suffers from draughts. Be realistic about your choices! Analyse them as you go along. Keep plans, sketches, rough ideas, and details of your work. When you have finished, evaluate your results.

2 a Carpet labels must indicate fibre content. Suggest *one* other piece of information that might be found on a carpet label.

b '80% wool/20% polyamide'
The above label is attached to a carpet. Give *two* reasons for mixing these fibres. *(Welsh Joint Education Committee)*

3 Appropriate heating and types of floor and wall covering are among points which should be considered when planning a bedroom for a new baby. For each of these points, name a suitable example and give a reason for your choice.

a Appropriate method of heating the room

b Type of floor covering

c Type of wall covering *(Northern Examining Association)*

Now look again at the objective at the beginning of the chapter, and check that you have achieved it.

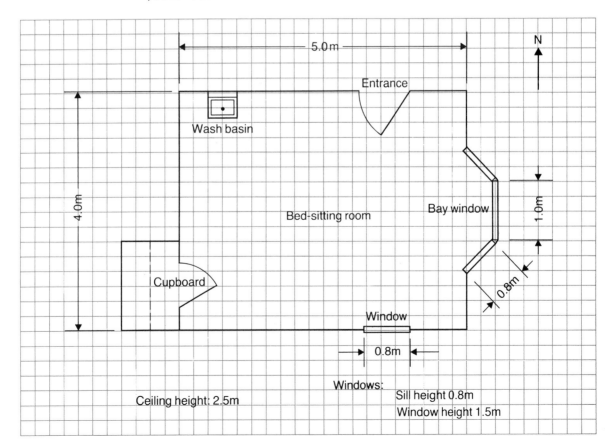

14 *H*ome management

By the end of this chapter, you should be able to:

- identify personal and family resources.
- demonstrate time and energy saving skills.
- recognize the uses and limitations of appliances.

- understand time and energy management.
- draw up plans for home management.

Can you manage time?

Answer the following by writing for each 'Agree', 'Disagree' or 'Don't know':

1 I am always on time.
2 I am often late.
3 I am often bored.
4 I am seldom bored.
5 I dislike having to wait.
6 I never know how to fill in spare time.
7 I never have any spare time.
8 I like to waste my time.
9 Hobbies are a waste of time.
10 Work is a waste of time.
11 Sleeping wastes time.
12 Television wastes a lot of my time.
13 Homemaking tasks waste time.
14 Computer games waste time.
15 When I start a task, there is never enough time to finish it.
16 I plan my time so I avoid a last-minute rush.
17 I spend half my time looking for things.

18 I know almost exactly where everything is.
19 I wish I could spend more time on myself.
20 Adults worry too much about time.
21 Most adults I know work too hard.
22 Some teachers never seem to have enough time.
23 Being a parent means being short of time.
24 I would like a job where I am not rushed.
25 I would like a fast-moving, hectic job.
26 I seem to have more time and energy than others.
27 I am getting old.
28 I am still very young.
29 I have all the time in the world to think about time.

1 Imagine you only have 15 minutes of life left. In their order of priority, write down the things you would most want to do. Keep your choices realistic – there must be time for them all.
2 Imagine you have unlimited resources and all the time in the world. State, with reasons, what you would choose to do to improve the quality of your life, or the life of others.
3 Time is one of our most precious resources. From your responses, try to work out the value you put on time.

Time as a resource

Time is a non-human resource. Each person has the same amount of this resource within a 24-hour day. Is time a limited, or an unlimited, resource?

Using graph paper and a bright colour, create your own **time log**. A time log is a written record showing the expenditure of time for specific activities. Do not use separate colours for separate activities – those which take less than 15 minutes each can be grouped together, so that, for example, washing and dressing can be marked in with eating breakfast.

Think of all the demands upon your time, such as sleeping, eating, travelling, school hours, homework, etc. Make a rough estimate of the time these take, and block in the periods on the graph. You may have to do homemaking tasks, fetch a younger sibling from school, care for an elderly relative, or help in the family business. If so, block in this time. What about a Saturday job? sport? an aerobics class? other classes? Block in any other demands upon your time.

How much time have you left? Do you think you will have more, or less, spare time in 10 years? Why? Do you agree that time is a precious resource? Why?

Saving time?

Gary saves time by missing breakfast. He wipes his face with a flannel instead of thoroughly washing off the grease on his skin. He mislays his books and arrives late at school. He cannot concentrate as he lacks energy, and is angry at being given a half-hour detention. After the detention, he spends an hour in the chemist's trying to decide which spot cream he can afford.

Harmony gets up early, has breakfast, and thoroughly grooms herself. She arrives at school early and sorts out her work. After school, she tells a time-wasting friend who wants a chat that she can do it on the way home. Her friend calls her a prig and walks off.

Identify those demands on your time which cannot be altered. What are the goals of **a** sleeping, **b** eating, **c** travelling, and so on? Do you value these goals? What might happen to your physical and mental development if you tried to reduce these times?

1 What do you think is meant by a 'time-wasting' person? Do you know any? Are you one yourself? Do you approve, or disapprove, of Harmony's behaviour with her friend, and why? Discuss the time Gary 'saved' by missing breakfast. What is the value, if any, of good grooming?
2 Which of the two people do you think invested time in themselves? Give reasons for your answer.

Developing a work plan

Do tasks waiting to be done bother you, and cause you stress? **Flexitime** is a plan which allows employees to choose specific working hours in a day. Do you think this a good idea? Why? Discuss the home life of workers you think most likely to benefit from flexitime. Can you 'budget' your spare time and energy in much the same way as you budget for flexible costs (p. 90)?

Ned's exams start in two weeks. He worries about all the things he must do before then. His teacher thinks he looks tense. Ned says he cannot fit in all his tasks. 'Make a list', his teacher advises. 'And don't forget to budget for spare time.'

Revise for exam.
Go to library for a needed text.
Buy clothes for interview.
Visit teacher for character reference.
Speak to careers teacher again.
Apply for sports club.
Take bike to be mended.

Buy fruit and magazines.
Visit friend in hospital.
Make dental appointment.
Buy notepaper and stamps.
Apply for that job.
Reply to friend's letter.
Fix bedroom light.

At this stage, Ned gives up. 'I'll never get it all done.' His Dad snorts, 'I have to fit that in, and with a full-time job.'

When making a work plan:
a be realistic. Remove all non-immediate goals to the list for next week; and stop worrying about them.
b put your immediate goals as top priority for demands on time and energy. Which do you think is Ned's top priority?
c set limits – 'revise for exam' is too vague. Ned should slot a period of time each evening for his revision, and stick to it. Knowing you are working to a plan stops worry and stress. A worried brain cannot absorb information at the optimum rate.
d cross off each task as you tackle it. This gives a feeling of confidence that you are being productive, and reduces stress.
e keep to your plan. Do not stay at one task for much longer than you planned, so you have time or energy left for the next.
f stay flexible within your plan. Take any opportunity to do small tasks, such as shopping on the way home from school.
g budget for spare time. Brain cells which are rested and relaxed before sleep work much better the next day.

1 What has Ned not planned for? Is this a wise choice, and why?

2 Assuming he gets home at 4.30 p.m. and goes to bed at 10.30, develop his work plan for the next two weeks.

Energy as a resource

Energy is a human resource. In some ways it is like time: only a certain amount is available for use each day. But the supply of energy varies from person to person. Within each person, the amount of available energy can often be raised.

a Where does energy come from?
b What happens when you forget to eat?
c Does the amount of sleep you get alter your available energy?
d Devise a task to find out whether you work better over a long period of time with or without a break.

Does it sometimes seem that minutes crawl by like hours, or that hours flash by like minutes? Try to think of examples of each. What were you doing at the time? Remember, energy is needed for every activity, even lying on your bed and simply day-dreaming. The way people perceive time depends on what they are doing – the way they are using, or not using, their energy.

A healthy diet, lots of exercise, and the right amount of sleep can increase your energy level.

Discuss the following two sentences in detail:

- People feel bored when they use energy for activities which **a** are repetitive, **b** seem unending, or **c** seem to bring no reward.

- People feel fatigued when their energy levels are reduced by **a** physical action, **b** mental exertion, **c** emotional stress, or **d** using their energy in boring ways.

List some homemaking tasks you think fit each of these descriptions. Give reasons for your choices.

Working in groups, plan, carry out, and evaluate a comparative study of the time involved in some of the following. Note the amount of human energy invested in each task.

a chopping vegetables by hand or machine
b preparing a soup or sponge-mix by hand or blender
c cooking by microwave, pressure cooker, or conventional oven
d balancing a budget by hand or computer
e cleaning carpets by hand brush or machine
f stitching a seam by hand or machine

1 Which produced the quickest results? Which used least human energy? Which produced the cleanest/most satisfactory results? Do these answers match? Which machines were stored, requiring time and energy to set up? How much time and energy was required to clean either yourself or the machines after the task?

2 What might be done with any time or energy saved by **a** an elderly person, **b** a young parent, **c** a single person?

3 From your findings, state which machines you think might be top priority for each of the above groups, and why.

Saving time and energy?

Do machines always save time and energy? What happens if they break down? Has any student a sad tale of a machine breaking down at exactly the wrong moment? Or waiting for a service engineer who does not show up? List which machines, if any, you think a household should be able to fix.

Some days you expend more energy than others. Some activities can be called high or low energy. Describe a high energy day and a low energy day for you. Do you find that school work makes high or low demands on your energy?

List some materials which it is not appropriate to clean with machines. Is there any satisfaction in doing them by hand? Can you do low energy activities at the same time, such as chatting to others, enjoying peace and quiet, listening to the radio, studying a book, and so on? Devise, plan, and carry out a task to test this.

List twenty of the homemaking tasks most frequently done. Divide the list into those which take:

a a lot of time.
b a high level of energy.
c a little time.
d a low level of energy.

Do some tasks appear in the same lists? What conclusions can you draw? What can you add to the priorities you need to think about when choosing between machines?

Collect: time- and/or energy-saving tips from magazines.
a Investigate one of your choice.
b Discuss what other values might have influenced your choice.
c Were any goals lost, such as satisfaction or pleasure in the task?
d Were there any other factors which might cause a homemaker to be reluctant to try 'your' tip?
e Would the tip be useful for a child of primary school age who enjoys homemaking? Give reasons for your answer.
f Could a handicapped person use 'your' tip? If not, could it be modified or changed in some way? Give details, and state how.

Visit a furnishing store and examine bedding and coverings. What features would you look for in a bed if you were not strong enough to move it yourself? What type of coverings would you choose to save time and energy in bed-making?

A case study

Ms Parker begins her task of setting the table for the evening meal. From the wall cabinet she gets the dishes and glasses needed for the family of five, and carries them to the table in two separate trips. The cream to go with the dessert is taken from the fridge, and placed on the counter while she goes to the wall cabinet and gets the sugar bowl. Both are then taken to and placed on the table.

From the cutlery drawer she gets five knives, forks, and spoons, and places them on the table. Napkins are obtained from the back of the base cabinet behind the baking dishes, and she folds each as she places it under the fork on the table.

It is now time to remove the food from the oven, and place it on the table for serving. The roast pork is placed on a large serving platter that she had to get from the wall cabinets above the refrigerator. She gets the serving bowl for the apple sauce from the wall cabinet, and goes to the warmer drawer of the oven to get the apple sauce. She puts it in the serving bowl that is on the counter, and then takes it to the table. Ms Parker strains the broccoli and places it in a hot serving dish, after going to the drawer to get an oven glove. She returns to the drawer to get a heat-proof mat and places it on the table. Then she carries the broccoli to the mat on the table.

The family is called for the evening meal. After everyone is seated, she remembers the butter, which is in the fridge, and gets up to get it. As soon as Ms Parker reaches for the apple sauce, it is evident there is no serving spoon, so she goes to the cutlery drawer for it. As the meal progresses, Tommy asks for more fruit juice, and Ms Parker goes to the fridge again to get it.

After the meal is concluded, Ms Parker cannot seem to find the energy to get up and begin cleaning up the kitchen. One of the children is assigned the job instead.

Using this case study, list eight ways in which Ms Parker could have prevented fatigue and increased the amount of energy she could use for the task. Note positions and movements which cause fatigue.

Counting the costs

Chantal designs her own 'dream' kitchen and buys the appliances, cabinets, fixtures, and fittings. She is proud of her homemaking skills, and would like to fit up the kitchen herself. But her job is demanding on her time and energy – she earns £100 a day. She reckons she can do the work in six days, but she will need to take this amount of time off from her job.

She asks a handyman how much it will cost to fix the electrical appliances to their own circuits, plumb in the machines, attach the cabinets to the walls, and do all the other necessary tasks. He estimates it will take him four days at a cost of £60 a day.

a Work out how much it will cost Chantal to hire the handyman.
b Work out how much it will cost Chantal in lost wages if she does the job herself.
c Which is the more cost efficient choice for Chantal, and by how much?
d What other factors does Chantal need to take into account before making her choice?
e Which choice would you make if you were Chantal, and why?

Chantal's father offers to help her do the job if they can spread the work over six Saturday afternoons. In return, she can help him modernize his garage over the six Saturdays following the completion of her kitchen.

Chantal is tempted to choose the option offered by her father. She feels it will **a** help them become closer friends, **b** be a superb opportunity to practise her homemaking skills, **c** give her enormous satisfaction to have participated in the task herself, and **d** be an opportunity to spend Saturday evenings with her mother, whom she does not see often enough.

The drawbacks to this choice include **a** having a mess in her kitchen for six weekends, **b** having to eat out for that period of time, **c** having to spend time and energy constantly cleaning the flat because of the dust and dirt, **d** not being able to entertain at home for six weeks, and **e** having her weekends tied up for three whole months.

Choices are not easy! Do you agree, and why? The factors Chantal is trying to take into account include not only her time, energy, skills, and money costs, but also her emotional needs and those of her parents, plus the satisfaction levels she might herself obtain.

Write an imaginative essay on Chantal's choices. Describe her short-term lifestyle if she decides to **a** do the work herself, **b** hire the handyman, and **c** work with her father.

Co-ordinating the work

Many homemaking tasks can be co-ordinated – done within the same time span. Co-ordinated tasks can be divided into three groups:

a a **cluster** includes tasks which are done in the same place, such as cleaning a fireplace, vacuuming the floor, and tidying and dusting the room.

b an **overlap** includes tasks which are part of another task, such as preparing a meal, washing dishes, and cleaning surfaces as you go.

c a **dovetail** includes tasks which are done at the same time, such as putting onions to fry/sorting laundry and loading the machine; preparing meat in a casserole/putting laundry in the dryer; preparing vegetables/folding clothes.

Some tasks are independent – they can only be done on their own. These include cleaning windows, completing homework, etc. They are usually large, involve a high level of time and energy, and require a work plan of their own. For example, you have three subjects to complete for homework – one is difficult, one is easy, and one involves drawing skills. Would you **a** tackle the difficult work first while your mind is fresh? **b** do the easy one first to get it out of the way? **c** use your drawing skills first because you enjoy this most?

● Independent tasks usually require full concentration and cannot be dovetailed with other tasks.

Do you agree, and why?

Using resources, find out and practise how to fix a dripping tap, and clear a blocked sink. Explain some health hazards in not doing each of these tasks.

Using a stop watch, carry out the above tasks consecutively. Then do the same tasks together – co-ordinate them. Compare your findings. Which of the groups does each task fall into? Why?

1 Put the following tasks into their groups:
- While sitting under a dryer, Ms Parker plans next week's menus and balances her cheque book.
- You take the last egg from the fridge. While it is boiling, you add 'eggs' to the shopping list, and check the rest of the contents of the fridge.
- In the bathroom, you clean the bath first, the sink next, then the toilet bowl. You finish by cleaning the floor.
- In the morning, you tidy your room, mend your shirt, and then help weed the garden. You do your homework in the afternoon.

2 In what ways might listing tasks in groups help **a** the manager of a hotel, and **b** a homemaker?

Saturday morning

'Women's work!', scoffs Arty. 'Anyone can do that!' 'Very well', replies his mother. 'Do my Saturday morning chores.'

Arty devises his work plan:
  50 minutes to clean the windows.
  15 minutes to vacuum the carpet.
   5 minutes to dust surfaces.
  10 minutes to change a plug.
  30 minutes for favourite television programme.
  10 minutes to make beds, and tidy rooms.
  15 minutes coffee break.
  15 minutes to clean breakfast dishes.
  30 minutes to prepare lunch.

Arty cleans the windows just on time. He drops the bucket and cleaning cloth by the sink. He starts to vacuum, but the bag breaks. It takes ages to clean the mess and fix on a new bag. For some reason, there is dust everywhere and water on the kitchen floor. He ignores this. It is television time.

After the programme, he decides to prepare the vegetables before doing the bedrooms. Halfway through, there is a telephone message for his father. Still holding the sharp knife, he dashes to the living room for a pen, and trips over the vacuum lead. By the time he has cleaned and bandaged the cut, the caller has rung off.

Arty is bewildered by the state of the living room. He decides to take his coffee break, and work out what is going wrong. He dumps the half-scraped vegetables into the food processor and, too late, remembers that was the plug he had to fix!

1 Discuss all the things you think were wrong with Arty's plan from beginning to end. How would you tackle his tasks?
  a Make a plan which is realistic.
  b Check it with available resources.
  c Act promptly, but without rush or stress.
  d Concentrate fully on each stage of each task.
  e Avoid interruptions, if possible.
2 Learn and practise the skills of changing a light bulb, mending a fuse, stripping a flex, and wiring a plug to a new appliance. What is the correct way to pull a plug out of a socket? Explain why sockets can get loose. Are moveable appliances, such as irons and hair dryers, more at risk of frayed flex and loose plugs? Why? What are the health and safety factors involved?

Sharing the work

Go back to your list of twenty homemaking tasks (p. 172). Take each task in turn and discuss why it must be done. What would be the consequences if nobody did it?

In a family of two adults in full-time employment and three children aged 9, 13, and 16, state, with reasons, whom you would expect to do the following evening tasks:

- preparing the meal
- washing up
- mopping the floor
- paying the insurance bill
- treating a cut
- feeding the pet
- cleaning the bath
- changing a faulty plug
- tidying the living room
- ironing the shirts
- fixing a stuck zip
- sewing on a button
- polishing the shoes
- changing a light bulb
- locking up at night

A small child needs routine.

Compare your list in class, and be prepared to discuss your choices and reasons.

Name the health and safety hazards of not doing at least six of the above tasks.

Imagine you are a parent and one child keeps 'forgetting' his or her tasks. You do not like punishments, and want to tackle the problem by other means. Discuss this in class and think up a 'reward' for the student whose solution seems best.

Toddlers can go through stages of being highly organized – teddy must be seated in the same place, the bowl and spoon must be laid in same way, and it is very upsetting if things are changed around. This outward need for order is calming, and helps the child cope with inward stress from developmental change.

In a reverse way, older people with disorganized lives can show signs of stress. Outward panics over not being able to find things cover the inner panics of what is really going wrong. So much time is spent searching a cluttered room for schoolbooks, keys, or a shoe that there is no time to search mentally for the real problem.

1 If one parent is a full-time homemaker, how many of the tasks listed above would you expect him or her to do, and why? Do you think he or she should **a** pick up toys and clothes left on the floor, **b** mop up the bathroom each time it is used, and **c** tell the bedtime story each night? Why? In what way can the parent's behaviour as role model help the children to be effective at managing their own lives?

2 Do you think a disorganized home can lead to accidents? Why? (See Chapter 15.)

What is home management?

Each home has a limited amount of human and material resources. To achieve optimum growth and development for each family member, these need to be used in the best possible way. Because material resources at home are used all the time, they need to be cleaned or replaced (or renewed/repaired) on a fairly regular basis. Home management is a way of using human and material resources so that family members have a chance to achieve some of their goals.

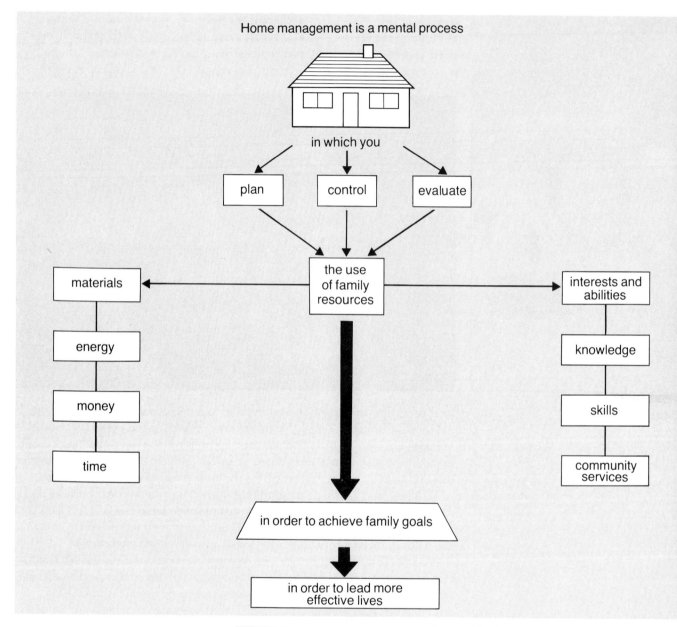

Home management is a mental process

in which you

plan · control · evaluate

materials · energy · money · time

the use of family resources

interests and abilities · knowledge · skills · community services

in order to achieve family goals

in order to lead more effective lives

---

1 Do home management plans need to be fixed or flexible? Why?

2 Are the values of family members likely to conflict at times?

3 Are their overall goals likely to be the same?

4 Do you think it better if one person or all family members are involved in the plan-making stage? Why?

5 Should only one person control the plans, or should all family members take their share of responsibility? Why?

6 Evaluation of plans helps people to lead more effective lives – to achieve their goals.

Do you agree? Discuss this statement.

Further work on Chapter 14

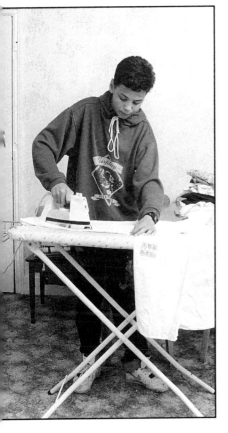

1 It is 3 p.m. You are to collect 4-year-old Tom from playschool (a 5-minute walk from your home), give him a nourishing snack, and prepare the evening meal. You have a date and need to wash your hair, iron a shirt, shower, and be ready by 7 p.m. when the family comes home. Plan your tasks to allow you to complete them without rushing. Allow 'emergency time' and 'quiet time'. Take into account that you have responsibility for a small child's health, safety, and welfare.

2 'Nobody has time to do the ironing these days.' Test the accuracy of this statement by a survey of at least three people from different household groups. Pool the class findings, and use appropriate graphs to present a fairly large survey.

3 Because roles are no longer clearly defined in the home, it is even more important that tasks are clearly defined.
   Do you agree with this statement, and why?

4 'A woman's work is never done.' Discuss what is meant by 'woman's work', and give your opinions of this statement.

5 A home without management is like a football match without a ball – you can't make goals!

   Comment on this.

6 'Procrastination is the thief of time.' Find out the meaning of this adage. Are you a procrastinator? List some tips you would offer to a person who wanted to use time more effectively.

7 Imagine you have moved into a flat with two friends.
   a Look at the list of tasks below. How often would you do each of these tasks?

Tasks	Daily	Weekly
making beds		
preparing meals		
vacuuming carpets		
cleaning bathroom		
washing dishes		
shopping for food		
ironing		
changing sheets		
tidying living room		
cleaning kitchen		

   b Choose *one* of the tasks you think should be done every day. State why it needs to be done every day.   *(Scottish Examination Board)*

8 When producing meals it is essential to be able to manage both time and money. Discuss this statement fully.   *(Midland Examining Group)*

Now look again at the objectives at the beginning of the chapter, and check that you have achieved them.

15 Protection

By the end of this chapter, you should be able to:
- identify the major causes of accidents in the home.
- make the connection between behaviour and accidents.
- develop your First Aid skills.
- make a choice between drugs and independence.

Safety in the home

The table shows the main kinds of accident in the home.

Category	Number	Per cent
Falls	24 124	44.8
Cuts	10 018	18.6
Struck by object	6 699	12.4
Burns/scalds	3 202	5.9
Poisoning	1 385	2.6
Choking/suffocation	705	1.3
Electric current	64	0.1
Others unknown	7 698	14.3

What is the main type of accident in the home? What percentage of people who have accidents at home are injured this way? List ten objects in the home which can cause falls. Name two groups of people who may be unsteady on their feet.

Babies are born curious, with a powerful urge to learn. Toddlers get frustrated because they cannot see above their height. List ten different objects a child might climb on to see what goes on above head height. How safe are these objects? How safe is the child?

It has been suggested that the word 'accident' is a misnomer. It implies chance, fate, or luck. Is it 'chance' to pass a hot drink over someone's head? Discuss this common cause of terrible scalds. Is it 'fate' to risk choking by not cutting up a toddler's food? Discuss this. Is it 'bad luck' to step on the edge of a jagged can? What should be done with all used sharp objects? Do appliances or furniture act as 'enemies' in your home, waiting to injure, perhaps kill, you or your family? Discuss. People interact with their environment. From the appallingly high data above, list some attitudes or behaviour changes families need to consider, to protect themselves from each category of harm.

1 Comment on these sayings: 'Polished floors and mats that slide – that's the way that Grandpa died.' 'Toys and stairs and dismal lighting cause more broken bones than fighting.'

2 Find out about the Green Cross Code. Role-play teaching a child how to cross the road.

More about accidents

Accidents cause about 3 per cent of all deaths, but the number of people injured is about 500 to every death. Using resources find out:

a Where do the majority of accidents to the under-5s happen? Who do you think is responsible for these accidents, and why? Name some ways in which a toddler could **i** choke, and **ii** suffocate.

b Which other group has the most accidents at home? Discuss some reasons for this.

1 Aunt Kim Wong, aged 76, hurried downstairs when she heard the front door opening. She woke up in hospital suffering from a broken leg and severe burns. How did this happen? Correct all the hazards you can find.

2 Parents and older members of the family have to be the safety 'eyes and ears' of a small child. List all the hazards in the bathroom. State clearly the danger of each. Sketch the same bathroom with the hazards removed, or corrected.

3 Kerin, aged 16, is reading in bed when the bedside light fuses. Name all the hazards he faces before he can switch on the overhead light. Clearly explain how each could have been avoided.

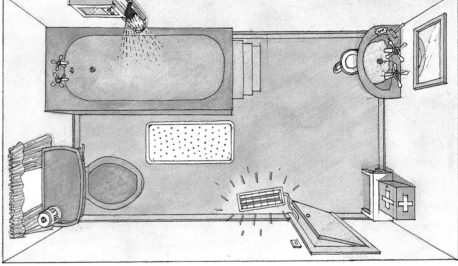

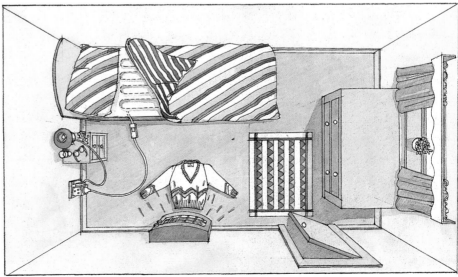

Heat and fire

The controlled use of fire is an important chemical process in our lives. The uncontrolled force of fire is a deadly destroyer of human life. The **point of ignition** – how the fire actually starts – is where human behaviour and the risk of fire meet. The table on the left shows the main causes of ignition in 1984.

Causes	Number	Per cent
Cooking appliances	20 800	45.8
Cigarettes	6 200	13.7
Electrical equipment	5 900	13.0
Matches	4 600	10.1
Space heating appliances	4 500	9.9
Electrical wiring	3 400	7.5

In these accidents, 262 people burned to death, 553 died from breathing in fumes, and 6947 people were rushed to hospital with severe burns. Fires produce choking smoke and deadly gases, mainly carbon monoxide. The combination of smoke and gases accounts for 60–90 per cent of all fire deaths. People are overcome by the fumes and cannot escape the path of the flames.

Collect: assorted fabric squares, a retort stand, a stop watch, and a taper.
a Hang a square by one corner from the retort stand. Light the taper and apply to the lowest corner of the square.
b Record your findings under: name of fabric; time to ignite; time to complete combustion; amount of smoke; smell; drip.

Nightwear for children can be treated for fire proofing, but all fabrics give only slight protection against heat and flames. Some fibres in furnishings are highly **flammable (inflammable** means the same thing), and burn fiercely, giving off a mix of deadly fumes. It is thought these fibres add to the problems of most urban fires.

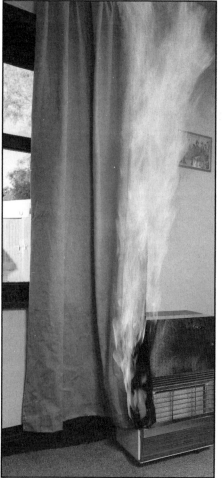

1 From the materials tested, choose two you would not use for nightwear.
2 Find out and list the paddings used in household furniture such as beds, armchairs, and head rests to make them more comfortable. Why should you not test the burning properties of these? The Fire Safety Officer may be available to give a demonstration and talk.

3 The point of ignition is where human behaviour and the risk of fire meet.

Discuss this, with reference to and comments on the above figures and the photos.

Life-saving skills

If someone collapses, the three life-saving checks are:
a is there a pulse and breathing?
b is there heavy bleeding?
c is the person unconscious?
Call for an ambulance immediately.

Brain cells die if they are deprived of oxygen for longer than five minutes. It is vital to start the heart beating and get the breathing going at once. Both skills can be dangerous in unskilled hands, so try to enrol in a course of First Aid.

Heart massage
Strike the lower chest once, to the left of the breast bone. Feel the carotid pulse (in the neck), as the heart might start beating. If not, apply the double heel of both hands low on the chest. Keeping the arms straight, rock back and forth once every second. For a child, use one hand, and press lightly 80 times a minute.

Mouth-to-mouth resuscitation
1 Check the mouth is empty and there is nothing blocking the airway.
2 Push the jaw up and back to prevent the tongue blocking up the airway.
3 Pinch the nose shut, breathe in, seal your lips over the mouth and blow out.
4 Lift your head to watch whether the chest falls as the blown-in air comes out.
5 Continue until help arrives, or the person is breathing normally again.

The recovery position
The First Aider's work is to make sure an unconscious person goes on breathing. In the recovery position, the tongue cannot fall down the throat and block the airway, and vomit cannot slip into the lungs and cause drowning.
1 Kneel at the right side halfway down the person's length.
2 Tuck one hand under the left knee. Grasp the left shoulder with the other hand.
3 Using the person's own weight, roll him or her gently but firmly towards you.
4 Turn the head sideways and upwards; tuck a smooth fabric beneath.
5 Move the right arm and leg up so body weight is comfortably distributed.

1 Working in pairs, practise heart massage and mouth-to-mouth resuscitation on a dummy only. (These skills are called **CPR**: cardiac pulmonary resuscitation – biology students can explain.)
2 Working in pairs, practise turning to the recovery position.

Major and minor bleeding

If you cut yourself, the First Aid treatment is **stop the bleeding**. For a small cut, hold the wound upwards under the cold tap. Blood flows more slowly uphill, cold closes the blood vessels, and water cleanses the cut. If you are continuing with food preparation, always apply a dressing – find out and explain why.

For **heavy bleeding**, press down firmly where the blood comes from. Bring the edges of the wound together, and press. If there is a handy clean pad, cover the cut first. Do not worry about germs – you *must* stop the bleeding. Call for an ambulance. If you are treating someone else, reassure the person by staying calm and chatting gently about your work. Keep pressing down. Raise the injured part if possible. Do not lift the pad or make jolting movements; this stops the blood clotting. A person who is bleeding heavily may go into shock (p. 185). If there is a piece of glass, or anything, sticking out of the wound, *do not pull it out*. Press down firmly on either side of the wound instead.

Never give anything to eat or drink. If the wound needs stitching, an anaesthetic (painkiller) is needed, and anything in the stomach causes vomiting and choking at the operation.

The treatment for a nose bleed is to keep the person sitting forward and with a firm, pinching grip on the top of the soft part of the nostrils for 10–20 minutes. Children need comforting laps: tell favourite stories while keeping the head still.

---

1 Role-play treating and comforting a child with a nose bleed.
2 Working in pairs, practise how to stop bleeding.

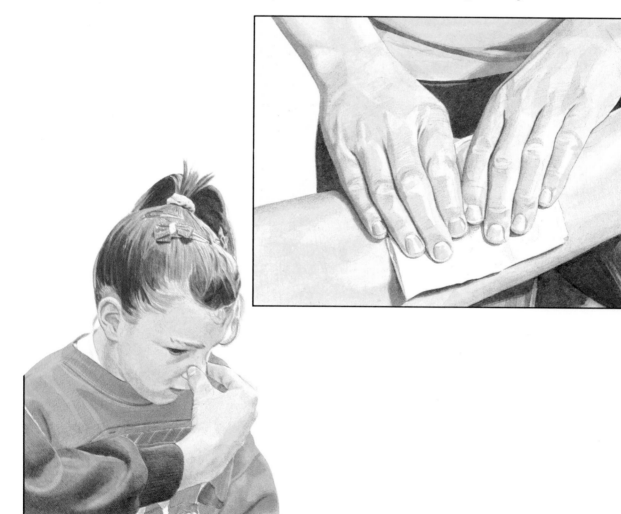

Shock and faints

Shock is a serious condition likely to follow any accident. It is the result of a sudden and severe drop in blood pressure. Not enough blood is pumped to the brain. Shock can be far more serious than the injury itself. You can recognize the signs of shock before the person collapses. These include weak or gasping breath, fast yet weak pulse, cold skin damp with sweat, and being deathly pale or a dark colour. Behaviour changes include restless and confused actions. Shock is worse if there is heavy bleeding – work out why. A person in shock must lie down.

The First Aider's work is to prevent shock.
1 If there is heavy loss of blood, first stop the bleeding (p. 184).
2 Raise the legs and feet to help blood flow back to the brain.
3 Turn the head to one side so there is no risk of the airway being blocked.
4 Keep the person warm, not hot. Cover with a light blanket. Never use a hot water bottle, as this draws blood away from the brain and increases shock.
5 Comfort and soothe away fears. A sudden collapse is always frightening. When the person is restless, anxious or upset, shock gets worse. A shocked person may be in great pain. Be as gentle, calm, and comforting as you can.

A faint is a brief collapse – you 'pass out' and fall down. It is caused by lack of blood to the brain. Once the head is lower than the heart, you 'come round' – try to work out why. People feel weak and giddy just before a faint. Why should they lie down with their feet up? Or put their head between their knees? It is not good for the brain to be short of oxygen, even for a brief faint. The other hazard is that the person risks injuries when falling.
a Elderly people can faint if they rise swiftly after bending or lying down.
b Getting up after a long illness can cause faintness. Move slowly at first.
c Very hot baths and spinning games cause dizziness, and should be avoided.
d Standing still in hot temperatures also drains blood from the brain.
e Not eating for a long period (for example, missing breakfast) reduces the amount of energy in blood to the brain.
f Sudden emotional surprises can cause faints – some people faint at the sight of an injection needle!

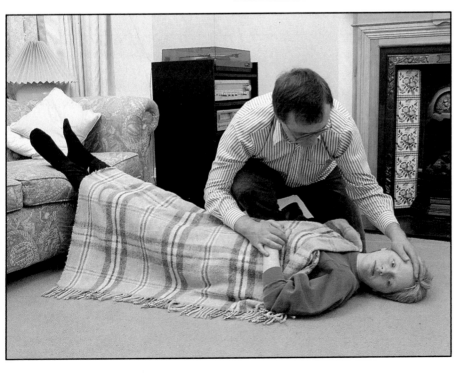

1 Working in pairs, practise First Aid skills for shock and fainting.
2 State, with reasons, some ways in which people can avoid faints.
3 Discuss the kinds of sudden emotional surprise which might cause you to faint.
4 In what ways is a faint rather like very mild shock?

Poisoning

Each year, around 10 000 children have to be treated in hospital for suspected poisoning. The cause of the poisoning is usually common household chemicals. High on the list are the cleaning agents – white spirit, bleach, metal polish, waxes for wood, shoe polish, cleaners for sinks, toilets and drains, paint, and paint strippers. Even washing-up liquid contains poisons, though it is unlikely to be drunk in such large quantities as to be a real risk.

Some of these 10 000 children suffer only mild effects; but even so, while they are in hospital they take up precious resources urgently needed for others, and parents suffer acute anxiety and guilt. Packaging and labelling Acts have been passed to make sure the warnings on toxic products are clearly marked. Medicine containers should be child proof. But the casualty rate is still high (p. 180). Discuss why parents feel guilty after accidental poisoning.

Collect: hair dyes, glues, insecticides, cleaning agents, and medicine containers.
a Study the packaging and the labelling. Comment on your findings.
b Select one you think could be improved. Design a container and labelling you think will protect against accidental poisoning.
c Evaluate your results.

A person suffering from poisoning may be unconscious – the thinking part of the brain shuts down. Breathing continues, but there is no power to think, talk, or move. There may be vomit or staining around the mouth. Call an ambulance at once. Treatment is specific to the type of poison swallowed. If the person is conscious, ask what happened. If not, search for the cleaning agent, alcohol, drugs, medicine container – any clue to identify the poison. Hand it to the ambulance crew so the correct treatment can be started immediately. A sample of vomit can be taken to hospital if the poison cannot be identified.

Some poisons are **corrosive** – there may be acid burns as red marks around the mouth. If there are corrosive stains on the lips, give large amounts of milk to drink to neutralize the acids. Give water if there is no milk handy to dilute the concentrate. You must only do this if the person is fully conscious, or the fluid will go into the lungs and cause choking. For all other kinds of poisoning, *give nothing by mouth.*

Do not try to make the person sick. Turn the person to the recovery position (p. 183).

Keeping dangerous household substances in old bottles is a common cause of poisoning.

1 A child enjoys a morning cuddle in Gran's bed. The tablets she needs during the night are on her bedside table. You are anxious the child might get to them before Gran is fully awake. Work out different ways to solve this problem.
2 Visit a toy shop and examine children's pencils and paints. Do they have the words 'non toxic' or 'lead free' clearly marked on the packaging or labelling? Examine some model construction kits. Are the glues, paints, and thinners safe?
3 All children need to be taught the dangers of toxic products. Design a bright picture to stick on all poisons in the home. Where should poisons be kept, and why?

Simple First Aid

Choking

Feel your airway – the rings of tough cartilage keep it permanently open. There is a busy junction at the back of the throat. Behind the opening to the airway is the **oesophagus** (gullet) for food and drink. When you swallow, a tough flap of cartilage, the **epiglottis**, slides over the airway to stop anything going to the lungs. If a mishap occurs, the **diaphragm** (a sheet of muscle separating the chest from the abdomen) causes huge splutters and racking coughs to force the obstruction out.

It is not really understood why death by choking is on the increase. Observe behaviour in school dining halls, play-groups, or nurseries, and evaluate the following possible reasons:

a People are so used to pulpy food they do not chew properly any more.
b People talk and laugh at the same time as they are trying to swallow.
c Parents think toddlers can chew properly when they get their first teeth.
d People eat meals in a hurry without noticing they are gulping lumps.
e People drink with food in their mouth and so wash unchewed food down.

Some obstructions are mild; a sharp pat on the back dislodges them. If food or a sweet is stuck in the throat, you may be able to hook it out. Turn the person so the head is below the knees. Banging on the back should bring the obstruction up.

Mild burns and scalds

These are treated by holding the area under the cold running tap for at least 10 minutes. This stops the burn going deeper, reduces the pain, and prevents blisters. Pat dry, and apply a loose dressing. Do not put anything else on the wound. For large burns, send for help at once. Keep the area in cold water until the ambulance arrives.

Insect stings

'Bicarb for Bees, Winegar for Wasps.' Remove the sting first with tweezers, then relieve the pain with antihistamine cream. If you have none, the above home remedy (bicarbonate of soda, or vinegar, applied to the area of the sting) works well. Watch the person for an allergic reaction to the sting. Call your family doctor if there is a reaction.

Find out everything a home First Aid box should contain.

1 Mary, age 9, bangs open the kitchen door showing you her wasp sting. Sam, sitting behind the door, chokes on his food. He is 3. As you move to help, your friend, age 15, drops a cup and scalds herself. Troubles come in threes! Plan the correct order and what you need from the First Aid box to help.

2 Working in groups, role-play your plan with First Aid skills. If necessary, adjust your plan as you go along. At the end, evaluate your original plan.

About drugs

Drugs are medicines used to cure illness, deaden pain, prevent the spread of disease, and maintain health. They may work on the body, the mind, or both. All drugs have some **side effects** – they affect other things as well as the illness. A '**safe dose**' is worked out for each different patient to have the fewest side effects. A 'safe dose' is not safe for anyone else.

Drug control

Drugs which are controlled can only be prescribed by a doctor. These include the **antibiotics**, which destroy bacteria; and the **narcotics**, used to deaden great pain. A **prescription** is the written instruction for a controlled drug to be made up. Any other way of obtaining drugs is illegal, and drug-trafficking is a criminal offence. As well as protection against drug misuse, there are important medical reasons why powerful drugs are controlled.

a **Addiction**   The body or the mind comes to depend upon the drug. A desperate craving is set up for more. This reduces the person to a state of dependency – an independent life free from the drug is no longer possible.

b **Allergy**   The body or mind can react dangerously to the drug. Some patients are allergic to the antibiotic penicillin. In a few cases, the person goes into allergy shock, and dies.

c **Resistance**   Germs are able to change structure, and build up resistance to antibiotics if frequently exposed to them. If the drug is used too often, it is powerless to help in an epidemic of disease.

d **Side effects**   Even uncontrolled drugs, such as aspirin, can have harmful side effects. In large doses, aspirin is fatal. In smaller doses, it can cause bleeding from the stomach wall.

e **Tolerance**   The body or mind becomes 'used to' a drug, such as a painkiller. At first, a normal dose works. As tolerance develops, much larger doses are needed to achieve the same thing. The increased side effects can cause death.

Studies show that many drug addicts come from homes in which they were given medicine at the first twinge of pain. The conclusion drawn is that families in which medicine is given too often and too freely may be encouraging children to misuse drugs in later life. Do you agree with this conclusion? In what ways might giving small children medicine for trivial things make them think illegal drugs will solve their adult problems?

Other factors which may lead to drug misuse are low self-esteem, poor relations with the family, and the availability of drugs.

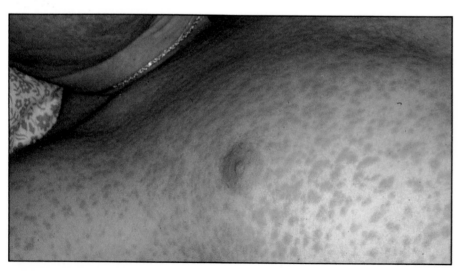

Most drugs which are misused deaden pain. But they cannot select only a few brain cells. They act like a sledge hammer – deadening and distorting great areas of thought, perception, and behaviour. Do you think drug control is necessary, and why?

Allergic reaction to an antibiotic

More about drugs

The Misuse of Drugs Act (1971) divides drugs into three categories. These depend upon the amount of damage they do to the person. Class A drugs are the 'hard' narcotics, and include heroin, cocain, methadone, morphine, opium, and pethidine. Class B drugs are mainly cannabis, cannabis resin, and amphetamines. Class C drugs are barbiturates – sedatives and hypnotics used to treat sleep disorders. In 1986, there were 29 800 seizures of drugs, nearly three times the number in 1975. The table below shows numbers of admissions of people aged 34 and under to mental hospitals in Britain as a result of drug misuse.

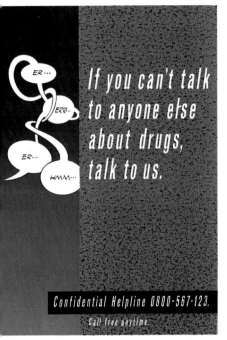

If you can't talk to anyone else about drugs, talk to us.

Confidential Helpline 0800-567-123.

Call free anytime.

	Age under 20		Age 20–4		Age 25–9		Age 30–4	
	Females	Males	Females	Males	Females	Males	Females	Males
1981	83	185	176	383	179	431	127	315
1982	90	208	201	435	200	439	131	416
1983	143	302	277	619	238	558	191	520
1984	149	341	334	872	291	628	193	529
1985	149	349	386	843	268	596	206	540

a Do you think all people misusing drugs are caught?
b Are people who try drugs only once or twice likely to become mentally ill?
c Is it likely many drug takers hide their addiction? Why?
d Do you think the figures for drug addiction may be higher than the above? Why?

Solvent abuse

Solvents are toxins in glue, paint, nail varnish remover, aerosols, and cleaning agents, used to keep these liquids fluid. Only a very small number of people misuse solvents, usually children between the ages of 10 and 16. If the solvent is sniffed or sprayed into the face, it acts on the brain very quickly. The sniffer has a 'high' – a strange, floating feeling rather like waking up after anaesthetic. Because the person feels strange, behaviour can be dangerous. The number of children who die each year from solvent abuse is estimated at between 30 and 40. Almost as sad are the children who suffer incurable brain damage.

Cannabis

Though cannabis is illegal, many young people try it out of curiosity. The physical effects are reddening of the eyes, widening of the pupils, a dry mouth, and big increase in appetite. The mental effects are much laughing, followed by euphoria – a feeling of extreme well-being. Perception alters: objects change size and shape, time speeds up or stands still. A nervous person can find these effects terrifying. If the dose is large enough, the drug-taker falls into a deep sleep.

Narcotics

Narcotics are injected directly into the blood stream. This is very dangerous. Drug addicts who share needles spread infectious diseases. The virus of the incurable and deadly AIDS syndrome is often spread this way.

1 Which gender misuses drugs more, males or females? Try to think of reasons for this.

2 In 1981, which age group were most drug misusers in? Which age group had most drug misusers by 1985, and by how much? Try to account for this change.

3 Why does drug misuse make some people mentally ill? Why can it kill others?

4 Discuss the data for the 30–4 age group.

Alcohol

Alcohol is the most widely misused drug today. After heart disease and cancer, it is the biggest single killer in the world. It shrinks the brain cells, hardens the liver (cirrhosis), and damages the heart and kidneys. It makes more people mentally ill than all other drugs put together. A third of all deaths on the road are caused by drunken drivers. It can break up families and marriages.

If alcohol causes all this damage, why do people drink it? The answer is simple – it makes them feel good. Like all drugs, alcohol is taken straight to the brain by the blood, so it works very quickly. It dampens down shy and nervous feelings; it lifts tiredness and anxiety. People stop worrying about their problems and cheer up. Surely anything which relieves unhappy feelings is good?

There is the same amount of alcohol in one glass of wine, one small sherry, one half-pint of lager or beer, and one measure of spirits. Spirits include whisky, gin, vodka, rum, and brandy. Each of these amounts of alcohol is called a **unit**. The safe maximum for men is two or three pints of beer no more than two or three times a week. Work out the equal amount in spirits. For women it is two or three units no more than two or three times a week. Some reasons why women are more affected by alcohol than men include their slighter build, lower water content in the body, different reproductive hormones, and greater liver sensitivity. Pregnant women have an especial problem as any alcohol they drink passes into the unborn baby's blood. Teenagers are not really safe if they have more than one drink occasionally.

Collect: advertisements for alcohol.
a How old are the people portrayed? Analyse their appearance.
b What effect do the settings of the advertisements have?
c Do the advertisements use humour?
d Discuss and write about their appeal.

Alcohol is a bit like fire: it makes a good servant but a bad master. If alcohol simply cheered people up, everything would be fine. The problem is that alcohol also dampens down people's common sense and affects them physically. After three units, drinkers lose their judgement – they cannot judge they should stop drinking. After five units, their senses are affected – speech becomes jumbled and slurred, and wild laughter or drunken fights may begin. After seven units, balance is affected – the drinker stumbles, bumps into furniture, and sometimes falls over. After ten units, the brain is so drugged that it has almost stopped working – the drinker may become unconscious, or fall into a heavy, snoring sleep.

In 1986, about 26 000 people died of alcohol-related causes in Britain alone. It has been estimated that, in world-wide terms, alcohol is more dangerous than heroin, cocaine, and AIDS put together – *then multiplied tenfold*. Most violence in the home is connected with heavy bouts of drinking. At football matches, violence erupts amongst drunken teenagers who cannot control their behaviour.

1 Sergei boasts he can 'drink everyone under the table'. Role-play how to refuse the drink he insists will do you good.

2 Many people think that advertisements for alcohol, particularly those aimed at young people, should be banned. Discuss this suggestion.

3 Habitual drinkers develop enormous tolerance of alcohol, and high dependency on it. Discuss dependency and how, together with increased tolerance, this might affect the daily life of an alcoholic.

Further work on Chapter 15

Tobacco smoke

Smoke from burning tobacco is noxious (harmful), whether it comes from pipes, cigars, or cigarettes. The things which do most harm are as follows:

a **Tobacco tar** is a **carcinogen** – something which causes cancer.

b **Carbon monoxide** cuts down the amount of oxygen carried in the blood and damages the heart and lungs.

c **Nicotine** is a drug of addiction. It causes overactivity of the heart and narrows the blood tubes of the body.

d **Passive smoking** means breathing in the smoke from other people's cigarettes. Cigarettes produce two kinds of smoke. **Mainstream** smoke is filtered through the cigarette before it is breathed in by the smoker. **Sidestream** smoke goes directly from the burning cigarette into the air around the smoker. It is not filtered, and so is full of high concentrations of tobacco pollutants. Smoking has been called 'self-pollution', but it pollutes the air around the smoker as well. For this reason, smoking is now forbidden in many public places.

Work through this section, and then evaluate the work you did on p. 23.

---

1 What is meant by a 'carcinogen'? Name the three main harmful substances in cigarette smoke, and state what damage they cause in the body.

2 What is meant by 'passive smoking'? Explain the difference between mainstream and sidestream smoke.

3 Use resources to find out **a** what percentage of **i** adults, and **ii** school-leavers do not smoke; and **b** what percentage of smokers die before they reach retirement age. How do these figures compare with those for five years ago? What conclusions can you draw?

4 **a** Find and name four public places in your community where smoking is banned.

b Draw the symbol for a no smoking area.

c Do you think the risk to non-smokers' health from passive smoking is unfair? Write a short essay giving reasons for your answer.

5 You might have an accident when you are hanging up the curtains. Give ways of preventing this.

(Scottish Examination Board)

6 It has been suggested that the advance in technology has made the home and its environment a more dangerous place. Comment critically on this statement.

(Welsh Joint Education Committee)

Now look again at the objectives at the beginning of the chapter, and check that you have achieved them.

16 *Food and family health*

By the end of this chapter, you should be able to:

- identify dietary goals and their relationship to health.
- interpret the nutritional value of given foods.
- apply dietary goals to family meals.
- analyse psychological problems of weight loss.
- identify the place of exercise in diet and health.

What are dietary goals?

Nutrients are substances in food which provide energy and the raw materials for healthy growth and cell repair. They are grouped into **proteins, carbohydrates, fats, vitamins,** and **minerals. Water** and **dietary fibre** are also essential for health.

The RDI is the Recommended Daily Intake of energy and nutrients, as listed by the Department of Health. This recommended intake is based on research into the needs of people of different body weights, age groups, gender, and culture. Energy is measured in **kilojoules** (kJ) or **kilocalories** (kcal – the 'calories' of many slimming diets). Find out and define what these measurements are. More or less kJ are needed depending upon how active people are – their energy output and exercise level. NACNE and COMA issue guidelines 'to improve the normal diet of the average British family'. They are called dietary goals, and include:

- Eat more whole natural foods and less manufactured foods.
- Eat less fats altogether, especially animal fats.
- Eat more plant protein and less animal protein.
- Eat less salt, sugar, and snacks high in both.
- Eat more fresh fruit and vegetables.
- Drink less coffee, tea, and cola.
- Drink less alcohol.

Nutrients interact with one another, too. For example: strong bones and teeth need protein, calcium, and vitamin D; for good muscle tone, you need calcium, salt, and the vitamin B group; and so on. Would your diet be 'balanced' if you cut out one food group completely? A 'balanced' diet means exactly what it says!

1 Find out what the acronyms 'NACNE' and 'COMA' stand for.
2 Find out about and discuss the RDI of energy and nutrients for teenage boys and girls. Try to work out reasons for the differences.

3 Do a survey of at least three families to find out the sweet-eating habits of today's children. Pool your findings in a class survey. What conclusions can you draw about whether or not people act on dental health advice?

Food and the emotions

How many people in the class eat their potatoes unpeeled? Nutritionists say that **a** the richest source of Vitamin C is just beneath the skin, **b** the skin itself is rich in fibre, and **c** for each potato eaten, there must be some energy output. Yet many people still choose to eat peeled potatoes and ignore the need for exercise. Why?

Food and the early emotions

The satisfying of our urgent hungers as babies is buried within our unconscious minds. Without realizing it, we link eating to some of our deepest sorrows and joys. As we leave childhood, we unconsciously resist advice on diet. We eat what we enjoy, and ignore any health effects.

Food as training

'Eat it up', 'Clean your plate', 'I hate a picky eater', and so on. Some parents show concern for their children by anxiety over diet. But children know the size of their appetites better than their parents. Children are often called 'good' when they finish food, 'bad' when they do not. This training also goes into the unconscious and results in muddled ideas about food.

Collect: packaging, advertisements, and menus for foods you regard as treats. List the tempting words which are used to describe the contents.

Food as a comfort habit

We associate eating with special 'treats' – biscuits for cuts, ice cream in hospital, barbecues, birthdays, feasts! During unhappy times, some people try to get back that comfort feeling of treats. They 'treat themselves' to a box of chocolates, tasty snacks, rich cream cakes, etc. Muddled ideas about food can lead to overeating, which causes **obesity**. Many health problems, such as heart disease and back pain, can be obesity-related. Obese people can have a constant battle with their weight. In fact, a few find slimming so difficult they have their jaws wired together so they can only sip liquids through a straw!

1 A friend's toddler refuses to eat the nourishing meal you have cooked. You worry in case your friend thinks you are starving the child. What can you do?
2 State, with reasons, why the nutritionists set dietary goals, not rules.

3 Have you ever 'punished' someone by refusing to eat when you were hungry? Discuss ways in which food has the ability to give sorrow or pleasure.

4 Obesity is a handicap as painful to the sufferer as any other handicap.

Discuss.

How much food is enough?

Body fat is measured by weighing people, submerging them in water, and reweighing them. This is not a popular method! Estimates are made based on the differences in density of fat and lean tissue. The BMI (Body Mass Index), based on large-scale studies, relates the ratio of weight to the square of height, and comes up with weight charts. These charts often do not mean much to teenagers, who are still at a developmental stage.

What is basal metabolism (p. 135)? You need about 4 kJ per minute for this. How much is that in kcal? How many kJ do you need **a** per hour, and **b** per day for basal metabolism? Using the RDI, find out how many more kJ (and kcal) you need for effective living – growth, development, cell repair, and physical activity.

Are you comfortable with your shape? Do you feel fit? Are you willing to eat more, or less, depending upon your reply? Any change in body shape should be accompanied by an increase in exercise to ensure skin and underlying tissue stay firm. Are you willing to increase your exercise level?

Eating (energy input) and exercise (energy output) interact to produce your shape. It is not really possible to discuss one without the other. If you have a hearty appetite and take lots of exercise you will stay lean. But if you do not take exercise, even the smallest amount of extra kJ will be turned into fat and stored in your tissues.

The findings of recent surveys for the Department of Health state that the majority of British teenagers:

- eat too many of the wrong foods.
- do not take enough exercise.
- have bodies which lack strength, stamina, and flexibility.

a Should strength be valued now there are so many machines to do the heavy work? Why?

b Do you value stamina – the ability to endure prolonged physical activity? Why?

c Do you value flexibility – having smooth supple movements? Why?

---

1 Who makes the choices about how much you eat? Do you think it takes mental strength, stamina, and flexibility to change your eating habits? Turn to p. 20 and re-read 'resisting change'. Is change easy?

2 What are the satisfactions you will get if you achieve the body shape you desire? Is this likely to be a short- or a long-term goal? Why?

Whole natural foods

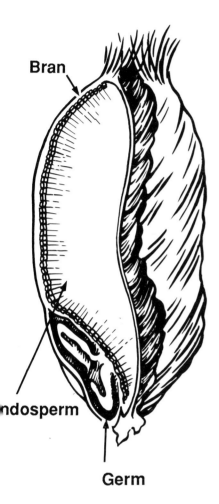

Bran

ndosperm

Germ

◄ whole wheat grain

In parts of West Africa, the population eat whole natural foods. They rarely suffer digestive diseases such as appendicitis, gall stones, constipation, piles, cancer of the bowel, or diverticular disease. All these painful conditions are common in the west.

Whole foods contain fibre. This is not a food, but the tough cell walls of plants which cannot be broken down. During digestion, a great deal of body fluid pours into the intestines. Fibre absorbs this water, becoming soft and bulky. This results in a feeling of fullness – without adding weight. The softened fibre and waste products of digestion are easily moved along the intestines. No damage is done to the lining and the person has soft bowel motions without any strain.

Collect: fresh and tinned peas, celery, and carrots, and a blunted knife.
a Chop both fresh and tinned vegetables with the knife. Which was easier? Are there any differences in the fibrous parts? Discuss.
b If you wish to increase the amount of fibre in your diet, would you choose fresh or tinned vegetables? Why?

The outside bran of a whole wheat grain contains protein, fibre, B vitamins, and important minerals. The germ contains protein, essential fats, B and E vitamins, and iron. The endosperm contains protein, B vitamins, and starch. When wheat is ground into white flour, both the bran and germ are removed. Which nutrients are lost?

Collect: labellings on loaves of bread, chapattis, rice, pasta, and breakfast cereals.
a List the ingredients. Tick those mentioned above. Is 'added vitamins and minerals' written anywhere? This usually means the natural ones have been removed. List words you do not understand.
b Write down what is meant by 'whole' and 'refined' foods.

Collect: fresh vegetables, dried cereals and pulses, and kitchen scales.
a Weigh fresh foods and record their weights.
b Dry out samples of both fresh and dried foods in a slow oven heat.
c Weigh and compare results.
d Which contains the most water? If you changed to a wholefood diet that contained a lot of dried cereals and pulses, would you need to increase your liquid intake? Why?

---

1 Name the nutrients in a meal of baked beans on wholemeal bread with salad. Would you recommend this meal? Why?
2 Do whole natural foods contain protein? In what ways can a vegan benefit from this information?

3 Mr X is constipated and is recovering from dental surgery. What foods does he need? How would you prepare them? Why?
4 For a healthy diet, eat more vegetable protein and less animal protein.

Analyse this statement.

Investigating fats

Using resources, list at least four functions of fats in the diet. Why are they essential for health?

Your diet must provide the **essential fatty acids**, as your body cannot make them. But too much fat in your diet may increase your level of **cholesterol**, a substance which can damage the heart and blood vessels. **Unsaturated** fats, found mostly in oils from plants and fish, are lower in cholesterol than **saturated** fats, found mostly in meat (especially red meat) and dairy produce. Foods to eat less of therefore include butter, cream, most cheese, full fat milk, coconut oil, and red meat, as they are high in saturated fats. But all fatty foods contain some saturated fat: there is, for example, 20 per cent in olive oil and soya oil, and 25 per cent in mackerel and plaice. It is more healthy to eat less of all fatty foods.

Collect: ethanol and a wide variety of natural and processed foods.
a Find out how to test for the presence of fats, and plan and carry out the test.
b List foods into those containing fats, and those which are fat free. Discuss in what way you might use this information.

If you cannot cut down on cream cakes or butter, increase your exercise level. This is because all fats are energy dense. They provide about 38 per cent of your energy output. What happens if you do not increase your energy output – if you eat lots of creamy, buttery goods without taking more exercise? There is nowhere else for the supply of energy to go except into storage cells – fatty tissue.

Collect: a variety of margarines and cooking fats.
a Study the labels. Do they state the percentage of saturated fats, especially those 'high in polyunsaturated fats'?
b Do you think people interested in health issues are being given sufficient information on these labels? Why?

Collect: a potato, bacon, a pork chop, a sausage, some liver, an egg, and a tomato.
a Prepare and cook a meal by frying these foods.
b Prepare and cook a meal with these foods without using the frying pan.
c Comment on the taste, fat content, and acceptability of both meals. State which you prefer, and why.
d Discuss whether knowing about the health risk of fatty foods might affect your choices as a parent when preparing food.

---

1 Find out and discuss what is meant by 'hidden' fats. Explain the difference in the fat content of an apple and an apple pie.
2 Unless you take exercise, eating foods high in fats makes you obese.

Discuss.

3 Find a list of obesity-related diseases. State, with reasons, why you should try to eat less of all fats.

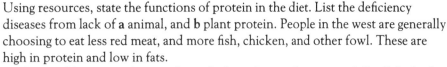

Proteins

	Men	Women	Girls 16–24
		Vegetarian (%)	
1984	2.1	1.6	2.6
1985	2.5	1.9	3.0
1986	2.7	2.1	3.4
	Eating less meat (%)		
1984	1.9	1.7	2.2
1985	2.6	2.1	3.0
1986	3.1	2.1	3.9

Using resources, state the functions of protein in the diet. List the deficiency diseases from lack of **a** animal, and **b** plant protein. People in the west are generally choosing to eat less red meat, and more fish, chicken, and other fowl. These are high in protein and low in fats.

The word 'vegetarian' comes from the Latin '*vegetus*', meaning full of life, fresh, whole. Is meat any of these things? Vegetarians get their full range of amino acids (which make up proteins) from non-meat products. Name some, and state why vegetarians must have them in their diet.

The table on the left shows the trends in giving up meat in Britain.

Vegans eat neither meat, nor animal products. List twenty foods they do not eat. Vegans risk a lack of Vitamin A, Vitamin D, and one another vitamin – name it, and state its deficiency disease. What are Vitamin D and calcium needed for? Why might vegans also suffer a shortage of calcium? What particular foods must they include in their diet?

Vegans must eat a wide variety of plant proteins to get all the amino acids they need, and they must eat them in the correct combination. Pregnant vegans may find it difficult to eat enough calories and iron for the growing baby. Vegan infants need breast feeding – why? Fortified yeast and B-12 fortified soya milk can be given later on.

Prepare a vegetarian meal. List all the nutrients. Evaluate your work.

1 Discuss the trend towards vegetarianism, especially for girls.

2 Find out which protein foods are not eaten by **a** Jews, **b** Hindus, **c** Muslims, and why.

3 Plan a day's vegetarian menu for Pam, aged 17, height 1 m 62.5 cm (5 ft 4 in), weight 51 kg (8 stones). You might choose to prepare one meal as a practical assignment.

Salt and sugar

Salt, in its natural state, is present in cereals, vegetables, fruit, meat, fish, and egg white. There is quite a lot of salt in milk. Table salt is called **sodium chloride**. The salt in baking powder and baking soda is **sodium bicarbonate**. **Monosodium glutamate** (MSG) is a heavily salted flavouring very popular in eastern cooking. Do you like Chinese take-aways?

Salt is essential for health, but too much can lead to high blood pressure, heart disease, strokes, and kidney and liver damage. In 1984, the average daily intake in Britain was 10.7 g for men and 8 g for women. Some nutritionists suggested this should be reduced by at least half per day. Find out and comment on the average intakes now. Why is salt added to food?

Collect: packaging of meat pies, sausages, sausage rolls, cooked ham, and bacon.
a Study the salt content.
b It is difficult to reduce the amount of sodium and potassium in meat products. More than just flavour would be lost, as salt **i** assists in the keeping qualities and safety of cured meats, **ii** interacts with the meat proteins to give tenderness and juiciness to the product, and **iii** when cooking, helps to keep in meat juices – it stops meat-loaves falling apart when sliced.

How can you test these statements?

Collect: packaging of various snacks and manufactured foods.
a Examine the labelling. Note the amounts of sodium, sodium chloride, or bicarbonate. Look for potassium chloride.
b Sodium and potassium interact – what is their function in the body?
c Name the snacks which are high in fats. Would you recommend snacks to a person who is trying to lose weight, and why?

Investigate snack foods for the presence of 'hidden' sugars.

Collect: recipes for biscuit and small cakes.
a Discuss alternatives to sugar in the recipes.
b Choose one alternative and test it out.

1 Prepare and cook some salt-free snacks. Test them for taste and acceptability.
2 As a practical assignment, demonstrate how the amount of sugar in a traditional cake or pudding can be satisfactorily reduced.
3 Compare the nutrient content and costs of take-away hamburger and chips with those you have made yourself.
4 Devise and carry out a survey of eating patterns among the class over the last week.

Checking your fluid intake

Average caffeine in some products	(mg)
Coffee (140 ml/5 oz cup)	
Decaffeinated	2.5
Instant	65.0
Brewed, percolated	80.0
Brewed, filter method	115.0
Tea (loose or bags, 140 ml/5 oz cup	
1-minute brew	26.0
3-minute brew	33.0
5-minute brew	35.0
Chocolate	
Cocoa (140 ml/5 oz cup)	4.0
Chocolate milkshake (225 ml/8 oz cup)	5.0
Milk choclate (28 g/1 oz)	6.0
Plain chocolate (28 g/1 oz)	20.0
Unsweetened chocolate (28 g/1 oz)	60.0
Fizzy drinks (336 ml/12 oz)	
Pepsi-Cola	38.4
Coca-Cola	45.6
Diet Coke	45.6

Were you allowed to drink coffee as a child? Perhaps you were not allowed to drink tea either? These contain the drug **caffeine**. In small doses, caffeine livens you up. It stimulates the heart muscle and the brain, relaxes the breathing muscles, and makes the kidneys produce more urine. Between 100 and 300 mg can produce this effect, depending on your age and weight. In some people, caffeine becomes addictive. Without their morning drinks of strong black coffee, they cannot start the day, have a bowel motion, or concentrate on their work.

Caffeine is also in many non-prescription and in some prescribed drugs (p. 188). It is used in pain relievers, energy drinks, cold medicines, and diuretics. These last are drugs to make you pass more urine – why is caffeine in them?

The health problems caused by too much caffeine are thought to include damage to the heart, blood vessels, stomach, breasts, and nervous and reproductive systems. Some studies link caffeine to cancers and to birth defects – the drug does pass from mother to unborn child, but these links are not proven. Until more research is done, some nutritionists suggest pregnant woman and all children should avoid caffeine.

The British cup of tea accounts for 45 per cent of all British fluid intake. On average, we consume 3.77 cups a day. If the tea is not strong, this amount does no harm. A daily intake of caffeine above 300 mg is not advised.

---

1 Some teenagers suffer from constipation. Many have a low fluid intake. Work out how much you drink **a** on a weekday, and **b** over a weekend.

2 Urine is 95 per cent water. Hot tea makes you sweat. In what ways does drinking tea or cola lower the body's water content?

3 You need at least 3 and up to 8 pints of non-diuretic fluids each day. Make up and taste some alternatives to tea, coffee, and cola.

Foods with additives

Advances in food technology mean that a wide variety of synthetic chemicals is added to most manufactured foods. All additives must be listed under their names followed by the code numbers of the chemicals; for example, 'flavour enhancer E621'. The main additives include:

preservatives, to protect against bacteria infection and keep food fresh.

antioxidants, to prevent fats reacting with oxygen and going rancid.

sweeteners, to give artificial taste without using refined sugars.

emulsifiers and **stabilizers**, to make foods containing different chemicals compatible.

cosmetic agents such as colouring, to put back things which are lost by processing.

Study the information on the packages shown here. By law, all ingredients must be listed in their order of weight.

a Which set of information do you find easier to read, and why?

b Write down all the chemicals (and other ingredients) you do not understand.

c Discuss and then give your opinion as to whether the public needs more information on synthetic chemicals added to foods.

Food allergies

This is a hot topic of debate! Many health problems are blamed on food allergies – the correct term is food **intolerance**. Expert opinion is divided, as there is not enough proof either way. But the known offenders which can cause severe health problems are mainly in natural foods. These include:

cow's milk – both children and adults can develop an intolerance to this.

wheat – this can cause digestive disorders, asthma, eczema, and migraine.

eggs – intolerance in young children tends to subside in adulthood.

soya beans – soya milk from soya beans can cause intolerance in infants.

cocoa – any food or drink containing cocoa can bring on a migraine.

additives – in 1981 the Commission of the European Communities stated that under 1 per cent of the population suffered from additives in food. Find out whether the figures have changed since.

The Food Intolerance Data Bank registers several thousand products which have been certified free from the main food offenders. It is put together by the Royal College of Physicians with the help of the food industry. A few people suffer from **multiple food intolerance**. What does this mean? They can be given a print-out of foods which are safe for them to eat.

1 If you suspected a mild food intolerance, how could you 'test' for it?

2 A single parent, with no time to cook, complains her 3-year-old is overactive because of 'poisons' in convenience foods. Draw up a daily menu which is a nutritious, b quick and easy to prepare, and c acceptable to a small child. You could choose to make one of the meals as a practical assignment.

Investigating slimming products

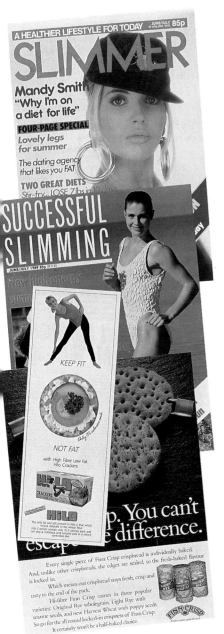

Slimming products include liquid meals, high protein diets, and fibre tablets or flakes. Many have added vitamins and minerals which make them sound nutritious. No slimming diet should be less than 1200 kcal per day for adults; and this amount is unlikely to be enough for development in the teens.

Collect: various diet sheets, and advertisements for different slimming products.

a Study a liquid diet. Which food is it based on? What is the daily cost? Could you make the same flavoured drink for less? Is the diet short on fibre?

b Study a high-protein diet. Is it low in both kcal (kJ) and carbohydrates?

   The idea of high-protein diets is to 'burn fats' and leave lean tissue. This produces high acid wastes which can cause digestive upsets, muscle cramps, and fatigue. Pregnant women and people with kidney, liver, or heart problems are most at risk.

c Study a diet with unrestricted kcal (kJ). Which nutrient is the diet low in? What health problems might this diet cause from the high protein and fats intake? Any weight loss at the start is only due to water loss – is this good for health? What, in fact, will the high kcal intake lead to over a period of time?

d Study a high-fibre diet. How does it work (p. 195)? Because nutrients interact, long-term fibre diets are linked to a shortage of calcium, zinc, and copper.

e Choose any one diet, and copy out the wording of hints or promises of sudden, dramatic weight loss. List the nutrients – are they in the right amounts for good health? What is the total daily kJ or kcal intake? Is it sufficient?

Create a slimming diet with better nutrients and as much chance of success. What do you think the success of any slimming diet really depends upon?

The way to slim is **a** eat less fat and sugar, so that **b** the stored fat then converts into energy, which is **c** worked off by exercise.

---

1 'Products made to help slimmers often fail to live up to hopes. Experience has shown that those which offer instant size and weight loss are invariably slim only in terms of proof.' Discuss this report in 1985 from the ASA (p. 99). How did the ASA know these products were failing the consumer? Why do you think the ASA warned the public while advertising the products? From your findings, state, with reasons, whether there has been any improvement in the products.

2 Slimming diets are placebos to stop the overweight taking exercise.

Discuss.

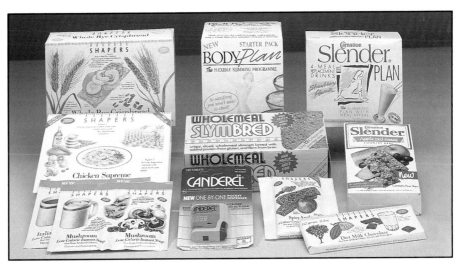

Planning your exercise programme

What is vigorous exercise? How does it strengthen the heart and lungs? Exercise is particularly important in the teens. It gives suppleness, stamina, and strength to all the developing organs and the outside frame. To change your body shape (and to lose weight), exercise must be:

- long enough – at least twenty minutes at a time.
- hard enough – to make you breathe heavily and sweat.
- often enough – at least three times each week.

The most important thing is that you must enjoy the exercise. Choose a programme you like, otherwise you may give it up! If you shudder at team games:

- join an aerobics class, or copy the programme and practise in your room.
- work out with yoga to develop suppleness, stamina, and strength slowly.
- dance to disco music until you feel ready to drop.
- pump sandbags above your head to develop stamina and strength.
- cycle or walk to school, if possible. Use the stairs, not the lifts.
- at the weekends, take a friend hill-climbing, ice-skating, or swimming.

---

1 Find out about isometrics – exercises you can do at almost any time.

2 Do an individual study on **a** posture in the teens, or **b** the correct way to lift weights. Resources: biology and health textbooks.

It's your choice

Only you can make choices about your diet. No single food is 'good' or 'bad'. What matters for healthy eating is the total diet over a period of time.

Summary

1 Eat more starchy foods for energy.
2 Eat more whole foods.
3 Eat more vegetable protein.
4 Eat more fresh fruit and vegetables.
5 Eat more dietary fibre.
6 Check your diet for iron.

Eat less fats, especially animal fats.
Eat less processed and refined foods.
Eat less animal protein.
Eat less canned and frozen foods.

Eat less salt.
Eat less sugar and sugary foods.

In short, your diet for sparkling good health should have more whole, natural, and plant food, and less manufactured, artificial, and animal food. Be proud of your appetite, your exercise programme, and your body shape!

Discuss the reports described in questions 1 and 2.

1 In 1985, an advertising company did a survey of the impact of healthy eating on food markets. From their findings, they divided consumers into:
   a the unconcerned – one-fifth of people who make no changes in their eating habits in spite of nutritional advice.
   b the aware – three-fifths of mainly female homemakers who know about health issues, but are confused between the latest ideas and their own common sense.
   c the believers – one-fifth of people who spend a great deal of time and thought over the family diet and who frequently shop at health food stores.
   Which of these groups do you consider you might belong to?

2 In 1987, an American report warned health-conscious parents not to become food fanatics. Doctors found that babies were starving because they were fed skimmed milk and raw vegetables instead of the high-energy foods they need. This undernourishment was slowing the babies' growth and development. 'We have noticed this for two years among fairly well-to-do parents', the report said.
   Has there been a similar trend in the UK?

3 Give sensible menus for *two* consecutive days for an office worker who needs to lose weight.
   (London and East Anglian Group)

4 What is the major role of protein in the development of a child?
   (Southern Examining Group)

Now look again at the objectives at the beginning of the chapter, and check that you have achieved them.

Useful addresses

Local business telephone directories are a good resource for addresses and telephone numbers. Contacting local resources is often quickest and most satisfactory. For central resources, always include a self-addressed, stamped envelope: availability of free literature may change from time to time. Magazines and journals provide information on technological advances in home design: furnishings, fittings, fabrics, lighting, appliances, and kitchenware.

Abbey National Building Society – free leaflets on mortgages
Abbey House, Baker Street, London NW1 6XL

Advertising Standards Authority Ltd. (ASA) – free leaflets on advertising standards
Brook House, Torrington Place, London WC1E 7HN

Advisory Unit for Computer Based Education (AUCBE)
Endymion Road, Hatfield, Herts AL10 8AU

Air Improvement Centre Ltd. – free pack on humidifiers, house plants
23 Denbigh Street, London SW1V 2HF

Anything Left Handed Ltd. – mail order catalogue
65 Beak Street, London W1

Association of British Insurers – free leaflets
Aldermary House, Queen Street, London EC4N 1TT

Association of British Laundry Cleaning & Rental Services – free leaflets
Lancaster Gate House, 319 Pinner Road, Harrow, Middlesex HA1 4HX

Barclays Bank plc – free leaflets on all aspects
Group Public Affairs Dept., 54 Lombard Street, London EC3P 3AH

Belling & Co. Ltd. – free leaflets on electric cookers, cameras
Bridge Works, Southbury Road, Enfield, Middlesex EN1 1UF

British Agencies for Adoption & Fostering – free leaflets
11 Southwark Street, London SE1 1RQ

British Gas Education Service – free leaflets on appliances, safety factors
PO Box 46, Hounslow TW4 6NF

British Gypsum Ltd. – free film loan on plasterboard
Westfield, 360 Singlewell Road, Gravesend, Kent DA11 7RZ

British Standards Institution (BSI) – practical projects
Education Section, 2 Park Street, London W1A 2BS

Building Research Establishment – wood treatment and care
Publication Office, Garston, Watford, Herts WD2 7JR

Careers Research and Advisory Centre (CRAC) – materials on careers
Hobson Publishing plc, Bateman Street, Cambridge CB2 1LZ

Community Service Volunteers – resource packs on the family
237 Pentonville Road, London N1 9NJ

Consumers' Association – publishers of *Which?* magazine
14 Buckingham Street, London WC2N 6DS

Creda Ltd. – free leaflets on washing appliances
Advertising Dept., Blythe Bridge, Stoke-on-Trent ST11 9LJ

Design Council – the Design Centre is worth a visit, if possible
28 Haymarket, London SW1Y 4SU

Development Education Centre – pack on family values
Gillett Centre, Selly Oak College, Bristol Road, Birmingham B29 6LE

Dr Barnardo's – speaker, films on disabled children in the family
Tanners Lane, Barkingside, Essex 1G6 1QG

Electricity Council – free leaflets on understanding electricity
Educational Service, 30 Millbank, London SW1P 4RD

General Dental Council – free loan video and film on dental hygiene
37 Wimpole Street, London W1M 8DQ

Gingerbread (pressure group for one-parent families) – leaflet on support work
35 Wellington Street, London WC2

Health Education Authority – see telephone directory for local office
78 New Oxford Street, London WC1A 1AH

Help the Aged, Education Dept. – pack on different life styles, caring needs, nutrition
16–18 St James's Walk, London EC1R 0BE

Her Majesty's Stationery Office (HMSO) – publishers of *Social Trends*, an annual book of statistical information
49 High Holborn, London WC1V 6HB

Home Laundering Consultative Council – free information packs
7 Swallow Place, London W1

Inland Revenue Education Service – free leaflets on tax affairs
PO Box 20, Wetherby, West Yorkshire LS23 7EH

Ministry of Agriculture, Fisheries and Food
Lion House Publications, Willowburn Trading Estate, Alnwick, Northumberland NE66 2PF

National Society for Clean Air – free pack on air and noise pollution
136 North Street, Brighton, East Sussex BN1 1RG

National Youth Bureau – free catalogue of leaflets
17/23 Albion Street, Leicester LE1 6GD

Noise Abatement Society – information on noise pollution
PO Box 8, Bromley, Kent BR2 0UH

Office of Fair Trading – free leaflets
Information Room 310c, Field House, Breams Buildings, London EC4A 1PR

Physically Handicapped and Able-Bodied (PHAB) – ask about PHAB clubs
Tavistock House North, Tavistock Square, London WC1

Pictorial Charts Educational Trust – wall charts on families from different ethnic groups, values, digestion, health
27 Kirchen Road, London W13 0UD

Prestige Group plc – free packs on kitchenware
Prestige House, 14–18 Holborn, London EC1N 2LQ

Royal Association for Disability and Rehabilitation (RADAR) – information on care needs
25 Mortimer Street, London W1N 8AB

Royal Institute of British Architects (RIBA) – local educational resource centres
66 Portland Place, London W1N 4AD

Royal Society for the Prevention of Accidents (RoSPA) – free leaflets
Cannon House, The Priory Queensway, Birmingham B4 6BS

Sainsbury's – free speaker, information packs in your area
Stamford House, Stamford Street, London SE1 9LL

Shell Film Library – films on pollution, free loan
Unit 2, Cornwall Works, Cornwall Avenue, London N13 1LD

Shelter, National Campaign for the Homeless – free information pack on leaving home
157 Waterloo Road, London SE1 8XF

Simplicity Product Advisory Service – free leaflets on puberty to menopause
Dept. M, Kimberly-Clark Ltd., Larkfield, Maidstone, Kent ME20 7PS

Solid Fuel Advisory Service – free information packs
Coal House, Lyon Road, Harrow on the Hill, Middlesex HA1 2EX

Spode – history of ceramics tours, museum
Church Street, Stoke-on-Trent, Staffordshire ST4 1BX

Unilever Educational – management, marketing, advertising
PO Box 68, Unilever House, Victoria Embankment, London EC4P 4BQ

Unit Trust Association – leaflets on investing money
Park House, 16 Finsbury Circus, London EC2M 7JP

Vegetarian Society of the UK Ltd. – free consumer leaflets
Parkdale, Dunham Road, Altrincham, Cheshire WA14 4QG

Welsh Consumer Council – educational consumer newsletter
Castle Buildings, Womanby Street, Cardiff CF1 2BN